MY WAR GONE BY,
I MISS IT SO

MY WAR GONE BY,
I MISS IT SO

Anthony Loyd

Atlantic Monthly Press
New York

*Originally published in 1999 by Doubleday—a division of Transworld
Publishers Ltd.*
Printed in the United States of America

An Irish Airman Forsees His Death by W. B. Yeats is reproduced by
permission of A. P. Watt Ltd. on behalf of Michael B. Yates.

Maps of Bosnia and Hercegovina and Chechnya are courtesy of the U.S.
Central Intelligence Agency.

FIRST AMERICAN EDITION

Library of Congress Cataloging-in-Publication Data

Loyd, Anthony.
    My war gone by, I miss it so / Anthony Loyd.
      p.   cm.
    ISBN 0-87113-769-0
    1. Loyd, Anthony. 2. Yugoslav War, 1991–1995—Bosnia and
Hercegovina. 3. Yugoslav War, 1991–1995—Personal narratives,
British. 4. Bosnia and Hercegovina—History, Military. I. Title.

DR1313.3.L69   2000
949.70321—dc21
                                                      99-043963

Atlantic Monthly Press
841 Broadway
New York, NY 10003

00 01 02 03   10 9 8 7 6 5 4 3 2 1

Mojim drugovima – For my comrades

Glossary

APC:	armoured personnel carrier.
armija:	Bosnian government's predominantly Muslim army.
Balije:	pejorative term for Bosnian Muslims.
BiH:	government army of Bosnia and Hercegovina.
BMP:	Soviet APC.
Četniks:	traditional Serbian term for irregular troops (from *četa* – 'unit'). In the latest war it referred to Serb nationalist fighters, though it became a label used by Bosnian Croats and Muslims to refer to all Serb soldiers.
DF:	DF 118s are prescribed heroin substitutes in tablet form.
drug:	comrade.
Gastarbeiters:	guest workers in Germany.
hajduk:	frontier guerrilla.
Herceg-Bosna:	self-styled Bosnian Croat independent state.
Hercegovina:	southern Bosnia.
HOS:	Croatian paramilitary force.
HV:	Croatian regular army.
HVO:	Bosnian Croat army.
imam:	Muslim prayer leader.

JNA:	Yugoslav People's Army.
Kuna:	Croatian currency.
MIA:	Missing in action.
NDH:	the Croatian fascist puppet state, which incorporated most of Bosnia, from 1941 to 1945.
partisans:	Tito's communist guerrilla army of the Second World War. Though dominated by Serbs it was a multi-denominational Slav force.
RPG:	rocket-propelled grenade.
šehid:	martyr.
smrtniks:	Chechen fighters committed to death rather than withdrawal once in battle.
Turks:	pejorative term for Bosnian Muslims.
UNHCR:	United Nations High Commission for Refugees.
Ustaša:	Croatian fascist movement led by Ante Pavelić during the Second World War.

Serbo-Croatian Pronunciations

The pronunciation of the language and its names are simple and phonetic with the following exceptions:

C is pronounced 'ts'.
Č 'tch' (as in 'scratch').
Ć like 'tch', but more similar to the 't' in 'future'.
Đ (đ) 'j' (as in 'jab').
J 'y' (as in 'Yugoslavia').
Š 'sh'.
U 'oo' (as in 'mood').
Ž 'zh' (as in 'Zhivago').

Definition of 'Bosnian'
The people of Bosnia are predominantly southern Slavs. Though still a contentious definition, as a generalization it is true to say that those whose ancestors converted to the Orthodox Christian religion are known as Bosnian Serbs, while those who took the Catholic faith became known as Bosnian Croats. The majority, who inherited a loose form of Islam, are known as Bosnian Muslims. For simplicity in this book they are termed Serbs, Croats and Muslims. More recently the term 'Bosnian', or Bošniak, usually refers to Bosnian Muslims.

Bosnia and Herzegovina

- International boundary
- Inter-Entity Boundary Line (IEBL)
- ★ National capital
- Railroad
- Expressway
- Road

0   20   40   60 Kilometers

0   20   40   60 Miles
Lambert Conformal Conic Projection, SP 40N/56N

Serbia and Montenegro have asserted
the formation of a joint independent
state, but this entity has not been
formally recognized as a state by
the United States.

Base 802520 (R00399) 1-97

Chechnya

0 25 Kilometers
0 25 Miles
RUSSIA
Caspian Sea
Zelenokumsk
Achikulak
Kochubey
Dagestan
Stavropol' Kray
Kamyshev
Kizlyar
Staryy Terek
Kargalinskaya
Mozdok
Prokhladnyy
Terek
Kalinovskaya
Novyy Terek
Kabardino-Balkaria
Chechnya
Nadterechnaya
Malgobek
Chervlënnaya
Ingushetia
Sunzha
Groznyy
Gudermes
Sulak
Khasavyurt
Argun
Beslan
Nazran'
Bomut
Shali
Urus-Martan
North Ossetia
Alagir
Vladikavkaz
Kirovauya
Sovetskoye
approximate boundary
CAUCASUS MOUNTAINS
Argun
Assa
Mqinvartsveri (Kazbek) 16,558 ft 5,047 m
Botlikh
GEORGIA
Andiyskoye Koysu
Avarskoye Koysu
P'asanauri
Dagestan
RUSSIA
Karachay-Cherkessia
Kabardino-Balkaria
Ingushetia
North Ossetia
Chechnya
Dagestan
Black Sea
GEORGIA
T'BILISI
TURKEY
ARMENIA
YEREVAN
AZERBAIJAN
0 100 Kilometers
0 100 Miles

735708 (R00672) 5-95

Nor law, nor duty bade me fight,
Nor public men, nor cheering crowds,
A lonely impulse of delight
Drove to this tumult in the clouds;
I balanced all, brought all to mind,
The years to come seemed waste of breath,
A waste of breath the years behind
In balance with this life, this death.

W.B. Yeats, 'An Irish Airman Foresees His Death'

MY WAR GONE BY,
I MISS IT SO

Prologue: The Forest

Srebrenica, Summer 1996

There were places among the crowded trees where the birdsong dropped away to nothing, shaded clearings with a sound vacuum: once you had stepped in no noise could reach you from the outside world except the rustling summer breeze, and you did not want to listen to that too carefully, for if you were alone your mind began to play tricks and it was more than just the grass that you heard whispering.

The bones lay strewn for miles through this woodland, paper-chasing a rough path eastwards across the hills from Srebrenica, the trail breaking then restarting in a jumbled profusion where a last stand had been made or a group of those too wounded or exhausted to go on had been found. The whole area was saturated with the legacy of the killing. There were mass graves in the valleys where prisoners had been herded, executed, then covered with a casual layer of earth which one year later was still heavy and reeking with decay. Elsewhere, more poignantly, there were solitary skeletons hidden in the undergrowth, individuals who had tried to make it out alone but had been hunted down and their lives chopped or shot from them. Even the roadsides bore tributes to the events of the previous summer. Beside one junction a skeleton in a pinstripe suit lay tangled around a concrete post. Among the bundle of collapsed bones fast being reclaimed to the earth by brambles and moss you could see that the man's arms had been bound to the post with wire. Whatever had happened to him, it was unlikely to have been quick or painless.

If a chart could be made of ways to die then Srebrenica's dead had ticked off most of the options. Some had gone by their own hand in panicking despair; others in confused gunbattles with their own troops or those of the enemy; many more had surrendered, taking a last long walk in the summer sun to stand in rows with their comrades, the languid working of machine-gun bolts behind them the final sound they heard, except perhaps for a few last whispered words of love or contrition.

The Serbs avoided the forest whenever they could. There was still a heavy cult of the dead in the villages of eastern Bosnia, a belief that the spirit hung around the body after death. So the last thing a Serb woodsman would want to do was go into those dark woods alone, especially as most of the locals were, at the very least, complicit in the orgy of killing that had gone on beneath the canopy of leaves.

It was not only the Serbs who got the spooks. A recce troop of US soldiers from the NATO forces in Bosnia had been tasked to secure the site of a mass grave so that war crimes investigators could carry out an exhumation. More than a hundred Muslim dead lay buried in the slope of a bank capped by an earthen track leading to the hamlet of Cerska, one of numerous clusters of broken, long-abandoned buildings that huddled within the trees. The Americans were not really expecting trouble, but if it came then fire would be met and – as their staff sergeant stated in a way that left no room for doubt – 'most certainly overwhelmed' with fire. They had a large array of hardware with them which if put to use could have levelled most of the remaining hamlet ruins and a lot of the forest. Somehow, though, it was the staff sergeant himself who seemed their most threatening asset. He was a large man, down to his last few months in the army, and everything he did and said was coated with the slick confidence and assuredness you find in men comfortably affiliated with taking life in a professional way. He had been a paratrooper for his first tour of Vietnam, a doorgunner with the aircav for his second. His men called him the Anti-Christ and unflinchingly obeyed his every instruction, while senior officers moved about him with wary respect.

Yet on the first night of their task, when the time came to send a foot patrol out into the trees, a tall black trooper from Mississippi refused to get out of his Humvee. He said he could hear voices coming from the bottom of the bank where the work of the investigators had scraped away the topsoil to uncover the first few bones. His mama had told him all about that stuff back in Mississippi, he told the staff sergeant. He would soldier against any enemy anywhere in the world, but there was no weapon in their arsenal big enough to deal with what he heard going down at the bottom of the bank.

The other men sort of laughed, but it was a dry sound that quickly faded into the night. There was none of the usual ragging and they shuffled their feet drawing unseen patterns in the stones of the track, not catching one another's eyes. The black trooper chewed his lower lip, hung his head and held out his hands. 'No, Staff,' he mumbled, 'I am not fucking around with you.'

A less experienced commander would have made an issue of it, forcing the trooper into a position where he would refuse to soldier and his fear would spark among the other men, clouding the mission in the days and nights ahead. But the staff sergeant did not have to prove his authority and, more pertinently, understood the way superstition can grip soldiers in the field. There are certain vibes that even the most modernized army in the world ignores at its peril. So he made the trooper hold his own gaze, broke the connection himself for a few seconds to look into the forest, then looked back into the frightened man's eyes. He ordered the man up to take over the .50 cal mounted on the Humvee and sent the white boys out into the trees. The pressure subsided so fast you could hear it hiss.

The war had been over for nine months. There was still enough of it in the atmosphere to fuel my memories and feed a sorrowful nostalgia. I reran the reels of the past four years through my mind feeling depressed, constantly seeking out friends to post-mortem the whole thing again and again in the hope of recapturing even a tiny part of its heady glowing rush, of putting it into some kind of context. The Muslim dead who still lay where they had been killed afforded a direct transfusion back to those times, a link that juiced up the whole engine again.

For several days I watched the work of the war crimes team as they dug at Cerska, my brain ceaselessly delving into the past like a tongue probing an ulcer. The smell and the flies got worse each hour but it was the patronizing tone of the team's spokesman that finally did for me. He seemed incapable of communicating without delivering some holier-than-thou aside, twinning piety with pathology in a mix that would have had a saint reaching for a bucket to throw up in. He could make the connection between the victims at the bottom of the bank and the absent killers that pulled the triggers. Anyone could do that bit. However, the links fell apart between himself and 'the beasts' he demonized. He seemed to think it took something really special to kill prisoners.

It was always difficult when people who had not been in the war started voicing their opinions on it. While I loathe the way some men act as if they are a kind of higher being simply because they have seen a bit of action, nothing is guaranteed to anger me more than some Johnny-come-lately who turns up when it is all over and starts getting large with the hows and whys. Listen to some of the revisionist junk being spouted by the post-conflict generation of journalists and NATO representatives in Sarajevo and you begin to wonder if they are even talking about the same war.

So when a friend of mixed American and Yugoslav blood asked me if I would like to go back into the forest with him to find the body of a relative, I readily agreed. Anything was better than listening to the war crimes spokesman. My friend was fine company, having hung out in Bosnia for much of the war, which meant I could be sure that he would not grate my nerves with sermonizing. He had a Yugoslav's insight and New York humour; throwaway slang and expletives rolled through his dialogue in a combination that cracked you up, the more so as the speaker appeared completely oblivious to how funny they were. A survivor of Srebrenica had given him directions of where his wife's cousin was last seen, apparently already wounded and being carried by two others. Yet the details were typically vague. Never ask a Bosnian where something is. The answer will either be a riddle that takes hours to unravel, or such an unformed generalization you feel embarrassed to ask for further clues.

And so it was that the friend and I ended up stumbling around in a vast segment of forest looking for 'a fallen tree'. Of course we never found the dead relative, though there were scores of others there. The dead have never lost their fascination for me.

There was a time at the beginning of the war when my curiosity had often been tempered with sorrow, shock or horror at the sight of the state of bodies. Brutal mutilation would stick in my eyes like a thorn for days, or else the expression or posture of a corpse would evoke sadness and anger within me. But as you lose count of the number of dead you have seen, a hidden threshold of sensitivity is raised, neutralizing most of your reactions. Only the curiosity remains. Some of it is borne out of my inability to connect the thought of a living, breathing person with the discarded husk death leaves, even when I have seen the whole transition from life to death. There is no God behind me, and I have strong doubts concerning the existence of a soul these days, but when I look at a corpse it always seems as if there is more than simply life missing. There have been a few disturbing exceptions when death gives more than it takes. I once saw a dead Russian girl. In her early twenties, long haired and lithe, she had caught a bit of shrapnel in her chest, one of those tiny wounds that you would not believe could take a life but does. In death the rude sun-burnish went from her skin, retreating before an ethereal blue glow. Alive she was strikingly pretty. Dead she was so beautiful you could have raised an army to sack Troy just for possession of her casket. I had not wanted to look too far into that reaction within me and walked away from her presence, unnerved for days.

Many of the dead in the forest had their ID cards with them, scattered by looters around their bones, and the one-dimensional black and white faces on the photographs seemed so abstract as to be almost irrelevant. But even if their owners had still been alive, those ID pictures would probably have been obsolete. Anyone who stayed in Bosnia during the war had their face change on a level beyond the purely physical. Even the war crimes spokesman might have had something different glowing in his eyes had he been there when it was all on. It would be so trite, so inappropriate to say that the eyes lost something as they witnessed the whole madness of it all, to talk of empty stares and children with hollow gazes. But it was not what people lost in Bosnia that you noticed in their eyes, it was what some of them gained. Whether it is your own or someone else's, the taste of evil leaves an indelible mark on the iris. You can see it flickering in moments of introspection as the muscles relax. I do not know if I would have recognized the pre-war picture on my own ID card – the open baby face, tousled hair and curious innocence – had I seen it lying on the forest floor that day. I find that man almost a stranger now.

The sun sank lower in the sky, the shadows deepened and my mood darkened. I had only been clean for a few days, kicking my heels through a succession of sleepless nights in a hotel in Tuzla and, as always in the opiate backblast, I felt raw and hyper-sensitized, thoughts surging and abating like the swell of the sea. I have sweated through withdrawal in a variety of obscure war-torn hovels, but that forest had to be one of the strangest.

My friend kept talking but my responses grew more distant. Their dead; my dead; necro-fascinations and gravediggers that did not get it at all; nationalism, fascism, level killing fields and equal guilt; all the crap you hear talked about Bosnia. You can break it down and build it up any way you want, throw on the cloak of interventionist or appeaser and spout the same words in a different order to broker your justifications for whatever standpoint you wish until you sicken yourself just thinking about it; pull up those bones like a Meccano set and make whatever you want of them until you find it is they, the dead, that are pulling your strings. You have to relinquish a lot until the reckoning comes, you snap off a twig in time, examine it and realize it's just the relationship between yourself, killers and victims that counts.

Look some more and you see there is not much gulf at all between the three. Close your eyes, open your fingers and discover you are a hybrid. Open your eyes again, look in a mirror and someone else looks back: someone older and degraded. People call it wisdom but it is just a substitute for hope.

Before he took an icy dive into the Miljacka River and out of my life, Momćilo had once explained to me the mentality of Bosnia's killers in a few short words: 'In the morning they hate themselves, in the afternoon the world.' So, Momćilo, where are you now? For your words come from a different time, a Neverland era long past when it was all so different. Did you take that swim before the words applied to you as well? You might have warned me.

Faces, sounds and lights began to move in my mind over the dark screen of the foliage; there was the crackle of flames and screech of shellfire; Darko and The Jokers; an old woman with her broken teeth falling bloodily down her chest; a girl's severed ear; the last letter in its blue envelope; Hamdu, the Tigers and the final attack; frightened soldiers, the reek of smoke and clatter of a gunship. My war gone by, I miss it so.

1

There was a Bosnian government army sniper positioned in one of the top floors of the burned-out tower block overlooking the Serbs in Grbavica. He was audio landmark to our days. We lived in the street below at the edge of Sarajevo's ruined parliament building in a small strip of the city sandwiched between the front-line Miljacka River and the wide expanse of Vojvode Putnika, the street dubbed Snipers' Alley soon after the war began. The area had a few benefits but they were purely relative in the overall scheme of Sarajevo's war.

Our proximity to the Serbs meant that they were seldom able to bring down heavy artillery fire upon us for fear of dropping short and hitting their own troops on the other side of the small river. The tight clustering of buildings afforded protection from automatic fire, provided you knew which alleys to run across and were not unlucky with a mortar round. It was only if you chose to leave the claustrophobic confines of this narrow template in search of food or as a release from the stifling boredom that your troubles really began. There was no way around it, if you wanted to go anywhere else in the capital you had to deal with Vojvode Putnika. Empty your mind, fill your lungs and kick out for the centre knowing that if it happened then you would not hear it, merely get smashed forward onto your face by a mighty punch. Some people never bothered to leave the area. They waited for others to bring them food, growing paler and madder with frustration by the day. Others never bothered running. They said that they were fatalists but I think they were just tired of living, exhausted by the mental effort of dealing with the random nature of the violence. Kalashnikov rounds and shrapnel might have been the city's new gods but there was no need to hand them your destiny on a plate. Even so, however fast you beat the ground you knew that it would never be faster than a speeding bullet. But most of us kept making the effort anyway, hoping it would cut us a bit of leeway with the reactions of the men on the hills above us.

I was sitting with Endre with my back to the wall of our house. It was late morning and the March sun was high and moving slowly south-west, leaving us in the wedged shadow of the building. We were indulging in Sarajevo's greatest wartime activity: smoking and hanging around hoping nothing would happen to us but that something would happen somewhere, anywhere, to break the monotony and give us a sense of time progressing, of anything progressing. The war had been going on for nearly a year and had no end in sight. The city's inhabitants were sinking into a sense of hopelessness which was catching, even for a foreigner with a way out. Our conversation followed the usual pattern: I asked lots of questions to try to get my head around the situation while Endre, a Hungarian Yugoslav, listened attentively and then began his answer. He did it the same way each time. 'Well, Antonio,' he would open ponderously, 'it's like this . . .' The sudden bullwhip crack of a bullet interrupted us and we looked at the tower block. The government sniper was obviously back up there, though we could not see him, and had taken a pop at something he had seen across the river.

The two sides of the tower visible from our position almost never changed their appearance: the front was a wide expanse of black and twisted window frames, the southern side a concrete Emmental of shellholes from tanks. There was only one time I can remember it ever looking different. Some Muslim soldiers had crawled up to the top at night and unfurled a long banner down the side of the building that directly faced the Serbs. 'DON'T WORRY BE HAPPY' it read vertically in letters each a metre high. The Serbs shot it to ribbons the next morning. I could never work out if this meant that they had got the joke or not.

After a few seconds' silence our conversation continued. Then another shot rang out. Endre paused again, this time raising an index finger in expectation of something. Across the river a machine-gun fired a burst back towards the tower, its dull popping sound following only after the whacking of the bullets chipped off bits of concrete in harmless-looking grey puffs above us. Still Endre held up his finger, waiting for something else. Again the sniper fired, only this time there was a scant second between the crack of his shot and great explosive smashings and sparks as an anti-aircraft gun riddled the top storeys of the tower in a nerve-jangling roll of sound. Silence followed the last detonation. The sniper would not fire again that day. Endre lowered his finger and turned to me smiling. 'Well, Antonio,' he began, 'that is what we call "educating fire".'

*   *   *

11

Sarajevo was a schooling such as I have never had. At the time of Endre's words I had been in the city only a short while and still knew almost nothing of war though the subsequent days queued packed in line to throw their rocks into the still pool of my naïvety.

Aside from the deeper reasons behind my being there, my path to the Bosnian capital was marked in equal parts by co-incidence and intent, milestones which stretched from a prophetic warning on the day Tito died over a decade before to a stoned conversation with a Serb deserter in Marrakech in the late spring of 1991. By the summer of 1992 I had finished a post-graduate course in photojournalism. My CV, updated with the new qualification, swarmed through London mailboxes. I wasted four months before giving up on a response. There was no specific moment when I suddenly resolved to go to Bosnia alone, though I do remember having felt an accelerating motiva-tion earlier that year when transfixed by a photograph in a British newspaper of a Serb fighter, cigarette in one hand, kick-ing a dead Muslim civilian in a town called Bijeljina. The photographer himself was to have a part in the final endgame of my war experience, but that was far away then; part of a future I could not have even guessed at.

I knew if I went I would not have much money with me, certainly not enough to hire an interpreter, so I rang up the Serb restaurant in Notting Hill and asked if there was anyone there who could teach me Serbo-Croatian. A surprised voice the other end of the line agreed to meet me at Notting Hill tube to discuss the prospect. Waiting for the rendezvous there as bedraggled commuters hurried in silent groups past me in the cold gloom of the winter evening I saw a beautiful girl waiting by the station's entrance. She had long straight hair that fell halfway down her back, its blackness matched only by the dark of her eyes, and was smoking a cigarette, hauling deeply on it as if it was the last she had. Mima was from Novi Sad. Her mother was Croatian, her father Serbian. She had left Yugoslavia to escape the sanctions, and hated the Milošević regime. She agreed to try to teach me the rudiments of her language. Her advice on Bosnia she repeated to me like a mantra throughout most of our evening lessons: 'There are some very crazy people there. Very crazy. Most of the intellectuals have left. The scum have risen to the surface. You must be very, very careful.' The last lesson was different. She asked me if I would marry her as the Home Office was giving her grief.

In the New Year and with the end of winter in sight I felt ready for what lay ahead, my formless concept of war. Mima introduced me to some friends of hers in Hammersmith, Omar and Isidora, a Muslim–Serb couple from Sarajevo. Isidora's parents still remained in the city. She asked me if I would take a parcel of medicine and money together with some letters to them, and told me that if I wished to stay in their flat I would be a welcome guest. She drew me a little sketch map of the city, X marking their house. The X was a little close to the thick red line she had used to indicate the front line but it seemed rude to bring that up at the time. Sarajevo seemed an obvious place to begin my journey and I was glad to be given a contact there.

However, I still waited hopefully for an employer to end the drumroll of my preparations. The thought of going off to a war without the cloak of a professional guise was a little unnerving. Without a contract there would be no aim to fulfil other than my own, and that was fairly vague: merely to go to war using, if possible, journalism as an open-ended ticket to remain in Bosnia for as long as I wished. I felt I needed at least some kind of contractual blessing to go, some practical and mental safety net to justify myself if it all went wrong. None came. I was left having to face the full responsibility of my own actions.

Two friends from college were leaving London for Moldova in a battered Skoda, hardly the golden chariot of my dreams. They were driving via Budapest, which was not far from the Croatian border. I tried to balance reason to produce an answer that would tell me 'Go'. I failed. My plan was not reasonable. So I thought fuck it and went anyway, throwing my bags into the Skoda one cold morning. It was not a decision that had anything to do with courage, but more an absolution of self-responsibility, a releasing of myself into the hands of chance.

The journey across Europe in the Skoda passed like a week-long Last Supper culminating in a seedy but otherwise empty bar in Budapest where my two friends and I got drunk together before going our separate ways. At some stage in the evening the juke-box had fired into life as if operated by an unseen hand and a young Hungarian girl walked in and up to our table. She wore a short black dress, had slanted green cat's eyes, pale skin and blue-black hair so clean it smelled like gun metal. Without a word she beckoned me up, put her arms around me, pulled me close and began to dance, swaying slowly to U2's 'Cruel'. I felt young and lucky. It seemed like we danced like that for a long time in absolute silence before the music stopped, I sat down and she smiled and walked out of the door. I try to fight superstition with the power of reason, but with the drink and smoke and significance of that last night I could not help but feel that she was some ghostly omen of good fortune. Then again, maybe she was just bored and between tricks.

From then on I was alone, taking trains and buses until I reached Split on the Dalmatian coast. At the UN office in the airport I flashed around a covering letter of accreditation made out by a friend in London which suggested I was a photographer. In return I was given a UN press card, the ticket for passage on a Hercules flying aid into the besieged Bosnian capital. I had no conception of mortal fear then, just apprehension at what lay ahead.

There was no slow spiralling of descent. The plane just nose-dived suddenly and through one of the windows I saw Sarajevo rising up beneath us. Acres of small ruined houses marked the western end of the capital, giving way to a narrow linear run of taller buildings and apartment blocks caught between high ridges of ground to the north and south. From the ruined airport complex a Ukrainian APC took me to the PTT building, the city's central communications centre and at the time a main UN base. From there onwards my UN press card lost its power. There were a couple of young Frenchmen from an aid organization waiting around at the PTT so I asked if I could ride with them back to the city centre. I tried to appear nonchalant as nothing invites refusal so fast as the smell of innocence. Though I clutched the dog-eared sketch map given to me in London by Isidora, it seemed a better idea to check into the Holiday Inn, then Sarajevo's one functioning hotel, for the first night in the city. There I could at least work out my bearings and get a feel for what was going on before I blundered into trouble. The Frenchmen eyed my baggage warily for a minute, then loaded it into their car. We roared off at speed and in silence, the city rushing past me on either side of the straight road in a dirty grey blur.

The war was the best thing that could have happened to the Holiday Inn. It had given a token vestige of character to what would have otherwise been the twin sister to a motorway service station: an empty, ugly transit centre of soullessness encased in a square of lurid yellow and brown paint, complete with terrible food and grumpy staff. Though the southern face was un-inhabitable due to the damage inflicted upon it by the Serbs across the Miljacka, it was a safe enough place to stay. There was either some tacit understanding within the Serb command that the hotel was the focal point of the media in Sarajevo and should be left untouched or possibly there was a deal to ensure its security. Occasionally a government sniper would use the top floor or roof as a position, provoking more 'educating fire' in response, but by and large it was untouched after its initial baptism. I got a room and lay on the bed smiling with delight. I was there. At last, a real full-on war and I was in it. As if on cue a burst of automatic fire rippled away elsewhere in the city. I laughed and laughed. It meant nothing to me and I did not understand what it might mean to anyone else.

I knew that I would have to get across Vojvode Putnika somehow to find Isidora's family, but was not exactly sure what happened on the other side as the details on the map were vague. However, the next morning a young man hanging around in the hotel foyer offered to take me to the address. Jasmin asked for nothing in return, and even when I later offered him a bit of cash he refused it determinedly. Those who have never been there may have the impression that Bosnia was simply a morass of hatred and killing. At times it could be. But it is the only place I have been to in the world where I know as an absolute certainty that if I stopped in a strange town, night or day, within an hour I would be accepted as a guest in someone's house, fed whatever food they had and plied with drink, with no expectation of anything in return. As long as you stayed clear of topics such as religion, war or politics, hospitality was seldom a problem in the Balkans. But, though Jasmin may have given me my first glimpse of Bosnian warmth, he also gave me an insight into their irrational obstinacy. As we walked to the edge of the hotel, our final cover before Snipers' Alley, he told me that he would not run across to the other side, explaining that he 'never ran for those people'. Even as a newcomer I could see that Vojvode Putnika was certainly a place to run if anywhere was: not a soul in sight, the empty road littered with debris and the Serbs only a few hundred metres away on the high ground overlooking us. It would not need the skill of a sniper to kill us, anyone who could pull a trigger could have managed it.

I was in a dilemma. To run across alone would be unforgivably rude and craven in the face of Jasmin's kindness. Yet to walk the stretch and risk being shot on the first day for the sake of politesse seemed equally stupid. The compromise was uncomfortable and a little ridiculous: as he strolled slowly across, face raised to the hills, I kept abreast of him walking sideways like a crab, first one way and then the other, hoping that anyone who wanted to shoot us would take out the easy target first.

We reached the other side and, after ducking through a narrow alleyway, walked through the door of a large four-storey house, its façade a bubbling plane of peeling plaster. Inside, the stairwell was dark and cool and for some minutes we used matches to check the names on doors as we ascended the stone stairs. Isidora's parents were not overly surprised when we finally knocked on their door. The war had bred a particular ingenuity to all who remained stuck in its confines and somehow, through a Gordian knot of communication I did not really understand that involved ham radio and distant phone connections, warning of my possible arrival had reached them from London. And as an entity from the outside world, part of a peaceful normality Sarajevo had long lost sight of, and a link to their family in London, I was welcomed like the prodigal son. They clutched at me for news from the outside and I felt the inadequacy of the half-learned language I had picked up from Mima. For the first but not the last time, I found myself moved by something in that flat. As they tore open the letters that had accompanied the small parcel, there was a few minutes' silence during which I felt a strange emotion welling within me. It was difficult to define and carried with it a sense of great awkwardness and humility. Suddenly I felt very sad, a feeling I struggled to explain to myself while the skin on my back shivered as if with presentiment.

Three people lived in the flat. Isidora's father, Petar, was a Serb from Montenegro who had lived in Sarajevo for twenty-eight years. As a partisan during the Second World War he had fought everybody, he told me later, Četniks, Ustaša, Italians and Germans, and raised his hands to click the trigger of an imaginary rifle as he explained. He was sixty-eight years old, but could have passed for much younger, small and compact with fitness, his black hair betraying hardly a trace of grey. His eyes shone with an energy I never saw diminish until a moment three years later. Even then it was only to dim for a second. He was a mathematician, as eccentric and stubborn as anyone in the Balkans. There was no way he was leaving his house for any war, even if it was on his doorstep. Yet it was obvious even in those first few minutes of meeting that his wife, Yelena, was not so easily able to resist the pressures of the conflict. She was a Serb born in Croatia, and there was a great sadness about her, visible in her downcast eyes, the paleness of her skin, and the way she tilted her head wistfully to one side as she spoke. Afraid and deeply depressed, she had only left that little street twice in the eleven months since the war had started.

With a face like a young decadent David Bowie, thin frame and slick mop of black hair, the third figure in the room lounged in a threadbare armchair, cigarette dangling precariously between long fingers, looking like the Thin White Duke obscurely transplanted from an underground Berlin nightclub. Momćilo was some kind of cousin, thirty-five years old, a natural ally who for me came to embody the spirit of resistance to the war and its madness, a quality that you found in ever dwindling numbers of

18

people as time went by and most were forced into taking one side or another by the erosive propaganda, or else just ground down by the energy and pain required to keep an open mind. He had fled from his hometown of Cisak in Croatia when the war started there in 1991, for although he was a Serb, Momćilo wanted to fight for neither side. He had escaped to Sarajevo, seeing it as a bastion of multi-ethnicity that no war could ever reach, a misjudgement he still laughed over when I first met him. He spent his mornings selling copies of *Oslobođenje* at a point near the state hospital, which meant he had to run the gauntlet of Vojvode Putnika every day, though ironically the bullet he had taken in the calf he had gained collecting firewood on the other side of the house. In the afternoons he hustled for black-market deals or short cuts in the handout of aid, always with one eye cocked for opportunity, the other for the approach of the army press-gangs that stalked the city. He was one of Bosnia's natural survivors and quickly became my 'droog', comrade, my guide and mentor.

Their flat was a one-level affair with seven rooms, two of which had a direct view of the front line. These were bullet-scarred and had been unused since the start of the fighting. The main room, in which we spent most of our time, moved in an L shape through an incongruous circular arch of Sixties-style architecture. At one end of it was a small kitchen and dining area, around the corner some chairs and a gas stove. Outside, snow still lay on the ground in icy grey scabs. The warmth of the small stove with its sometimes feckless flame became the focus of our conversations with the coming of darkness each night.

The local community was predictably close-knit under the circumstances and of such mixed religious definition as to deny you the possibility of making any judgement as to who – Serb, Muslim or Croat – made up the predominant group. At this stage of the war there were still up to 60,000 Serbs living in Sarajevo, a little under a quarter of the total population that remained. Some had joined the government army and fought bravely alongside their Muslim neighbours against what they saw as the forces of nationalist aggression that threatened their beloved city; others, including Petar, remained because they did not want to leave their homes and hoped the war would end soon; a lesser number actively sympathized with the men who shelled the city but were trapped in their houses by the gelling of the front lines that had encircled the capital.

Our discussions around the stove were a forum for arguments from every strand of the spectrum and frequently became hot-tempered affairs of raised voices and wild gesticulations. At this time I had no real foundation for an opinion of my own concerning the war. Of course it was obvious that the city was suffering, and that terrible deeds were being committed elsewhere in Bosnia. Yet my impressions of the conflict prior to my arrival had been moulded by Mima's tutoring and in general she blamed all sides equally. So in debates I acted as a kind of muted umpire. Angrier exchanges were often halted as if to protect my sensibilities, bestowing me somehow with a passifying role. I listened with interest to what I heard.

Momćilo was in favour of foreign intervention and massive air strikes upon the Serb forces around the city. He was convinced that this would bring the war to an early close, leaving some hope for a continued form of co-existence between the various religious denominations. He was supported in this opinion by Endre, a friend and neighbour whose knowledge of the English language helped me to grasp details in the debates that otherwise would have been lost on me. However, Endre was not in favour of lifting the arms embargo that hamstrung the Bosnian government's ability to fight. He believed that the consequent withdrawal of UN troops would lead to an immediate Serb retaliation that would swiftly overrun Sarajevo's fragile defence lines. Petar opposed both air strikes and the lifting of the arms embargo. He said either move would lengthen and intensify the war. Though he was no lover of the political or military strategy that emanated from Pale, the ski resort town east of Sarajevo that the Bosnian Serbs had styled their 'capital', in his heart he was a Yugoslav, and division of that creation was not something he saw as desirable. If pushed, his loyalties lay ultimately with the Serbs.

The city's war was a strange experience, far more abstract than I had expected. First, you never saw the 'enemy'. The metal that scythed through people's lives came as sudden barrages of noise and dust, combustions of energy that it was hard to equate with invisible men pulling triggers or cords. As the days slipped into weeks there were times when we could laugh it off from the sanctuary of our seven-room womb. Petar would chuckle and nod his head from side to side as a gunbattle grew in intensity outside, while Momćilo would roll his eyes and smile, as if to say 'same old shit again'. We were seldom hungry, though the quality of the food we had varied tremendously. Sometimes, if Momćilo had linked up with one of his contacts inside an aid distribution centre, we would find a meal of pasta, meat and eggs as we gathered in candlelight around the dining-room table. At others we supplemented the handouts with whatever we could gather in the overgrown gardens that bordered the surrounding buildings, on one particular evening enjoying a real delicacy of boiled stinging nettles and fried snails. There were nights when Yelena could offer little more than a lump of hot fat, and we would slither the greasy chunks onto our plates trying not to catch each other's eyes.

But war is not dismissed so easily. There were times when our feelings changed, as if synchronized by a hidden clock, and the noise of the fighting outside reached into us. Except for Yelena's murmurs we would stare at the burning ash of our cigarettes or into the gas stove as bullets and shrapnel whacked into the walls of the house, clawing at our moods, drawing us into a dark shadowland where we existed only as helpless beings whose sole aim seemed to be to shoulder the grim, sometimes fearful tedium of just getting by, carry on living until something so far away as to be invisible arrived and altered things.

For me there was always a way out. I could go to the airport, flash that UN ID card and get on a plane to Split. I could be in London the same day if I timed it right, and that knowledge protected me from the despair that affected Sarajevo's people. But it was not a move I wished or chose to take, and in the close proximity of that flat, sharing their life with them, I found myself susceptible at least to the moods and emotions of the people with whom I lived. After a time I discarded the bullet-proof vest I had bought in London. I had worn it because I was aware that it was easy to die in those streets – especially as a stranger new to the rules of the fighting – and realized that life was not something to be treated flippantly there. Yet I soon found it more of a barrier, in my own mind at least, between myself and those who befriended me than between my body and bullets. Its heavy weight ceased to be reassuring and instead brought only shame to me in the presence of people I knew, people who had no avenue of escape. I began to leave it in the room in which I slept, where it finally gathered dust.

On the streets outside, however, the war's lessons were less subliminal; harder, more immediate physical entities. Within a few days of arriving I was shot at. With my growing confidence I had walked off alone to see the old town. Sarajevo was then only a vague series of impressions in my mind. I wanted to know it better. Names of places and hills were still alien, as was the overall physical perspective of the city, which I had only glimpsed during the first day for a few seconds through the window of the Hercules. As a pedestrian you seldom travelled anywhere directly, but took instead a zigzagging route that gave you cover from fire.

I approached a junction where two old women were preparing to leave the corner of a building. They presented a fairly comical sight, both small and round with fat, slightly bowed, their bodies encased in thick black coats drawn across their stomachs with long belts of material to keep out the cold. Between them they pulled a child's wooden cart laden with potatoes.

Their shuffling pace did not alter as they left the cover of the wall and stepped into the open intersection. Momćilo had already advised me to run across this area because it presented a clear gallery to the Serbs in the buildings to the south. I broke into a jog and had nearly drawn parallel to the old women and their cart when around me the still winter air broke into a cacophony of fluttering zings, smacks and whistles. There were sparks on the tarmac, a sudden cloud of dust from the wall that provided a backdrop; a small wheel blew off the cart and chips of potato flew everywhere.

It was over in seconds. I passed the old women at speed. They seemed incapable of going any faster and steadfastly refused to relinquish their grip on the cart which now scraped along the ground on three wheels. Puffing and swearing indignantly, they joined me as I stood on the leeside of the distant wall. I felt outraged. Someone had just tried to kill me for no reason at all. I was not even carrying a gun. They had also shot at two people whose silhouettes, whatever the range, can have suggested nothing other than what they were – a couple of old bags pulling a go-cart. I expected the women to share my surprise, recrimination and anger. Yet they barely looked at me. They examined their cart for a second, said 'yoy' and 'fuck', 'fuck it', 'fuck him' and 'fuck his father', swore 'on his mother's cunt', then said 'yoy' again a few times before trundling off dragging their scraping burden behind them. The women's indifference annoyed me even more than the gunman's bullets but when I told the story to Momćilo he simply smiled tolerantly, shrugged and opened out his hands, palms up. 'It's like that now,' he laughed. 'It's . . . normal.'

Sarajevo's 'normality' came in many guises. The city was full of hidden traps, structures of power and allegiance that were far from obvious, even to those who lived there. The fighting had first broken, then obliterated the old hierarchy of authority and social structure. Within weeks of the outbreak of war, while the lines of confrontation were still fluid, thousands of people had fled the city, to be replaced by refugees from rural areas who brought a new brand of culture to the capital and with it new tensions. In the absence of a professional army, the only groups with any real organization, weapons or structure were the city's criminal gangs, and so they took over the task of defence. For a long time the government's strategy was in the hands of men like Juka Prazina, Ćelo and Saco: hard, enigmatic criminals with localized cult followings and a taste for killing. Later that year, battles would be waged not across trenchlines with the Serbs, but within Sarajevo itself as the government sought to wrest control from the hands of these splintered mafia groups by establishing a central, legitimate body using loyalist special forces and police groups.

In the meantime these urban barons and their subordinates held supreme power. Usually it was easy to spot the men of authority as they moved around the city with their cortèges of bodyguards, but there were exceptions. One afternoon, as I returned home from my wanderings, the streets' atmosphere changed – as it so often did before something bad happened. Sometimes the change came with no warning at all, but usually there was a sudden sensation of unease, a brooding electricity that emptied the pavements of people. The sense of foreboding mounted in intensity, like the gathering movement of an orchestra, the pressure and silence cranking your nerves until you were almost desperate for the noise to rend it all open again. The feeling was soundless but it crackled. You could not see it, but it was black. Then it would come: the double concussion-sound kerrump of shellfire and the air-cutting crack of bullets. It almost brought you relief but it had a reverse side: times, stretching to a week, when as if by unspoken agreement everybody knew it was safe to promenade down Sarajevo's thoroughfares in full view of the Serbs. Such periods would inevitably end in blood and weeping as the resumption of fighting would reap inordinate casualties among the vulnerable crowds.

I hurried into the ruined Bosnian parliament building for cover, lit a cigarette and waited. Inside there was the usual huddle of soldiers – they too silent and smoking – and a new unit of men in black uniforms who formed a group of their own in the shadows. Explosions erupted from behind the twin Unis towers to our north, followed quickly by heavy automatic- and rifle-fire to the east. Once it had begun the tension subsided and the soldiers began to talk in lowered voices among themselves and someone laughed. A couple of the black-clad strangers approached me to ask who I was and what I was doing. There was no menace in their words, merely curiosity, and they seemed happy enough with my answers. But then a small fat man wearing a pink T-shirt, camouflage trousers and bedroom slippers walked up. He was unarmed but carried a walkie-talkie. He jabbered away at the two fighters too quickly for me to understand, stabbing his finger in my direction to emphasize his words. The two soldiers changed, becoming cold and formal. 'Where are your papers?' they demanded. I showed them my passport and a Bosnian accreditation card I had picked up but this did little to satisfy them.

The fat man in the pink T-shirt continued talking. It seemed obvious to me that he was just some insignificant troublemaker who had nothing better to do than sow suspicion in the minds of bored troops. I weighed up the odds and decided that a display of resolution might restore things in my favour; he seemed the sort of loud-mouthed bully who would wither in the face of confrontation. I took a breath, rounded on him sharply and told him to 'fuck off'.

The bullets were still raining down outside as two of the soldiers carted me off to the police station. As the fat man's shouting receded into the distance the men dropped their hostility, though there was no point arguing with them. One held my arm above the elbow but his grip was not hard, more like that of a B-movie villain hustling someone into a car, knowing that he has a gun in his pocket to back up the authority of his fingers.

The door to the police station was on the other side of the road. Behind us was the ongoing gunfight, and the overspill of Serb fire smacked around the doorway and pavement outside. A car slewed round the corner with a mixture of policemen and soldiers inside, took two rounds in the door, then bounced off the kerb as it squealed away. We stopped and my arm was released. The soldiers looked at each other then across the road at the doorway. I could not believe that they were considering crossing the road to reach it. 'Listen,' I said, realizing the whole misunderstanding was getting out of control, 'we can sort all this out later. Why don't we just go back to the parliament building, have a smoke and return when this is all over?' The man who had held my arm looked like he might have gone for my suggestion, but the quizzical glance he gave to his companion drew only a shaken head in response. Whatever authority the little pink shit had was obviously greater than the fear of the Serb fire. No-one said anything for a second as we all looked at the far wall and its narrow door while the fire still sung around us. 'When we say run, then run, you understand?' one of the soldiers said. I immediately thought this was a sick plan conjured up by the fat man; on the given word it would be me alone who ran out into a hail of bullets – a bit like the final scene of *Butch Cassidy and the Sundance Kid*. But I had little choice. You can only argue so far with armed men. I grumbled without much hope that they had both better come with me, before one shouted, 'Run.'

The three of us belted across the road, for a second jamming together in the doorway in a tangle of thrashing limbs. It must have looked hysterically funny to the Serbs. Inside, anger lending me strength, I turned on them: 'I don't fucking believe you made me do that.' They just laughed, though the tinge of relief in it spoiled their display of bravado, offered me a cigarette and escorted me upstairs to an office.

I was invited to sit down by a stern-looking grey-haired police officer who sat the other side of a large wooden desk. He was wearing an immaculately pressed shirt and seemed to be of some rank, though since pink T-shirts and slippers obviously carried such clout I could not be sure whether the bars on his epaulettes meant anything. He asked me my name and a few other mundane details before starting to talk about London. He had a daughter who lived near Islington, he said, and had visited the city in the late Eighties. He asked if I liked Sarajevo and what I thought of the war. We talked in this way for about an hour before he smiled and said that unless there was anything else, I could go. Puzzled,

I told him that I thought I was under arrest, explained to him what had happened, right up to the road crossing, and said that I would need at least a letter from the police, some document I could produce in case of a similar incident. He waved a hand dismissively and shook his head. But what about the fat man, I said, who was he anyway? 'The commander,' I was told, as though that explained everything. As I got up, shook his hand and turned to leave, I asked who was in fact responsible for the parliament building area. He just looked at me, smiling like I was a dumb child too young to understand, and shrugged. 'Listen,' he told me with slow deliberation, 'these are difficult times here. Some of today's heroes are yesterday's criminals.' Then came the words I was to hear a thousand times during the conflict, the short-circuit dismissal of any attempt to analyse the confusion, the air of resignation accompanied by hunched shoulders and raised hands: 'What can you do?' he said. 'It's war.'

2

Marko was doing his best to kill somebody for my benefit. Twenty-four years old, trilingual, well educated, he was a sniper for the HOS, the extremist Croat militia which was still managing to maintain a loose affiliation with the government army in Sarajevo. We had met in the city's one remaining nightclub, the BB, a sweltering basement venue that afforded an outlet for easy pick-ups among Sarajevo's youth as the war stoked desire with one hand while unbuttoning restraint with the other. Curfew meant that once inside you were there until dawn unless prepared to risk a night in jail, a delight I had discovered once already in the continuing saga of my relationship with Bosnian 'law'. The black-market beer served at the bar was so foul it produced a hangover whose chemical legacy left its taste on your brain, and the fumes from the generator seemed to threaten mass asphyxiation, but for sheer atmosphere the BB was unsurpassed. The fashion accessories included Scorpion machine-pistols strapped to the ankle for the men, thigh-high black suede boots for the vampiresque women. On a good night there was even shellfire to pick up where the bass left off.

Despite such easy kicks the war was beginning to impress its cruelty upon me as I witnessed my first casualties prefiguring a darker incident that was to cause me finally to leave Sarajevo. There was a slow build-up to my initiation in the physical suffering of others. At a party given by some friends of Momćilo I had noticed the crutches stacked by the door where there should have been coats. There cannot have been more than twenty people in the room, but there were at least four pairs of crutches there, left by the wounded as they hobbled in to sit down. Casualty figures in Bosnia have become a bitter topic since the war ended. The claim of 250,000 dead is frequently contested, usually by quasi-academics who were never there but whose revisionist figures are glibly bandied about by politicos to justify and exonerate their policies of non-intervention. But if you stuck around long enough at the time, the dead and wounded piled up so quickly they squeezed one another off the narrow platforms of your memory.

Some children showed me my first body. I had bumped into them outside our house, a tough little street gang of ten-year-olds led by a kid with a revolver. We smoked for a while before one asked if I wanted to see a dead Četnik. They took me through a small labyrinth of looted flats on the front line, clambering over the toppled masonry and crunching glass before beckoning me towards a room. Torn blue curtains flapped idly in the breeze, gates to a frameless window that overlooked the Vrbanja Bridge and the Serb-held bank a mere stone's throw beyond. 'You must be quick,' they warned, 'or the snipers will get you,' and directed my gaze to a body lying in the roadway on the other side. It felt like I was sharing an odd childhood experience with them. At that distance the corpse was a shapeless lump in a military overcoat, though one swollen white hand was visible poking out of a sleeve. Later I asked Momćilo why the Serbs had not removed it under the cover of darkness. 'It's a very bad place,' he said, 'you send some men there at night to get one body, maybe in the morning there are three bodies.'

I saw my next casualties while talking to a doctor I had met in the state hospital. An elderly couple were rushed in on stretchers. They had been walking together in the old town and shot with an anti-aircraft gun. Great lumps had been blasted out of them leaving ghastly injuries, gaping wounds of bone sliver, blood and tattered flesh. The old man – he must have been over seventy – was moaning and trying to reach out to his wife who made a gurgling sound, like water going down a plughole. One of her legs seemed to be the wrong way round; the stretcher began to drip with blood as I watched. She was not going to live. It was the first mutilation of the body that I had ever seen, and stuck in my mind for a long time afterwards, an unwelcome memory that would spring up unannounced like a hideous blood-soaked jack-in-the-box. I felt as upset by their age as by their injuries. I imagined all the hurdles they must have navigated successfully to be able to stay together all their lives, then blam blam blam, someone blows them away with a gun designed to bring down a jet aircraft.

Even the dead were not beyond the gracelessness of the war. A few days after the shooting of the old couple I wandered into a funeral service. It was taking place on a football pitch that had been converted into a cemetery to cope with the excess of dead in the capital. I had never seen a Muslim funeral and I was curious so I attached myself, at a distance I thought respectful, to the cortège of twelve people. The body had not even been lowered into the ground when someone opened up on us with a machine-gun from a distant hillside. My memory recalls it as a frozen

31

moment of absolute stillness: a gravedigger on his belly before me staring upwards, shovel still in his hand; the imam and others sprawled wide-eyed among the cover of the graves; the crude wooden coffin abandoned askew on the newly turned earth. Only the sound moves, a soundtrack of zings and putts as the bullets hit the earth around us.

There was a crucial element missing in all this: 'they', 'them', 'those people', as Jasmin had called them. I had never seen a Serb fighter. Nor had I any understanding of what it really was to see a human being in a sight and pull the trigger. I had been in close proximity to fighting, it happened around our house almost every night, but it was an unmoving, faceless sound and presence. I wanted to know what it was like to shoot people. I felt it was the key to understanding so much more. I had to find out.

Then I met Marko in the BB. He was drunk, had bumped into me as he swayed to the bar and apologized. We struck up a conversation, drank some more and it transpired he was a sniper. Then he asked if I would like to go up to the front with him. A couple of days later I met him at his unit's base, an old school-house near the bakery. His comrades were a strange collection, a mixture of hard-faced elder veterans, many of whom had fought the Serbs at Vukovar in Croatia two years before, and teenage recruits already experienced in the fighting around Sarajevo. There were two women with them. One was ugly, large and wounded. She said she had killed five men and her commander told me she was the best shot in his unit. The other was the most beautiful woman combat fighter I have ever seen. She was in her early twenties, blonde and pale-skinned with a figure that could have graced a models' catwalk in Rome. The HOS had a fanatical ideology which, if fully realized, would have made all of Bosnia, right up to the Drina, part of Croatia, at the expense of every Serb living there. I could not believe someone as beautiful as this girl could be party to such sectarianism, especially after I discovered that she had lived with Serbs until the start of the war. Hoping to find at least a trace of humanist compassion within her, I asked if she really hated each and every Serb. 'I hope that the only ones I see again are those I am about to kill,' she replied.

As the sun began to drop Marko and I, together with two other marksmen, left the base and walked out of the city's confines up the green slopes to the north, heading for the lines that over-looked the Serb-held suburb of Vogošća. En route, as the darkness collected, we dropped into a field headquarters located in an abandoned house. There we were briefed on the latest situation by a government army commander. It had become increasingly obvious to me that the war was an unequal contest. The outgoing fire was only ever a fraction of the incoming, some-thing apparent even before Endre had made his cynical quip about its educating values. The government soldiers I met on the lines near our house always complained about how little ammu-nition they had and most were lucky if they even had uniforms, let alone boots. The commander in this headquarters looked totally exhausted, his eyes sunken so far back into his head as to be almost invisible. As with so many Bosnians, he was keen to talk to a foreigner and hear another opinion on the war, almost desperate that the words coming from the world beyond would make sense of things, perhaps offer a glimmer of hope where there was none. I fear they were always disappointed by what I had to say. In turn I asked this man what most angered him as a commander. 'I am sick', he replied in a tone so sorrowful I wished for a moment that I had not asked, 'of sending my boys into the line with barely a magazine a man, and having to ask them to conserve their fire.'

The three snipers went separate ways after the briefing. I stuck with Marko. After another twenty minutes or so we crawled into a damp fold of earth overlooking the Serb positions some 200 metres beyond. A vague misgiving flittered through my mind as I wondered how much Marko's attention to his task was intensified by my presence. From our position on the hillside, among trees whose spring blossom appeared to glow in the bright starlight, we had a panoramic view of the battlelines and sporadic firefights that erupted in the valley below us. Periods of silence were punctuated by clattering bursts of fire; purple-red tracers drifted and bounced between the slopes with curves of inimitable grace; choreographed flashes of light followed by resonant thumps marked the impact of mortars; from the Serb-held ground an anti-aircraft gun spat single repetitive streaks of fire upon a perfect, unchanging axis into a position to our left. It was truly beautiful.

Marko appeared unimpressed. After about an hour he grunted and turned to me. 'Hey, English, you want a look?' he murmured, handing me the wooden stock of his rifle, a Kalashnikov sniper variant. Through the starlight scope I was witness to a speckled green world of surprising clarity, in which the tracers left time-delayed imprints like the tails of comets. Scanning along the Serb positions before us, the trenchlines stood out as vivid scars in the landscape, interrupted by the shadowy bunkers and broken, doll-like houses. Then a small black blob stirred from the ground beside one of the bunkers, stood up, and took the shape of a man.

I stopped breathing and pulled the sight closer to my eye. I wanted to pull the trigger, to erase the faceless shape in the sight. It would be no different from shooting sparrows as I had done in the garden as a child. It was not a question of killing; there seemed nothing human in the exchange, only the need to achieve a conclusion to the trigger-bullet-body equation. It would be so easy.

I did nothing. My detachment faded with the coldness of the

trigger. A nameless Serb fighter scrambled back into position, for ever unaware of his predicament. But Marko had noticed a change in my posture and wanted to know its cause. 'Can you see something? Here, give it to me . . .' He snatched at the rifle.

Momćilo laughed for a long time when I told him what had happened, rocking around in the armchair repeating 'You saved one Četnik' over and over again. Thinking of how close I came to pulling the trigger, how absolutely meaningless that little black blob had been to me, my return grin was a little lopsided. But I had not fired the shot. It was not my war and I had no excuse or reason to kill anyone.

At that time I still had such values.

For a while longer my life in Sarajevo went on in much the same way and I adapted easily into the rhythm of each day. Sometimes we were afraid, sometimes depressed. We laughed a lot, and were often bored. We drank enormous amounts of coffee and smoked thousands of bitter-tasting Drina cigarettes. The sound of gunfire lost some of its novelty for me. Once you have been shot at a few times even the first thrill of that begins to pall, leaving you with a realization of how pointless it could be to be gunned down for nothing on the streets of a strange city.

Then something happened which broke the comfortable ease. I was leaning out of the window one afternoon having a smoke, looking at the destruction and daydreaming vacantly. A mortar round exploded by the side of the house nearest the parliament building, then another, then a whole clutch of them. The sound of a woman's keening bit the air, its low wail making my skin crawl. I ran outside. A young woman was dead, slain by the first explosion as she stepped out of the building onto the grass below. The mortar had landed close by, killing her immediately. Her mother was holding her. It was she who cried.

'Get your cameras,' a neighbour called out. His voice was neutral as if he was just making a statement. But I could not take a picture of this. I knew the dead girl. I knew the people around her body. I was part of this, yet detached. A feeling of great confusion came over me. There was nothing I could do. She was dead and that was it. Often I had talked with her in the apron of tatty garden on the far side of the parliament building. There was nothing between us; she was just a friendly face who was always ready with a smoke and a story, a blonde-haired girl in her twenties. It was not even that I felt especially affected by her death in the immediacy of those moments. It was the issue of the cameras that really got to me.

I walked away. I walked through the city for hours, full of self-hatred, the security and ease of my life in Sarajevo falling away from me like a shed skin, my mind a turmoil of questions. Why was I here? There had to be a reason. I was not a Bosnian stuck in Sarajevo, I was a foreigner who could leave. So why did I stay? Was I a sluttish dilettante day-tripping into someone else's nightmare? Maybe. And if I wanted to be a journalist, what then? I could not even pick up a camera when it really came down to it. My time in the flat had cosseted and lulled me. I must have been mad to think that such days could go on for ever. No past history, no impression from the words of others had preceded me to the house so I had arrived as an open book to those who lived there. As a stranger in the war only the present mattered as to how you were judged. Your past was irrelevant. In my desire to learn of war I sought only the cloak of anonymity in the community in which I lived. I had ended up not wanting even to carry cameras, let alone use them. Like the bullet-proof vest, the camera was a barrier. Yet it was impossible to integrate totally, unbelievably stupid to think that I could have managed it. The words 'get your cameras' re-identified me as the outsider I was. And if I could not accept that status, if I could not use my cameras, then I should not be there. I could not stay on and feed off the misery of people who had become my friends just to 'see a war'. I had used the warmth shown to me in that house to shackle and deceive myself. I had to break away. I had to be alone without support.

I despised myself that day; everything I had ever proved to myself was suddenly nullified. I could not even talk about it with Momćilo. It was too difficult to explain and I would have felt too ashamed to do so anyway. So I left Sarajevo. It was a hard moment for me, full of guilt at leaving the three of them. I did not really say goodbye as I resolved to return when I could. There was a new war breaking out in central Bosnia, this time between Muslims and Croats. I did not know the details but decided to go there.

3

Hercegovina, Summer 1993

I met an HVO fighter in a bar one night who told me a story. It was as if he had handed me a blank canvas that each subsequent day filled in, brushstroke by brushstroke. It was not until nearly a year later when the last shots of the Muslim–Croat fighting finally added a signature that I could see it all and understand what he meant. The soldier was drunk and morose, sweat-stained fatigues clinging to his body with the familiarity of an aged lizard's last skin. His eyes had the transient blank stare you often notice in men who have just come out of combat, a one-dimensional emptiness normally seen only in baby animals or very old men. It never lasts long with fighters though, and is always replaced by something harder and meaner. But if ever you wish to hear a story as close to the truth as you can find, then speak to a man with these eyes, for you will find it in the stream of consciousness that pours forth with his words, before he has time to gather his wits and corrupt his account of reality with what he thinks he should have felt, or thinks he should have done, rather than telling what he actually did feel, or did do. This is what the soldier told me:

It was at the beginning of the conflict between Muslims and Croats in Hercegovina, where Croatian nationalism found such strong roots in the sun-blasted rock and the corresponding infertile set of the minds of the men who lived there. The fighter was part of a small unit of troops from west Mostar, old childhood friends. Their commander was a young athlete, renowned for his strength and prowess on the track. He was a good man, the soldier said, brave and strong. One morning, cleaning the ground of Muslims, as he put it, the men scrabbled down a slope northwest of the city through stunted bushes and sharp-edged grass, the only vegetation that seemed to grow on the hills there. They approached a small Muslim village and were met by rifle fire. The man said that all the civilians had already left the area.

The athlete broke cover first, leaving a shallow ravine to bound across some open ground towards the houses. There was a small explosion and he fell down. The front of his foot had been blown off by a mine and he lay in view of his comrades moaning and writhing with pain. His men were in a dilemma. To rescue their commander they would need first to clear a route to him free of mines, itself made impossible by the fire coming against them. They called out to reassure him and he replied. They then laid down a lot of return fire but were unable to locate the exact position of the sniper, nor could they tell exactly how many Muslim troops were in the village. All the time the athlete lay on the open ground, crying out and cursing. After a while one of the men, a particular friend of the athlete, began to crawl towards him, feeling for mines in the tufts of grass with a knife. It was only when this man had not moved for a while that the others realized he was dead, killed by a single bullet. The soldiers went mad with rage, and wasted a lot of ammunition firing on empty houses. Yet still they were unable to reach either man, and the fire against them seemed only to increase with the heat of the day. The athlete was aware that his friend was dead. Several times he called out to the remaining troops to abandon him. He must have been making his own appreciation of the situation lying out there, for suddenly he drew his pistol and blew out his brains.

'There are two ways to die here,' the fighter concluded. 'You can die doing the right thing for the wrong reason, or die doing the wrong thing for the right reason.'

I never asked if they recovered the bodies.

The Muslim–Croat war: it could really stretch your concepts of courage and cowardice to the point where your mind just jammed with trying to feel out values like right and wrong. Analysts now say that it was just a bloody side-show to the main event, the conflict between the Serbs and Muslims. They miss the point. As the war shed its cloth like a cheap strip artist, few could deny the contours of its flesh. The conflict had been started by the Serbs, who aimed to create a Greater Serbia out of the mulch left by the disintegration of Yugoslavia. Arranged against them was an alliance between the Croats and Muslims who still at that time wanted to live in a multi-denominational secular Bosnia independent of Serbia. For those who wished for co-existence – including many Serbs – the alliance was the hook upon which they hung their ideals. But it began to fall apart at the end of 1992, the decay spreading in the spring of 1993 and leading to all-out war. Even the most liberal, tolerant minds were faced with the choice of leaving Bosnia, though this was usually impossible for the Muslims who were cut off, or drawing on long-forgotten religious heritages to find whatever label would ensure survival. It was this second conflict which killed the liberal ideal in Bosnia.

There was no balance of guilt in the causes of the Muslim–Croat war. It began when opportunistic Croat leaders in Hercegovina saw in the inaction of the international community their chance to seize large swathes of Muslim territory. Fighting the Serbs had helped the Croats to perfect the methods they now employed in Bosnia – vitriolic propaganda, pogroms and massacres. Yet once the war was under way, trying to apportion blame often became as relevant as trying to find a copycat arsonist while the first firestarter is still at large, and all the while a city disappears into a firestorm.

If the war as a whole was some epic tragedy, then in ignoring the Muslim–Croat conflict you were leaving the theatre before the hero died. And that was some time before the final act even started.

I walked on just after the beginning, and soon got sent to jail. Again.

The Hercules from Sarajevo dropped down in Split beneath the skirts of a storm. There was only one other civilian passenger on board, a Bosnian in his late thirties with the cultured, aquiline nose of an academic. As an interpreter for a foreign newspaper in the city he had managed to get hold of one of the UN's precious press cards, his ticket out of the Bosnian capital. I doubt he ever returned. We walked out of customs together and for a while stood on the pavement outside the airport terminal in quiet vexation as taxi drivers and UN personnel hustled past us. When an aircraft suddenly plucks you from a war situation and deposits you into the confusing slipstream of peace it leaves you very alone.

Suddenly the air around us was rent by a terrific crashing as if an enormous artillery barrage had opened up. For seconds we stood staring at each other like the dumbstruck victims of a cruel joke, whom the war had somehow reached though it had no right to do so. Lightning broke our gaze, flashing out from the dark cumulus rolling in from the Adriatic. A storm. Only a storm. Laughter ripped out of our bellies, bending us nearly double, threatening to crush our ribs as we rocked off the pavement, slapping each other's shoulders in recognition of our shared fear and relief. I finally recovered but as I said goodbye and shook the Bosnian's hand I saw the skin beneath his eyes twitch and jerk, and mirthless tears break out from the palisade of his lashes and trickle down his face.

After Sarajevo, Split seemed like a lotus fruit to the senses, a blast of waterfront restaurants, light, space, wine and beautiful, unobtainable Dalmatian women. Yet I found it hard to relax during the two days I spent there. I had neither a car nor contacts, and in the absence of any alternative, my plan to reach central Bosnia involved first taking a bus to Mostar, itself now wracked by Muslim–Croat fighting, then hitch-hiking north-westwards across the battlelines that were growing in number and intensity by the day. Deep in Bosnia a town named Vitez had become the centre of media attention after HVO troops had massacred the Muslim inhabitants in the nearby village of Ahmići a month earlier. Its name meant 'knight' but when I eventually arrived there I found little chivalry in the ugly town. War had lifted Vitez from its dull anonymity, and it was now becoming a hub to the fighting in central Bosnia; action began to revolve around it like the spokes of a slow-turning wheel, scarcely braked by the presence of a battalion of British troops. It seemed a natural choice of destination, a place where I could see a war that moved, and maybe even use the cameras that seemed to have become the muted voice of my conscience.

Aware that the longer I stayed in Split brooding over my plan, the more intimidating it would become, I moved quickly, using the time to make decisions over what belongings I must leave in the small room I rented from a Croat family, and what I could carry on my back in an old rucksack for the indeterminate journey ahead. Once again the flak jacket proved an annoying encumbrance. It weighed a ton and took up space. For a while I thought about leaving it behind or else ditching its two ceramic plates. Finally it went into the rucksack too, plates and all. Then I rang home.

Home: I was only two hours from London. It seemed so far away. It was more my mindset than geographical position that accounted for my feeling of isolation. It was not necessarily a bad sensation, indeed at times I relished the liberty of my solitude. Memories of London, my family and life in England were almost abstract; the odd face and emotion whirling out of a vague and distant cloud. It was as if my recall stretched only as far as the moment three months earlier when I started the journey eastwards. Everything before that day was like a half-remembered dream. My emotions had lost their definition. It was not that I no longer missed those close to me, merely that I felt so detached as to be suddenly unaware of what I wanted or cared about outside the immediate realm of Bosnia, a kind of ongoing metamorphosis from which I had no way of knowing what would emerge.

I had left a girl behind in London. We had been together for a year before I departed for Bosnia. I loved her. I had tried writing to her from Sarajevo but after a time had not really known what to say any more, and my letters had stopped. Now I felt unsettled and guilty. The conversations in the PTT phone booth were more like exercises in what not to say than what to say. The task of communicating what I had experienced or felt to her, and to others at home, was completely beyond me. The 'Hi-how-are-you-I'm-fine' bit went all right, but it was followed by a ghastly mêlée of wooden dialogue and empty silences, all overshadowed by the certainty that I would leave the listener either worried and unenlightened, or else very worried and wiser. How can you condense war into an acceptable telephone recipe and leave the person on the other end of the line happy?

More distressing still, I found it difficult to grasp anything of what was going on in the lives of those in England. I was trying to equate listening to news from home with thoughts of crutches, killing and firefights; the inevitable domestics of peace versus the insular details of war. Irreconcilable worlds: try linking them up and it feels as if your head will blow off.

Brooding on the phone calls, running misunderstandings over in my mind, I hardly noticed the bus ride until the coach stopped at Metković on the Bosnian border. Croat customs officials there became unnecessarily suspicious of my British passport and called over the 'Special Police' to check it out. Either solitary foreign travellers were rare on this route or else the officials were so bored that the chance of a little power demonstration was too irresistible to miss. My protests were weakened by a looming sense of déjà vu. I was taken off the bus with one other passenger and escorted to an empty container shed. The vehicle pulled away leaving us sitting alone in the baking heat. I pulled out the ritual packet of cigarettes with a resigned grunt and offered one to my new companion of circumstance, a tough-looking young man in his twenties with a crew cut. He had quite a story, though the first instalment he gave me was brief and to the point.

Eric was a deserter from the French Foreign Legion's parachute regiment. A Canadian of Italian descent, he had become bored with the tedium and heat of his regiment's distant posting, and so had come to fight in Bosnia. He had already seen action with Croat troops fighting the Serbs along the Posavina corridor, way to the north, but found the stagnation of the lines dull after a while. Now he was en route to central Bosnia to get involved in the fighting there.

At this stage in our conversation he gave away little more than that. We smoked and let the subject drift into wondering what would happen to us next. We did not have to wait long to find out. Two cars appeared, each with HVO military police inside, and with scarcely a word we were driven separately to a barracks in Čaplina, in Bosnian territory. It is amazing how quickly you get accustomed to saying nothing when dealing with Bosnian authority. Very soon you realize that it is a waste of time trying to explain anything and that it is better just to shut up and see what happens.

Much of the barracks was damaged, the result of fighting with the Serbs the previous year, but the separate cells we were given in the guardroom were untouched, save for the predictable scrawl of jailbird graffiti on the walls: a pastiche of naked women, obscenities, dates, names and a Croat flag, all carved crudely into the stone. I was neither particularly surprised nor disturbed by the turn of events. Only weeks before the HVO had turned on their Muslim allies in the region; we were close to the fighting, and the atmosphere was tense and ugly. The appearance of a couple of strangers, both of military age, was bound to have caused some reaction. I peered out of the tiny window at the back of the cell into the yard beyond. There were two small units of regular Croat troops, identifiable by the flashes on their arms, who waited quietly at the edge of the yard being briefed by officers. More boisterous were the forty or so Bosnian-Croat HVO soldiers. They were all heavily armed and appeared to have just completed an operation. A few of them threw themselves down on the ground and began to doze in the sun while others shouted and jostled each other, gulping brandy from bottles. Their leering faces and swaggering shoulders were the first examples of the porcine brutishness I was to see so much of in the months ahead.

After about an hour I was taken out of the cell and led to a small room where I was questioned by an HVO officer. He had one of those intransigent spade-shaped faces common to ex-communist officials, the kind that lets you know immediately that nothing you say or do will influence the outcome of a decision which has been made in advance anyway. So I went through a minimal preamble explaining I was on my way to Mostar, before letting him drone on about a betrayal of the Croatian people by fundamentalist Muslim hordes, a speech he rounded off by telling me that my documents were not in order and that I would be taken under escort back to Croatia.

To my surprise Eric and I were put in the same car for the journey back to the border. The fact that he had served alongside a Croatian unit that still remained loyal to the Bosnian government army was enough to provoke the HVO's suspicion, so he was due to be deported too. There was only one policeman in the car, though, and scarcely had we pulled out of the barrack gates when Eric launched into tales of his days fighting the Serbs and proclaimed his desire to serve again with the glorious HVO. Within a mile the driver accepted cigarettes from us; minutes later we had him laughing; a few miles further and he simply pulled the car over, let us out, indicated the road to Mostar, then left us standing at the verge.

The sun was low in the sky so we lay down our bedrolls in a clearing among the scrub, shared some bread and wine that was stashed in our baggage, and exchanged our stories. Eric's plan was a little more complex than he had at first let on. It turned out that after his experience in the Posavina corridor, he had spent time in Zagreb where he had stayed with a group of Arab aid workers and learned of the plight of the Muslims in Bosnia. Rather than joining up with the HVO, Eric was in fact trying to reach central Bosnia to link up with the government forces, the BiH armija.

His world was divided into two categories: 'good' mercs and 'bad' mercs. Good mercenaries knew their profession and got on with it, bad mercenaries just bullshitted each other about it in bars. Eric said he knew that 'good mercs' had a short life-expectancy, so he planned to fight in a few wars before quitting the profession to write a book on his experiences. He did not rate the competence of the local fighters very highly and described the ease with which he had carried out night raids upon the Serb positions around the Posavina.

'Both sides hardly ever went out into no man's land,' he explained matter-of-factly. 'They became so confident that the only threat was from shelling, after a while they never even bothered posting sentries at night, and in the winter just used to pack into their bunkers and drink. One evening I got so fucking bored that I crawled out of the trench with an RPG and one other guy. We made it up to the Serb lines, heard voices from a bunker, and hit it with the RPG. We heard the wounded screaming and shouting and ran back to our own positions, which the Serbs then shelled in retaliation. After that I began to wait in no man's land after hitting a bunker. It was better to hang out there, maybe even have a cigarette, while the Serbs shelled our lines. But it got stupid after a while. The officers would encourage me to go out on raids but a lot of the guys I was with got pissed off because they knew every time I went out with an RPG they would get shelled. I mean, do they want to fight a war or what?'

I laughed. I could well imagine the attitude of many of the men in the trench, farmers and townsfolk who had ended up in uniform through no choice of their own, content to have a quiet time of things until some gung-ho legionnaire turned up and began spoiling it all. Eric spoke with the kind of naïve assurance and frankness, devoid of bravado, that carried with it the ring of truth. I had no reason to doubt him; he was not trying to impress me, merely tell it as it happened.

I had a dreamless sleep beneath the open sky, and with dawn no more than a pastel glow on the horizon, we hit the road again. After several miles we came to another town, Čitluk. The light was still the peaceful blue-grey of early morning, and the streets were deserted except for a few stretching dogs and a pair of HVO soldiers who passed us hunched and silent, bleary-eyed with sleep. Lights shone from the ground floor of a small hotel on our right, so we stopped there for some coffee, pulling up a couple of chairs to a table still damp with the night's dew. The moment remains so clear in my mind: the stillness of the town in its waking moments, the distant cry of a cockerel, the sense of easy intro-spection in our mood, the feeling of unfolding and limitless adventure, the flippant shrug of shoulders with which we agreed on the venue to drink coffee. It was all in such total contrast to the significance that moment would have on my companion's life.

We had scarcely been there five minutes when three uniformed men walked out of the foyer, sat at a nearby table and laid their assault rifles across their knees. Two of them were barely out of their teens; one tall and blond, the other stocky and brown-haired. The presence of the third man so dominated the small patio I barely noticed their features. He was tall and slender with a whipcord leanness that dispelled any suggestion of weakness. He wore the Legion's green beret pulled down low over his forehead so that for a time only his mouth was visible out of the shadow. Yet when he looked towards us a pair of burning ice-blue eyes stared out of the darkness, seeming to look straight through us to some point in the far distance. Here was a killer of men. The winged dagger of the Deuxième Régiment Étranger Parachutiste, Eric's regiment, glinted dully above one eye beside the small red and white chequered shield of the HVO. On noticing it Eric took a breath and walked over to the man's table.

They spoke for a couple of minutes, the man at the table firing short questions at Eric in a flat voice then staring keenly at him while he answered. Finally he gave out a bloodless white smile and shook Eric's hand. It was quite a handshake. With it went Eric's intention to join the government army. He had just thrown in his lot with the HVO. I joined them at the table where my presence was met with neither hostility nor undue interest. They asked me what unit I was with. I said nobody's. They asked me if I wanted to join. I said no thank you. They asked me what I did and where I was going. I said I was a photographer and was going to central Bosnia, but I would be interested to see Mostar first. They asked if I would like a ride in. I said yes.

The legionnaire was French, his tall companion Dutch, the shorter man Irish. I gathered they were going to a briefing at an HVO headquarters in the city. Their transport was a Red Cross lorry. They explained that the emblem provided useful protection against Muslim fire on a particularly vulnerable corner of the road as it began to descend to the city. I jumped in the back with Eric and we sped off, baby food and spare ammunition bouncing around our feet as the vehicle lurched over the rough tarmac. It was a strange way to go to war, but I could not help grinning at the childlike sense of pleasure I got from violating the Red Cross taboo.

'Hey, I hope you don't feel bad that I won't be going to central

Bosnia with you,' Eric shouted above the noise. He did not look embarrassed at his sudden change of allegiance, nor had he particular reason to be, but he wanted to explain things to me anyway. 'It's just this guy was in the Legion, we know some of the same people and . . .' I brushed aside his apology. He didn't have to justify himself to me. He had come to Bosnia to fight, and whatever concept of cause he had subsequently discovered took second place to that. He had just met up with someone from his old četa, his martial tribe, the Legion. Unless his views of justice, right and wrong had been iron-cast by his encounter with the Arabs in Zagreb, then his new choice of loyalty was inevitable.

The lorry took a winding route alongside steep, barren hills and plunging ravines, before dropping sharply into the Neretva Valley, the arid linear crucible in which Mostar lay. With the exception of a few narrow government-held salients on the Croat bank, the river marked the front line: the Croats to the west in the larger sector of the city which we now entered; the Muslims jammed up in a shell-blasted ghetto on the east bank.

The mercenaries parked the lorry outside a tall building whose otherwise featureless grey face was fanned by an enormous Croatian flag. They waved vaguely eastwards to indicate the front line and suggested I join them for a drink later, then trooped into the doorway of the headquarters. Eric and I shook hands and he followed them inside. A passing soldier, with no more than a trace of irony in his smile, suggested I try the Hotel Ero as a place to stay and directed me to the edge of a long avenue. 'Just keep walking down there, you'll know when you get there,' he added, only then grinning wolfishly.

The same brooding electricity I had met in Sarajevo hung over the avenue, and intensified as I walked eastwards. Fewer people became visible, and those I saw were moving in a shuffling jog.

The sound of explosions and heavy gunfire came closer. It would have been easy to turn around, and I felt vulnerable and exposed, lumbering conspicuously down a now-deserted road with an enormous rucksack on my back. But if I allowed fear to take over it could carry me back to England on a plane, unfulfilled in any way, so I tried to control it, telling myself without much conviction that it was all to do with state of mind.

Turning a corner I saw a body, in civilian clothes but barefoot, lying headfirst in a ditch beside me. Ahead a burned-out lorry blocked the road. As I crouched and prepared to run back, the whooshing of an RPG sounded above me, exploding a short distance away, followed immediately by another, closer. A burst of machine-gunfire answered from a building behind me.

I was inside the ditch with the body, which was buzzing with flies and smelled terrible, when an HVO soldier leapt in beside me, a red flash of cloth all that distinguished him from the Muslim troops ahead. 'What the fuck are you doing?' he asked in English. I told him, rather sheepishly, that I was trying to find the hotel. He paused, catching his breath, grabbed me by the arm, and together we ran across some waste ground to a building beyond.

The sign outside read 'Hotel Ero' and I walked in, attempting to look sanguine and unconcerned. The scene was chaotic. The floor was a skidpan of congealing blood, broken glass and spent bullet casings, while through a haze of smoke and dust HVO troops fired Kalashnikovs in random bursts from the edge of windows on the other side of the foyer to unseen targets beyond. Every few seconds a round would smack back through the windows into one of the walls around us, sending everybody ducking in unison. It was obviously the place to be.

I no longer felt afraid, as the inside of the building felt a lot safer than the street I had just come from, besides which, bullets are seldom as unnerving as shellfire. It was logical that as long as you stayed away from the windows you would be unlucky to get hit, though the odd ricochet pinballed between the walls in an unpleasant series of whines and thwacks. So I lit a cigarette, dumped the rucksack, and installed myself in a suitable corner and watched what happened. The first thing I noticed was the way the fighters' faces seemed contorted: eyes wide, jaws clenched, mouths grimacing, skins oily with sweat. Nobody was still for more than a few seconds. It was as if small dust devils of energy would ripple one group or another into action, something close to a hysteria of juddering gun barrels, feverish concentration and tensed muscle, followed by an almost post-coital backwash when a firer would slide behind the cover of a wall, head lolling slightly, sometimes uttering an unnatural peal of relieved laughter, near to a giggle, to anyone who made glittering eye contact. Then the vibe would rip into another part of the room, and that would suddenly convulse into activity and noise. There were the occasional shouts, grunts and hoarse directives, all but lost to the overwhelming Kalashnikov-crackling tempo and the jingle of falling brass.

Accompanied by the soldier who had brought me in from the street, an officer was gesturing to me from the side of the room nearest the door. I walked over quickly. He was young, looked good-humoured, and asked what I was doing. Playing to his humour, I asked him as coolly as I could if I could have a room on the west side. All Bosnians regard the English as ridiculously indifferent. They even have a phrase for it, 'nemoj da se praviš Englez', meaning 'don't be as the English', which they use if urging someone to get real. Coldness is alien to Bosnians, and often bemuses rather than angers them. The officer laughed encouragingly, spoke for a second with the soldier, and told me he would see what he could do. Minutes later he reappeared, now looking serious, with a more senior commander who could have been the pasty-faced twin of the officer in the jailhouse at Čaplina. The familiar refrain concerning absence of documents snapped from his lips and, as the younger man shrugged apologetically, I was led away, crestfallen. Two other soldiers escorted me through a succession of alleys to an HVO BMW with a complement of gun-toting fighters, who drove me to the outskirts of the city. Consoling myself with the thought that I had at least seen a proper gunbattle, I decided to continue my journey northwards.

The mercenaries were fairly drunk when I met them that night back in Čitluk, and talked freely of their experiences. The legionnaire, Luc, was a veteran of fighting in South America and Africa before joining the Croats for combat against the Serbs during the Croatian war of 1991. He was a sniper by specialization; with eyes like that he could not have been much else. He had met his two younger companions in Croatia, and when that war ended they had come to Bosnia together, again to fight the Serbs. The tide of the conflict now meant that his foes were Muslim, but he seemed comfortable with the change of circumstance.

'OK, so I have many Muslim friends, I don't have a problem with Muslims,' he told me. 'We all make our choices. Mine is to stay with the HVO. As it happens they fight the Muslims. It's that simple.'

In contrast the Irishman, Shane, the youngest at twenty-two, had had no military experience before arriving in the Balkans. The others said that didn't matter, that he had now survived two years of fighting, and that was knowledge enough. He was affable and amusing, the inevitable mascot of the team. After a while we retired to a room above the bar, shotgunned hash down a Kalashnikov barrel and drank a lot of whisky. They reminisced about the Croatian war, and speculated on Mostar's fate. 'Listen,' said Peter, the Dutchman, 'we don't fight for the money, and we're not in it for the killing. It's about camaraderie and, sure, it's about excitement. Some are bullshitters, some are psychotics. We are neither. We are here because we want to be, and if there is a price to pay, then we are ready for that too.'

There was little real difference between them and anyone else who goes to war voluntarily. In their case they had taken a side and were ultimately prepared to kill. Though my reasoning for being there was still in flux, at its simplest I was there to watch, and that gave neither of us the higher moral ground. Men and women who venture to someone else's war through choice do so in a variety of guises. UN general, BBC correspondent, aid worker, mercenary: in the final analysis they all want the same thing, a hit off the action, a walk on the dark side. It's just a question of how slick a cover you give yourself, and how far you want to go. If you find a cause later then hold on to it, but never blind yourself with your own disguise. I spent a couple of days with Luc, Shane and Peter, pumping them for information about the roads northwards and the state of the fighting on my route. Then I said goodbye and left.

Many months later I returned to the hotel in search of them. Their rooms were empty. As I walked out through the foyer I noticed a figure sitting alone in the deserted bar. He was in civilian clothes, had his back to me, and a kit bag by his feet. It was Peter. He gave me a dry smile as he reached out over his coffee to shake my hand. We talked for a long time. I was lucky to have caught him, for he was leaving Bosnia for good the next day. 'There was an ideal once,' he said and paused, eyes vacant and shiftless with fatigue, squinting slightly through clouds of chain-smoked Marlboro, 'but not any more.' He told me that Shane had been fighting near Gornji Vakuf when he trod on one mine and was blown onto a second. With both his legs gone above the knee, he had returned to Ireland for life in a wheelchair. Luc's girlfriend, a Croat nurse, had been eviscerated by an RPG on the front in Mostar. He had gone too. I hear that he is now serving a long stretch in Marseilles for armed robbery. Eric? Well, I had somehow known what would happen when I said goodbye. He was killed in action five days later. War bills.

GHOSTS

August 1996

There are teeth at the edges of the void left by peace. Srebrenica's forests brought them snapping back as bad as ever, angry winds howling between the gums. If I had hoped to purge some demons by returning to post-war Bosnia I was painfully disappointed.

It was not necessarily that I had 'found' myself during the war, but the conflict had certainly put a kind of buffer zone between the fault lines in my head. Without it, or any narcotic relief, they ground away with renewed vigour. After spending a few more days in eastern Bosnia I headed south, drifting through some old war haunts on the way down, desperate to recapture some kind of hit off the memory of action, but all I found were shadows and distant echoes.

Stopping in Čitluk before the final leg of the journey home to London and the sweet arms of oblivion that I knew waited for me there, I struck up a conversation with an ex-soldier in a bar. He mentioned to me that there was an Irishman living near by, a legless veteran in a wheelchair: Shane.

I did not believe it initially. The last I had heard, over two years before, was that he was living in Dublin. I quickly tracked him down in another bar in a nearby village. He had put on a lot of weight since I first saw him in the summer of 1993; he was drunk when I found him, drunker when I left and by the sound of things each day was like that. I knew the cycle so well.

His story was simple enough, and once it was finished I wondered how I had ever imagined that he could stay in Ireland. Isolated and alone in Dublin, regarded as a bit of a freak by one-time peers who barely knew where Bosnia was let alone what the war was about, he had returned to Hercegovina to live on an HVO war pension in the company of people he knew 'knew': the former Croat fighters alongside whom he had operated. Whatever else could be said about the HVO, they looked after their veterans. He had been given a small plot of land and enough money each month to keep him drunk.

Regret may have been something too painful for him even to allude to, or else a feeling too deeply submerged beneath the booze. Whatever the case, it never emerged in our conversation, though losing your legs is a good deal stronger a reason to feel it than merely suffering the sensation of continuous exile that I laboured under.

Yet he was certainly trying to track the path of whatever had brought him to Bosnia and cost him his mobility. 'Why am I here?' It is a big question to ask oneself in someone else's war, and I for one never really bothered until it was too late and the bill arrived.

Shane did not have many answers to his own motivations at that point, but when I finally managed to stagger upright and shake his hand goodbye he said that when he was a boy his grand-mother told him that her grandfather left Ireland to become a *longrider in the States, fighting around the Mexican border. He didn't know any more details. At that moment it was all he had to go on.*

Back at Heathrow twelve hours later I made the usual call before collecting my bags, scoring the gear before I even reached the flat, the luggage suddenly weightless in my hands as I strode upstairs to my room, already strong on anticipation.

A few scrambled seconds of torn foil followed until the hit bust into my lungs and the bad feelings in the pit of my stomach vaporized, replaced by a blissful sensation of anaesthesia and a rush of mental clarity, so clear it was almost crystalline.

Habits tend to live longer than wars, though one keeps me stuck in the other and I find it harder each day now to differentiate between the two: both are conflicts, one played inside, the other out. And that is just the beginning of it. Start digging away at the death-trip angle and all you see are a set of incestuous Siamese twins joined at the neck feeding and fucking one another: perfect symmetry and balance.

War and smack: I always hope for some kind of epiphany in each to lead me out but it never happens. You think you have hit the bottom many times then always find something else to lose, till after a while what once seemed like the bottom is an altitude that you are trying to scrabble back to. Even in my deepest moments of fear, retreating or withdrawing it's all the same, when I see those flashes of hope and swear never again, promise I'll keep away from the front or stay clean tonight, I know they are just illusions, flotsam in the river I pull myself up onto just so I can catch enough breath to last me for the next dive down.

There are many advantages to living on the foil, though. You can think without feeling, and that bestows upon you a certain black power. If you cannot see your way out, at least you can see how you got to where you are, track your own spiralling descent instant by instant. So back in West London that day I thought again of Shane, and his longrider ancestor, had another hit and turned the light back into my own eyes.

We think we have freedom of choice, but really most of our actions are puny meanderings in the prison yard built by history and early experience. Looking back with the hindsight of years, the laying of the foundations that were to send me to Bosnia floated past me like sticks in a river, some thrown by myself but most by others, many of them already dead. I had no idea until after the war how carefully I had dried and stacked this tinder, using it to torch so many of the bridges behind me. If one distant American cowboy was enough to send an Irish son to a Balkan war then my own fate should hardly have come as a surprise.

I still remember the day Tito died, though the significance of that moment was to lie dormant until an incident in Marrakech more than ten years later resurrected it and the sound of a ticking clock grew louder.

On 4 May 1980 I was standing on a stone bridge over a flowing Hampshire chalk stream. It was a Sunday. My grandmother, a tall elegant lady given to easy laughter and explosive swings of mood, was talking with particular vehemence to my mother. Her tone distracted me from a trout lying under one of the arches which I was making plans to lift that night, and I turned to listen to her.

'They say he died today, but who knows?' She paused dramatically. 'They may have kept it quiet for days to try to hold it together.' I ambled over and asked what had happened, assuming some old family friend had died. 'Tito has died,' she said gently. 'There will be the most terrible trouble, mark my words. He was the only man who could stop Yugoslavia falling apart. It's a desperate situation.' She liked that word 'desperate', always drawing it out with particular emphasis. I walked back to look at

the fish. Eastern Europe was of no great interest to me though it played a great part in the mind of my grandmother, who was no stranger to Balkan affairs or fratricidal conflict. However, if the places of my grandmother's past were of little concern, the characters that dwelt there had created a great impression upon my mind. My father had left home for another woman when I was six and, in the intervening years before my mother remarried, much time had been spent visiting my grandmother, listening to her tales in the glorious wild of her rambling garden.

Her father was born of a liaison between a Belgian barrister and an Egyptian bellydancer. Raised largely by his stepmother and Irish grandmother, Adrian Carton De Wiart was educated in England and was studying law at Oxford when the Boer war began. He ditched his studies and ran off to fight. He was not a British subject and would have been happy to join the Boers if the British army had refused to take him. He was wounded twice in action, going on to fight the Mad Mullah in Somalia where he lost an eye. A man of violent temper, he had scant regard for the frailty of the body. Laughing with pride, my grandmother often told me how he had duped a medical board into passing him fit for service once more by wearing a glass eye which he then pulled out in a London taxi, threw out of the window and replaced with his trademark black patch. Wounded again, again, again and again in France during the First World War, on another occasion he pulled off what remained of his left hand in front of an aghast surgeon who had refused to amputate it in a field hospital.

As an expression of solidarity with such fortitude, my grandmother years later refused all attempts to give her an anaesthetic to have her appendix removed. Citing her father's example, she forced an exasperated London surgical team to operate as she lay there fully conscious. Her father had led his men over the top at the Somme, by this time missing part of his arm, and with the tiny

60

band of survivors that managed to get as far as the German lines had stormed and held an objective against great odds.

Adrian Carton De Wiart must have sometimes pondered his loyalties. Shortly before the First World War he had married an Austrian countess, my great-grandmother. Although she lived in London during the war, her family fought for the Kaiser. When he went to collect his VC from the king, Carton De Wiart remarked that it was strange to win such an award when he was not even a British citizen.

After escaping from Poland at the start of World War Two he went on to fight the Germans in Norway. En route to Cairo in 1941 to be briefed on leading a special mission to Yugoslavia where he was to link up with Tito's partisans, his plane crashed off North Africa. He was taken prisoner by the Italians, and after Italy's capitulation went to China as Chiang Kai-shek's personal emissary from Churchill, dying, finally, in Southern Ireland three years before I was born.

Adrian Carton De Wiart was always a presence in my grandmother's rural cottage. A portrait of him hung in the drawing room, where he glowered from the wall at newcomers, one-eyed, the wound stripes scaling his empty sleeve like the rungs of a ladder. Yet it was never as if we lived in his shadow. He was just one of a number of strong characters in my mother's family history. It was not until years later, and in a war of my own, that I thought deeply about him at all. Besides, he had separated from his wife not long after his second daughter was born, and became almost estranged from my grandmother when as a young woman she abandoned the Catholic Church. He was a strong fatalist, believing death would arrive at an 'appointed moment'. I can never see it like that, though wish I could.

The Second World War lay fresher seeds in my childhood memories. My grandmother, having spent her youth in Austria, married a shy Englishman in the early Thirties. I remember him well: a tall, studious man wrapped up in a scientific mind and love of nature. He joined the RAF when war broke out, becoming the navigator in a bomber crew. As the war progressed so the bombing raids on Germany grew larger and casualties among the British aircrews rocketed to a rate that still remains a contentious issue among military historians. Deep over Germany one night my grandfather's Lancaster was badly savaged by enemy fire and lost the rest of the squadron formation, leaking fuel heavily.

What were those moments like? My impression of war is so geared to the 'them and us' scenario of land battle that I can barely stretch my imagination to take in my grandfather's situation: the concept of disembodied death suddenly smashing through the tube of the fuselage around you; the shock; the tension; the awareness that you are in mortal danger, and that as navigator you must salvage the lives of the crew around you – men whom you know and understand, maybe even love, better than your wife; the crushing pressure of time as the fuel sprays out of the tanks; the frantic calculations to work out where you are in the darkness of the night . . .

He got the plane home and was awarded the DFC. After the war was over he never spoke of it to me. The medal was hidden and was a forbidden subject. He was always a quiet man but the few sallies I made on the topic when I was a young boy drew the shutters right down on him. My questions were met with brush-offs then silence. I do not know what happened to him up there in the clouds. Maybe it was, as my grandmother told me, simply his natural modesty that led to such reticence but thinking of it now there was something a little unnatural in his inability to speak of the war. He was a very sensitive and very intelligent man. I think, perhaps, that as Bomber Harris's strategy to bring Germany to its knees by destroying its cities was put into action so my *grandfather, along with all the other bomber crews, found himself having to deal with the knowledge that his efforts were geared to dropping apocalyptic quantities of fire upon women and children. For such a sensitive man that realization must have been hard to bear. More than any of the other men in my family who fought, it is him that I would most like to speak to now of war. His death from leukaemia robbed me of that chance before I was even in my teens. I am aware of missing his wisdom more today than I ever did.*

My grandmother hated Hitler passionately, and talked of the Germans' stupidity in allowing themselves to fall for 'such a ghastly little man'. Yet many of her family fought for the Führer. One cousin, Uncle Polde, was a German fighter ace awarded the Iron Cross for the number of his kills. Others were Wehrmacht soldiers who fought the British as well as the Russians. She visited two of them in POW camps after they were captured.

She spoke of them all with affection, told me they were brave men, and insisted that they were fighting for their motherland and not Hitler. Much later, long after she died, I discovered that some of her family were of Jewish origin. Centuries ago they had become entwined by bloodline into the Austrian royal hierarchy and had adopted the Catholic faith. They too had fought with swastikas on their tunics. I never really thought about it much until Bosnia.

My own path was obvious: I wanted to go to war, so I joined the army. There had never been any family pressure upon me to sign up. There never had to be. From my earliest recall I had wanted only to be a soldier. The legends of my own ancestors were motivation enough. Their medals were their identities. Though the German side seemed more 'the enemy', my family's complex web of nationalities and the differing causes its menfolk had served had undermined any sense of real patriotism in me. I was aware that I was a son of British culture but I knew my blood was mixed. I did not necessarily think that it mattered for whom or what you fought, just as long as you got into a uniform and fought bravely. Inevitably I was in love with the idea of war without even knowing what it was. In church on Sundays, barely old enough to walk, I was given toy soldiers by my mother to keep me happy during the interminable sermons. Loud, large battles were fought in the pews, my mother staring down anyone inconsiderate enough to sniff or cough disapprovingly. She brought me an air rifle when I was ten; within a couple of years my grandmother got me a bolt-action shotgun. Telephone pylons, neighbours' drainpipes, birds and animals: they all changed guise on the end of my sights and became the enemy, any enemy. I looked forward to the day when I would be a soldier and could do it for real.

Strangely though, when the moment arrived I regarded it with great suspicion. The only discipline I had really been exposed to was at school, and I had hated that. My education had been a disaster and the thought that I might have to relive a similar experience filled me with fear. When I was ten years old I was sent away to board at prep school. I loathed every minute of it and ran away at the first opportunity, more as a symbol of protest than with any belief that it would end the nightmare. I still don't understand how anyone can believe their children will become better people for being sent away from home at an early age. It seems a peculiarly English syndrome.

After prep school I went to Eton, which I hated even more. I was young for my year, solitary and insecure, and lacking the quick wit, charm or academic talent that could have enabled me to carve out an enjoyable niche. I was deeply unhappy and remember only vicious betrayal and scything mental cruelty when I think of my time there. Even in the worst despair of days that followed I have never felt the powerlessness and loss of belief in myself that I felt at that school. I resent it even now. It works for some people, but it did not for me. I learned only to spend as much time as possible alone and endured the rest miserably as it ground away at my confidence.

Caught in one of the biannual drug busts at the school, I was sent home for a month. I suggested that I did not go back and my fee-paying father, angered at the lack of any sign of progress in his son, readily agreed. I guess that was first strike for narcotics in my life.

Next I went to a co-ed tutorial college in Guildford where I inhaled deeply on the sudden freedom and space at the expense of my education. Less than a year and a half later, aged seventeen, I left with scarcely a qualification. I felt such bitterness towards the education system that I never even entertained the thought of university. Thinking it would be like school, I would not have gone to one even if I had the right exam results.

I had been brought up with horses and could ride well. It was a useful talent in Australia where I worked as a jackaroo on outback properties for several months. Afterwards, on the already well-trodden path up through Indonesia and finally into Thailand, I grabbed greedily at each and every opportunity for a new sensual experience to stock the empty larder left by boarding school. So I returned to England late in the summer of 1985 long-haired, fit and brown, feeling worldly and empowered, eager to feed more on what life had to offer.

Only one question remained in my mind. Did I still want to join the army? A loner, I still did not like the company of groups. More to the point, there was no ongoing war to go to. Long gone were the days when by joining up you could be guaranteed at the very least a skirmish in some far-flung colony or isolated frontier outpost. And South-east Asia had taught me what a good time there was to be had as a civilian. The possibility of sitting for years on some German plain waiting for something that did not happen appalled me.

There was other access to war. I had recently read Michael Herr's book on the Vietnam war, Dispatches, billed by John Le Carré as the best book he had read on men and war in our time. It had had a profound effect on me, and demonstrated that another tribe existed to whom discipline and authority were at best abstract concepts: war correspondents. Yet journalism itself had little allure, and I thought many years working for some local paper would be needed before I would be lucky enough to get a war assignment. The thought of working in an office was out of the question. Anyway, war correspondents did not get to fight unless they were very lucky. And fighting was the key to the whole thing. No point going to war unless you fought, was there? There were no medals given out for waving a biro at the right moment.

So after a period of teetering indecision I joined the army. The minimum term of service was three years. Though I was to end up serving five, at the time even that seemed a lot to ask.

Because of his absence, my father's family had not had the same influence on my childhood, but I knew enough to understand that they too had all been soldiers. My great-uncle's fate held special interest. He had been killed in France in 1917, a young captain in the 60th King's Royal Rifle Corps. Leading a forlorn attack, he had been slain by machine-gunfire. Word had stretched through the years to me describing how he had been hit more than forty times, as if that in itself was a special honour. As a boy I imagined neat red wounds clustered on his chest like rosettes. I did not see him strung out on wire getting shredded and pulped by lead.

The King's Royal Rifle Corps still existed, though it had been amalgamated with two other regiments to become the Royal Green Jackets, who together with the Light Infantry now made up the Light Division. They had a reputation for being tough, *professional infantry soldiers. I wanted to try for officer selection because that seemed to allow at least a bit more of the control of life I was so wary of giving up. The recruiting major at the depot near Winchester asked me why I wanted to join and I went through a well-rehearsed patter about the sense of challenge and responsibility. I could hardly tell this urbane man the truth, that I just wanted to go to any war as soon as possible. In retrospect perhaps I should have done so, for there is still much honour attached to the profession of arms in Britain and, ironically, once I was in the regiment I found that my real feelings were shared by most of the other young Light Division officers. Some were even more vitriolic than me, and came right out with it: 'We want to know what killing is like.' The words hang in my mind. If you are a young man of combat age frustrated by the tedium and meaninglessness of life in twentieth-century Europe, you may understand them. If not, you will probably think they come from a psychopath.*

The major informed me the regiment had a policy of making potential officers go through basic training as soldiers before they attempted the selection tests of the commissions board. I was given a date to join up with a new platoon of recruits. I decided that as the army would cut my hair anyway, I would not bother doing anything about it beforehand. The day arrived. I found a nervous queue of recruits waiting outside an office in one of the barrack blocks. The door was open and inside I saw a small, hard-faced man in uniform. He was sitting bolt upright in a chair, resting closed fists on the desk before him. There were sergeant's stripes on his arm. He seemed to be waiting with an air of expectancy but no-one stepped forward from the line of frightened teenagers in the corridor. It was obviously time to show a bit of the initiative everyone kept banging on about. So I pushed my hair back, slouched up to the desk and said, 'Hi.'

The small man seemed to explode, catalysed by some invisible force into a raging demon of apoplectic fuck words and bulging veins. 'Saunter in here like some fucking rock star do you, sonny? Well it's a different fucking style now . . .' I was a skinhead before I knew it. And so began the army.

4

Central Bosnia, Summer 1993

'Have you got any Muslim friends?' The man pulled back the hammer of his pistol to emphasize the gravity of the question and leaned forward so close the brandy on his breath seemed to gum our faces together. There was total silence from the soldiers standing behind me in the darkness of the container room, not so much as a cough or shuffle. My interrogator's companion, a shaven-headed bison with a dagger on his hip, folded his arms waiting for the judgement my words would bring me.

Fuck, I thought, how do I answer that one? I had just admitted to having lived in Sarajevo for a while, so they were sure to interpret a negative reply as a lie. Yet in the wake of the crazed bigotry I had glimpsed in the previous twelve hours, to say yes seemed an even worse prospect. It was like an evil game of bluff, and I was not sure what the stakes were. Was the man just playing with me or was I in as deep shit as it felt? There were a different set of rules here characterized by a rabid sentiment I had never seen before. The suspicion and hostility of these men were mediaeval, and their regard for human life at best minimal. Values like respect for foreigners were just so far out of the scheme of things as to be irrelevant.

I had tried hard to reach the shelter of a town before the night fell. As the day had progressed it became vividly apparent that the roads of central Bosnia were not a place to wander alone after the sun went down. I had left Čitluk at dawn and after walking a few miles had been picked up by a heavily built middle-aged Bosnian Croat woman. The rosary around her neck was so large it was more like the chain of an anchor, and you could have crucified an undersized dwarf on its cross. Naïvely I had imagined having to listen to tales of grandchildren or cats for the next leg of my journey. Instead she had launched into a tirade against Islam that gathered momentum with each dragging mile. There were thousands of Arab mujahidin swarming through the hills, she told me. They had radicalized the minds of the Bosnian Muslims who were now waging a jihad, a holy war, upon the beleaguered Croat people who for so long had been persecuted by the filth of the Ottoman empire. Bosnia was now Europe's frontier against the fundamentalist legions of Allah, the Croatian people the brave hajduk vanguard in the battle for christianity. As for the Serbs, not one of them would find salvation. Not one. Her demeanour changed as her monologue went on. Spittle began to fly like sparks from the edge of her mouth, and her hair managed somehow to escape the confines of its tight bun and flick Medusa-like across her face and shoulders.

I barely managed to get a word in until the ride ended. I thanked her kindly and hurried away, casually dismissing her as a nutter. My next lift was in a flash red VW with a thumping sound system. The shaven-headed HVO soldier who drove it did not seem especially bright, but at least he looked as if he would make more sense than the woman. Yet within five minutes I was hearing the same story: mujahidin, fundamentalism, the Ottoman empire, jihad, Turks, Christ. Suddenly I wondered if it was I who had missed some crucial detail of the plot. Perhaps the Muslims I knew in Sarajevo were completely different from those in the rest of Bosnia. Perhaps the hills were alive with psychotic Islamic killers intent on obliterating Christians from the earth. I subscribed to no faith, but I felt unnerved.

It was the key to so much of what was happening in Bosnia. If I, a relatively impartial foreigner with access to a free media, could be frightened by local scaremongering and propaganda, imagine what it was doing to the minds of isolated rural communities with no access to outside news, no experience of media impartiality, reliant instead on the voice of local authority for 'truth'. You could pop common sense from the minds of villagers in Bosnia like a pea from a pod. Make them afraid by resurrecting real or imagined threats, catalyse it with a bit of bloodletting, and you were only two steps from massacre and mayhem.

The soldier dropped me off at the far edge of Tomislavgrad, a small town at the foot of a menacing range of mountains and forest that rose darkly upwards to meet the northern sky. He made an encouraging throat-cutting gesture with his hand before squealing back off towards the town in a cloud of dust and throbbing bassline. It was by now mid-afternoon, and although there were several hours of daylight left, I had no desire to find myself stranded on a roadside at night with zealots of any denomination rampaging through the forest. I was considering walking back to Tomislavgrad and continuing the next day when in the distance I saw a large vehicle heading my way, the protesting whine of its engine and crunch of the clutch preceding its features by several minutes. It was a coach of sorts. Half the windows were missing and the axle was so damaged that the vehicle moved along the road in a kind of lurching three-quarter profile. I stuck out my thumb and it stopped.

On board were a handful of young HVO troops, two crates of beer, and an old fat baba – grandmother – warty-faced, dressed in black. The road disappeared into an unsurfaced track which climbed the mountain in diagonal rungs up which we ground at varying speeds and angles. One of the soldiers sidled up to me and asked for a smoke. I gave him the cigarette reluctantly as I did not want it to be the key to a new conversation. My fears were justified, only this man had an alternative intro to the theme.

'I cut their ears off,' he said knowledgeably and without any preliminaries. He slithered his index finger down an ear just in case I had missed the point. 'Sometimes their noses.' Up the finger went again. 'Or their lips. But never the señorinas. I never touch the señorinas.'

'Oh, well that's all right then,' I said dryly, but he was not to be put off.

'We, we are Ustaša.' He said it with great pride, as if it was something I should be impressed by. And so the new journey began, this time with a bunch of teenage killers whose version of history derived less from the Ottomans and more from the Second World War and homage to the Croatian fascist leader, Ante Pavelić. There was one exception among them, a doe-eyed kid who shook his head as the others' talk of mutilation, murder and burning grew in passion. I managed to speak to him for a couple of minutes before his comrades began the first jeering intrusions which ended up with him being poked, harassed and mocked. He had been born in a village near by but educated in Croatia. Bravely, considering the company, he said he thought the war between Muslims and Croats was 'shit'.

'We lived together for a long time,' he said, looking out of a crack-spangled window, 'we have no need to fight.'

I bet he is dead now. He had the vulnerable purity and courage that would ensure he was among the first to get whacked on the front.

The coach stopped for an hour or so by a Croat village at the edge of a small grass plateau, and I followed the soldiers into a bar tucked away in a cluster of houses. There any doubts I had had concerning their real beliefs were quickly dispelled. Ante Pavelić himself gave me the stiff-armed salute from a large photograph hanging on the wall immediately facing the door. Various smaller pictures, brown-edged with age, showed his Croat NDH troops in German coal-scuttle helmets that carried a large U centre-pinned by a cross on their front: Ustaša. Swastikas, Sieg Heils and Wehrmacht helmets: these were symbols I could understand. Some of my own family may have fought for this side, but these were still the emblems of gas chambers and goosesteps, the insignia of the enemy.

If I was to become so convinced of the inherent hospitality of Bosnians that I felt guaranteed of a room to stay in any town at any time, then there was one exception. Prozor. My first impression of the town, as dusk collected its shades of darkness, was never changed by anything I subsequently saw there. Prozor was the arsehole of central Bosnia. It was also the coach's final destination. The HVO soldiers had remained in the bar on the plateau, and I completed the journey there with only the silent fat woman as company. As the sun disappeared behind the mountains I felt optimistic that I would find somewhere to stay. Three seconds after my feet touched the ground, I wanted to leave the place.

There was scarcely a light on in the town, which lay like a tumbled urban rubbish pit at the base of another towering ridge-line. Many of the houses, Muslim homes, had been completely fire-gutted when their occupants were purged months earlier in the first pogrom of the new war. The empty doorways and windows gave smoke-stained yawns on to the dirty pavement and loitering groups of drunken HVO troops who hung around in the shadows. These men were the only visible presence. There was the sound of a breaking bottle; someone vomiting; a burst of gunfire; a fistfight; shouting.

It was not so much the sense of malice there, though it was palpable. It was the unremitting brute ugliness of the place that made me walk through it, eyes-front and silent, up the black slope north. If I had been truly desperate perhaps I would have tried to find somewhere to sleep there. I have never been that desperate, neither before nor since.

Distant patters of a gunbattle reached me as the tiring climb up the ridgeline progressed. By the time I reached the crest of the ridge the features of the land on either side of the road had long ago disappeared into absolute blackness, and I cursed myself for having mistimed this final stage of the journey so badly. Just as I was about to lay down my bedroll among some bushes to the side of the road I saw a dim light ahead. Walking towards it, I made out the shape of two small buildings: a wooden hut and a container. As I was not entirely sure what the situation was I approached with my arms held open from my sides and called out while still some distance away. Lurching up to surprised and frightened troops out of the dark with a rucksack on your back seemed like an easy way to get blown away before anyone had time to think about a question. But I may as well have done that for there was no sentry outside, just the murmur of voices from the container. I knocked on the door and walked in.

There were half a dozen HVO troops there, barely discernible through a fug of smoke from cigarettes and a wood stove. Their senses and speech were too slurred by brandy to allow them much surprise at my entry and they were fairly relaxed towards me. I gave them the simple cover story I had thought up during the climb to the ridge: I was a journalist whose car had broken down on the road before Prozor. I had an urgent meeting with colleagues who were expecting me in the town beyond, Gornji Vakuf, the next morning, and the company of British UN troops there knew that I had been forced to overnight in Prozor.

It was all total bullshit: nobody in the region knew I even existed let alone where I was, but the HVO were not to know that, and I hoped that if they believed other people were aware of my approximate location then anyone with the idea of cutting me in the night might have at least a second thought about it.

They accepted the story and everything went smoothly for a couple of hours. I was given a chair, some tinned meat, bread, cigarettes and brandy, and I listened with interest to what they told me of the next valley. Though they had checkpoint duties for the road, they were primarily a communications post responsible for monitoring the radio traffic of their troops positioned in the surrounding hills. One man permanently wore a headset and if anything important happened he let the NCO know, who then relayed it back to the HVO headquarters in Prozor on a field telephone. The fighting in Gornji Vakuf was not yet too bad, they said, though there was a front line of sorts that bisected the town. It was more a demarcation between the HVO and BiH – sometimes the scene of exchanged fire – than a confrontation line. On 'good days' civilians still went from one side to the other. The situation in the hills was different, of course. There units from either side jostled for control of the high ground with increasingly bloody confrontation.

Their words seemed to set the pattern for so much of the war to follow. Some local HVO forces, either unwilling or unable at that time to take on the BiH head-to-head, had adopted an unstable 'phoney war' strategy – a kind of tense Mexican standoff. Others, either hardcore outsiders sent in from faraway Hercegovina where the war was on full throttle, or indigenous nationalists, were happy to start fighting. When real action did occur it happened in the hills. Though there were to be instances of heavy combat in towns, and Gornji Vakuf itself soon became the scene of bloodier fighting, most operations in Bosnia involved a struggle for high ground. Whoever controlled that as good as possessed the towns in the valleys below. The sacrificial lambs in the strategy were the villages. They could be used as convenient, vulnerable targets for massacre, as happened in Ahmići, in order to polarize surrounding populations along religious lines, or sometimes they were simply over-run in surprise advances which left the occupants at the negligible mercy of whatever unit took control. Too often they were simply burned to the ground and their populace slain or purged.

I was relaxed and happy in a warm alcoholic glow when the door creaked open behind me. The conversation stopped dead. I turned around. There were two men in the doorway: the thug with the dagger and a smaller soldier, an officer with an Adolf fringe of black hair and creased olive face. I could not see what rank he was in the gloom but judging by the reaction of the other men he was a powerful figure.

'Who is this and what is he doing here?' Adolf addressed the NCO. The man shrugged defensively and repeated my story. He had got about three-quarters of the way through when he was cut off by a tirade of abuse. Adolf was nasty but not stupid.

'Some fucking stranger walks in here out of nowhere claiming he is a journalist and you sit him down by the radio? What the fuck do you think this is?' The NCO's shoulders slumped. Before he had time to say anything, new questions came.

'Does he speak Croatian? What has he been asking?' The

NCO was in a position whereby he could either stand up for me and take a lot of abuse for having allowed me in, or slide the focus of interest my way as a means of letting himself off the hook. He chose the latter option, and for the first time I realized my grasp of the language was a double-edged sword.

'Oh, well, he started asking about the situation around here and where our lines were,' the NCO replied cravenly, 'we didn't tell him much but he kept on asking . . .' The other men, getting in on the act, regarded me with a sudden flurry of suspicious frowns.

I was to see this situation often repeated. A group of Bosnians are either polite or indifferent towards you until one headcase turns up and starts causing trouble. Rather than being assuaged by the mood of the majority, the new arrival always seems to convert the atmosphere with the disproportionate power of madness, particularly if they are of any rank, and before you know it you have a real shitstorm to deal with.

The thug pulled me out of the chair, re-arranged it to face the doorway, then pushed me back into it. Before me was Adolf, who drew out his pistol; behind me were the other HVO troops, now all standing.

'Who are you?'

'Where are you from?'

'What are you doing here?'

'Who do you work for?'

'Where did you learn Croatian?'

'How long have you been in Bosnia?'

'Where have you been in Bosnia?'

'Where is your car?'

'What kind of car is it?'

The questions were rapped out one after another. If I had thought that telling the whole truth would make my position there less dangerous, I would have told it all. But it seemed inconceivable that, if I said I had hitch-hiked up through a zone most people were trying to leave, en route for Vitez just to see what happened, I would be safer for it. It went back to the thing of having an identity in war. Everybody needs a guise, an identifying word to satisfy authority. Tell people in power that you are just there to find out about it all for yourself and they will think you are a liar. Officialdom needs to put you in a categorizing box, and if it cannot then it is free to make its own verdict upon your status, which in the case of Adolf and his monkey was obviously not in my best interests.

Many of the questions I could bullshit him on easily. I could have told him I was a weatherman and he would have been pushed to disprove it. As for the car, even if I had owned one it would have been stolen within a couple of hours of breaking down. There was no way he could check up on that. However, it was a strange role I had to play and the men did not have to prove my guilt, merely suspect it, before I was in trouble. In true ex-communist style he thought I was a spy of some type and to allay his fears I had to answer quickly; act a little stupid, but not too stupid; be slightly offended, but not arrogant; respectful, but not afraid. The last point was crucial. The slightest whiff of fear brings out the vulpine nature in such men and they will give you a harder time just for the hell of it. And in Bosnia at that point a hard time could be anything from verbal abuse to time in jail, beatings or a bullet. Apart from that the situation felt not so very different from the questioning I had got at Eton when I was busted for smoking dope: heavy but manageable.

'Have you got any Muslim friends?' he repeated.

'Yes,' I replied. 'Of course I have some Muslim friends. I lived in Sarajevo like I said. You know how it is there. I have got Croat friends, Serb friends. This war is nothing to do with me.'

He paused, running my answer through his head, then lowered the pistol.

'I don't like you or your story.' He leaned close again. 'I don't want you here.'

I shrugged at him. The moment had passed. It was going to be OK. It was funny really. He had the power to shoot me but not the logistics to send me back to distant Croatia. A sullen soldier escorted me to a shed and I was shut in for the night. I was let out at dawn and walked away down the road towards Gornji Vakuf. The officer and his henchman had gone. None of the other HVO could catch my eye as I passed them.

5

The shaking, huddled mass of people cringed and moaned with every fluttering whistle of the incoming mortars. Crowded together in a grass gully, they were the survivors of three coaches caught in a BiH barrage intended for a Croat checkpoint outside Travnik. Bosnian *Gastarbeiters* returning home from Germany, they had become the latest unwitting victims of the fighting that had exploded that day between the HVO and government troops in the town. Terrified, many of them wounded, two of their number messily dead on the road, they were still under fire.

I was happy to lie on the ground among them, cameras clasped forgotten to my chest, until the whirring of a motor drive distracted me. Looking up, I saw the American photographer taking pictures. A little pale, not moving around very much, but taking pictures. Bastard, I thought to myself, realizing that his action was an unwitting challenge to my own, that I would have to betray my instinct and stand up. I got to my feet and started to shoot. This would be no repeat of Sarajevo. I was at last about to sell a picture.

I had finally arrived in Gornji Vakuf and managed to cross the still-fluid front line with the help of a local group of HVO, finally reaching the British UN base in the town. Though dishevelled and stinking, I was offered a civilized welcome by these troops, which included a shower and update on the situation. The whole region was being led down the same path as Mostar and the territory to the south, slipping into Muslim–Croat war. Village by village, town by town, the tenuous alliance against the Serbs was fragmenting into bloody conflict: Prozor, Vitez, Gornji Vakuf and Mostar were only the beginning.

With the help of the Brits through another set of lines I reached the village of Stara Bila the following day, a picturesque Croat stronghold on the high alluvial plain of the Lašva Valley. It was near Vitez, and the location of what was then the main British base in Bosnia. As it was at the centre of the rising conflict and buzzing with the sense of impending fighting, a large number of journalists had rented rooms from local Bosnian Croat families. I had only ever met about four journalists in Sarajevo, and those briefly. The media group in the Holiday Inn had been cliquey and remote. I had always felt awkward on the few occasions I had ventured back to the hotel after my first day in Sarajevo, feeling that the journalists there would dismiss me as a 'war tourist' before I became reconciled to the meaning. In any case, unless there is a real need, I do not like to impose conversation on those I do not know.

Now though, things were very different. The experiences of the past few months had instilled me with belligerent confidence, to the point that I felt almost dismissive towards foreigners with an organization and armoured cars to back them up. I believed that, although I hadn't got the overall picture, I knew as much or more of Bosnians than the average hack, and anyway I no longer cared what journalists thought. Besides, I was now convinced that they could call no-one 'war tourist' without first passing the same judgment on themselves.

To my surprise, away from the confines of the Holiday Inn they seemed like an affable clan of damaged children; a concentration of black sheep taking their chances in the casino of war. However sophisticated the veneer an individual wore, a little way beneath it you discovered personal tragedy and misfortune, the hungry appetite that motivated them to load up on more damage, each personal victory locking them further into defeat. Some carried the symptoms of post-traumatic stress disorder like an inconsequential sidebar to a deeper malaise. They could fight and fuck one another with the abandon of delinquents in care, but they also looked after each other, linked by the altruistic camaraderie common to any pariah group. I fitted in just fine.

I rented a room in a large three-storey house in the centre of the village owned by a childless Bosnian Croat couple, Viktorija and Milan. He lived there, she ran it. On the top floor, facing southwards, my room was spartan and clean, a single bed, wooden table and chair the only furnishings. Though I did not know it at the time, it was to be my home for most of the next two years. I installed myself, slept for a long time, then awoke and waited for the next spasm of war.

The land around me was a confusing kaleidoscope of different allegiances and confrontations, spirals of tension and loyalty imposed upon a landscape of breathtaking beauty. The valley was flat, fertile and lush with summer grass. Deciduous forest covered many of the surrounding hills, though to the west Mount Vlašić and its arterial ridgelines rose like a barren rocky monolith from the vivid green veil beneath. Ahmići, out of view to the east, had been all but burned down and its mosque toppled, yet Muslims still held out in the smallest enclave in Bosnia, Stari Vitez, the old town that formed the kernel of its namesake a mile from us. Nearer the house, a mere three hundred metres away, a little knoll of ground rose above the British base, marking the forward salient of a BiH front line. Sometimes, through the cool mists of dawn, you could see a small crescent flag fluttering above the BiH trenches, and watch the soldiers beneath it stretching away the coldness of the night. By afternoon Viktorija's northern balconies offered stall seats for the firefights that erupted there as the HVO tried to seize this ground, and we would cheer on the progress of these battles like Roman plebs at the amphitheatre, until the bullets started whacking into the roof above us, sending us crawling giggling inside accompanied by the crash of fallen chairs abandoned in the drunken panic.

Stara Bila had a strange atmosphere, an uneasy mixture of the good-humoured sanity that soaked out of the British school-house base, between the lines of white Portakabins that accommodated the troops, across the rolls of encompassing razor wire and into the Bosnian hills behind the tracks of their APCs, and the outright in-yer-face violence of the war. A drunken HVO soldier, nicknamed 'Postman Splat' on account of his pre-war job, had set up a mortar position behind Viktorija's house. Whatever the time of day, he seemed to fire at precisely the moment when your mind had switched to war-state autopilot; the illusion of relaxation that allows you to think of nothing much in particular, although behind the façade your nerves are pulled to the tension of a bow. Then bang, Splat fires his mortar and you hit the fucking roof. 'Outgoing,' some bright boy just in would say self-righteously, like he had known it all along, but you knew that the only reason he was still sitting was because he was fresh out of a London office and not accustomed to the cumulative strain bestowed by random death.

Fire went out around us, fire came in: sometimes mortars and rockets, more often bullets. The weapon system did not really matter, the result was the same: tissue-damage and death. Sometimes it was boring. Nothing happening. But when it changed, it was bad. Walk down the road to see a friend: oh look there's some old bloke been whacked by a sniper; shit, that cow got killed by shrapnel; man, did you see that kid picking cherries blown out of the tree by a recoilless rifle. Not even the Brits were safe. They had already taken their first fatal casualty down in Gornji Vakuf, and firefights along the camp perimeter were nothing new; then one night one of their interpreters, Dobrila, a tall, dark-haired Serb girl, was killed by a bullet in an officer's house at the edge of the Vitez base. The fire that killed her came from HVO lines, yet within twelve hours the locals had a different story. Another interpreter, they said, a Muslim girl, was jealous of Dobrila and had lured her to sit in a chair in sight of a Muslim sniper on the hill, who had then shot her as instructed. This was the mindset of the guilty in Bosnia: screwed-up denial and village cunning from small-minded bigots whose prejudices were given free rein by twentieth-century hardware and the failure of anyone to try and stop them.

The liberal and educated in Bosnia, whose attitudes became an enemy of the war whatever their denomination, had a term for it, *papci*. Literally it means 'trotters', loosely 'oafs'. A *papak* was an oaf. The word amused me when I had first heard Momćilo use it in Sarajevo to describe the Serbs who fired into the city. Then the word extended its meaning in my mind to encompass anyone who failed to understand what was at stake in Bosnia, as the forces of nationalism squeezed the tolerant victims into a nugget of territory before remoulding their leaders into their own likeness. *Papci* – I grew to hate them, whether they were local boot-boys or British diplomats who perpetuated the power of killers by talk of the war as 'an unavoidable tragedy'.

It was the beginning of a formative time in my own perception of the war. Sarajevo had laid down a field of anger in me, yet its focus was still shapeless and unformed, more concerned with 'the war' as an entity than with apportioning blame to any of those behind it. Many people found themselves carrying a gun whether they liked it or not. If you were of combat age, meaning only that you possessed the strength to fight, kill and possibly survive, then you were conscripted into whichever army represented your denomination, Muslim, Serb or Croat. So carrying a weapon was not in itself an indication of guilt. It was more the attitude of the armed individual that gave the clue to what was going on; and generally the Croats in central Bosnia, like the Serbs before them, were drinking more readily than the Muslims from the poisoned chalice of nationalism. There were many reasons why. Primarily it was far easier to resurrect nationalist angst in people who have a defined sense of nationality than those who do not. Both Croat and Serb leaders could bang the drum with images of their people's past persecution and military 'glory' to effect this. After the departure of the Turks in the nineteenth century, the Muslims lacked an 'ethnic identity' until 1974, when Tito recognized them as a separate entity in Bosnia, where they formed the majority population. They were no more than the descendants of Slavic tribes who had settled in Bosnia and converted to the religion of their rulers, the Turks. So the majority had no real sense of an historically rooted nationalism beyond being 'Bosnian'.

The identity of the Croats and Serbs had been borne out of their fights with the Turks. With their history Bosnian Muslims could hardly use the same template. Inevitably many had found a belated quasi-religious sectarianism as a result of their persecution in this war, though the majority remained infinitely more open-minded than their opponents. Most Muslims fought to preserve the right of their nation to exist along its established borderlines.

There were still many towns and villages in which the HVO and BiH maintained an uneasy alliance, strained more each day by the arrival of refugees from fighting in other areas or extremist groups sent in to radicalize the situation. At that stage the ancient town of Travnik at the foot of Mount Vlašić, with its seven mosques the one-time seat of the Ottoman viziers, was still held by both the Muslim and Croat units who shared a front line facing the Serbs across the village of Turbe, slightly further west.

In another universe from mine the Vance–Owen plan was on the table, intending to end the war in Bosnia by carving the state into an unequal three-way share. The proposed borders seemed so ridiculously advantageous to the Bosnian Croats that even they joked that HVO stood for 'Hvala Vance Owen', thank you Vance Owen. Bosnian Croat nationalists in Hercegovina were keen that the land allocated to them in this plan be incorporated into their self-styled state of Herceg-Bosna by force of arms, thinking it would grant de facto credence to the map before anyone had time to change their mind. Much of the area around Stara Bila, including Travnik, was included in the planned Croat sector, so tensions there rose even further, catalysed by the very diplomatic initiative that sought to end it all.

I was drunk in the sun on Viktorija's veranda, waiting for war to happen while talking a brandy-sodden mix of dreams and aspiration with Alex, a young Canadian journalist, when an American photographer burst through the door of my room.

'The shit's hitting the fan in Travnik. The fighting's started. Let's go.' We reached the outskirts of the town within minutes, driving fast in a Lada Niva down the vortex that characterizes every journey to ongoing action: first the noise, the distant kerrump doomdoomdoom, that rips into a crescendo as you get closer; then the visuals – the smoke, burning houses, debris, empty spaces where there should be people; then the time to feel afraid, the moment your life stretches out into a different plane, a sense of freefall without a parachute. Action – it feels like madness every time.

Angry, hostile columns of Croat troops withdrew ahead of the clattering gunbattles and crash of artillery in the town centre. Fleeting images through the haze of brandy: an enraged HVO soldier, puce-faced and with bulging eyes, veins like fat blue worms etched clearly on his neck, shouting 'Catholic or Muslim? Catholic or Muslim? Catholic or Muslim?' as he levelled his Kalashnikov at us; sprawling on the pavement as something exploded near by to the hysterical laughter of a Croatian woman soldier who sat camouflaged, long-legged and lithe on a wall – 'Outgoing,' she managed to splutter through the laughs while the mad fighter fired bursts over our heads, triumphing at our fear; more explosions, close; more angry, frightened soldiers waving us down, blood on the road, slick dark pools of it, the three coaches stationary and shrapnel-scarred, the survivors cowering near by; incoming, outgoing – there is nothing Zen about it; one draws the other, but the other can slice your legs away, eviscerate you, take your jaw off. Dying? That's the least of it sometimes. A whole different story anyway. The game you came to play.

Then the whirling tunnel in reverse, rocket-fuelled by the adrenalin you get when running from fire; careering off back down the road, the car screeching from side to side as someone gave us another burst, the American's words a jumble of life-affirming monologue 'yeah-fuck-you-you-fucking-arseholes-fuck-you-oooowee-fuck-I'm-scared-fuck-fuck-fuck . . .' He had had one of his balls blown off in Sarajevo the previous year when a mortar round landed right in front of him and killed the colleague behind him. David may have lost more than flesh alone that day, but in the small circles of war he cropped up in my life at various pertinent times, usually the lunatic prophet for something bad to come. Our journey that day was far from the worst we were to share together.

Later, sober, as the light faded into tracer-sparkling dusk through the hills around us, he developed my film in his garage laboratory at Stara Bila. He held the roll up to a light bulb, scanning each frame once, then again, happy to see me sweat. 'Nice shot. I'll have this one.' He indicated a single frame. On it, in a weird two-dimensional reversal of the reality that I had snatched from the grass gully, were four faces; those of an old woman falling in the foreground and three men crouched behind her. It was just before the impact of a shell they could hear inbound. They looked predictably terrified. I was given 50 Deutschmarks for the shot and felt elated. It was like Eric's handshake in Čitluk, an open-ended new loyalty with which I began to stop seeing the war from the inside looking out, and began to look from the outside in. The tatty document I still carried to keep UN officialdom happy by suggesting that I worked for a British newspaper was as much fiction as ever, but I had an identity of sorts, the cloak I needed. I was badged a photographer. No longer would I have to take a deep breath before answering the question 'what do you do here?' A four-syllable word could keep all but the most persistent out of my life. Neither the money nor the elation lasted long.

*   *   *

Within twenty-four hours my nerve deserted me. It was not a simple matter of feeling cautious and unsettled, but more a sensation of complete instability which led me again to question myself, only this time it was not a case of wondering whether or not I should be in the war, but the issue of whether I could 'stay' there. We had returned to Travnik, where the Croat resistance was in its death throes, though fighting still ripped through the town. Maybe it was something to do with a hangover, or maybe I had expended my quota of resilience for the time being, but as I stood with three journalists in a building listening to the bull-whipping crack of passing bullets and the shrieking of incoming shells, I knew that I could not walk out of the door into that, and that if I did so I would surely die. Mortal fear had just made its debut in my life, and it was far from welcome.

Of course I had felt afraid before, many times in Sarajevo, and again in Mostar and on the road north. That in itself had been a new experience, like losing control of a speeding car on a mountain road, or walking naked and blindfolded through a sawmill. The fear for your life, the fear of your death. This was different, not a sense that I might die, more that I would die. Once the feeling was upon me – a terrible asphyxiating dread with the first traces of panic snapping at its heels – my imagination went wild. I thought of the ripped limbs, blown flesh and casual mutilation of the war casualties I had seen, feeling worse by the minute. I looked around at my companions. They seemed unmoved. It was just me out there in that icy waste. Worse still I was convinced that my sudden frozen immobility and silence made my state of mind conspicuous to them. I was right. When the fighting subsided slightly we made it back out of the town in an armoured Chevrolet. Even then the fear reached through to me. 'Don't worry about it,' someone said quietly.

Of course I worried about it. Dread was never in my script.

What was it? Where did it come from? Would it stay? The concepts of war and courage left by my family never involved this. Surely my dead ancestors had never felt like this in action, they had just piled in with a cowboy's reckless abandon and returned for the laurels later. That was all I had felt I had to be, reckless. I thought it was the same as courage. The understanding of real fear, let alone dread, had never even crossed my mind in the army. I had sometimes wondered what it was. The only operations I had seen, Ireland and the Gulf, had given no opportunity for it to manifest itself but even if they had done so you are governed by such a different mentality as a soldier, dominated by the aim of fulfilling your task, that you are afforded a powerful barrier to fear's depredations. Your mind is so channelled to a particular purpose, its flanks shielded by concerns related to the position and action of your troops, that little else is allowed in. Besides, you have the beautiful cold weight of a gun with you and if there is time for a bit of individual thought on a job then it is geared to praying for the chance of using it.

The dynamic of my life in Bosnia, one that also fitted this newfound job as a photographer, was entirely different: unarmed, to reach the edge of the abyss in which people were getting killed, stay teetering there for as long as possible without dying, leave, then do it all again as quickly as possible. It was a solitary state whatever the company, and there were darker things than lead that could whack into you out of that void.

Maybe I was a coward? The thought was too awful to contemplate. As bad was the possibility that my nerve had broken like a bit of dry wood and would never be there again. I brooded for three days, and sank into introverted depression. I was totally unprepared for it.

On the fourth day, Gilles, a French war photographer with thirty years' experience, told me not to be such an arsehole.

'Listen,' he said, 'you can do this only so long through ignorance. Reality comes to everybody if they stay long enough. So now maybe you have seen it, don't waste your time dwelling on it. Learn that every day will be different; some days you can be "brave", and some days you cannot. Don't punish yourself with it, it's OK. It's normal. Cut down on your emotional output. You can carry on indefinitely if you stop thinking so much. There is so much shit talked here. Don't argue about anything unnecessarily. Don't get worked up, angry, sad, don't even talk about anything that doesn't matter. Conserve your energy. Whatever you know, you know shit. Each of us has the reaction. It is about different chemistry on different days. Each day is different for each person. You must understand that.'

It was no magical cure, but Gilles was revered for his experience and not the kind of man to roll out empty words of consolation just for the sake of making someone feel better. His advice was to come back to me many times and I see that day now without any sense of shame. It was as if a door had opened, slowly at first, to a new understanding. I did not learn to accept courage in a different form, I grew to see it as a meaningless term of glorification used by the ignorant to describe the actions of others whose real motivations are more often instinctive than altruistic. So began the long winter retreat of emotion.

I took it easy for a while. You could have a good time in Stara Bila that summer, providing you had not been born in the place. Congregated there were every type and nationality of journalist, photographer, cameraman, writer, producer and engineer – the wild, brash, bold and bland, their egos often disproportionate to their talent, if not fame. The fighting spilled further into the hills around us; they glowed with burning villages at night, and echoed with firefights by day. We sometimes watched it over barbecues.

91

At dusk, we would choose our company, load up on whatever was going, and party to excess. We would fade out what the war meant to us and turn up the volume on the generator-run sound system. Night after night the Stereo MCs told us to get connected but for the time being I for one was happy to have pulled the plug.

The relationship between the media and the British troops was close. At that time there was no coherent UN strategy governing its foreign troops in Bosnia. Different commanders in different sectors interpreted their task – to escort aid supplies into Bosnia – in very different ways. Any commander with sense could see the flaw in the whole thing, and throwing food at the victims of an ongoing and savage fight, risking your men's lives to safeguard the impotent moral cowardice of an organization that only perpetuated the war with its hamfisted ineptitude and indecision shamed officers of every nationality on whom the UN's blue beret was forced. Some had their troops close down behind their armour and sandbags and do as little as possible, hoping casualties would be minimal until it was either time to be relieved or the whole maelstrom ceased.

The British in central Bosnia had a unique asset: a twenty-seven-ton tracked shoebox of armour capped by a weasel-head turret, needle-pinned in turn by a Rarden 30mm cannon and the ugly stub of a 7.62 chain-gun with a rate of fire of over 600 rounds per minute. The Warrior fighting vehicle was the battlefield's equivalent of a mobile Kenwood Chef when its hardware was applied to flesh, concrete and metal; in terms of belligerence it was the most potent vehicle of any UN unit in Bosnia at that time. But with no UN strategy to guide them, the British were left to get on with things as they saw best.

'Aid' had become an asset of war. It fed civilians and soldiers alike, and its supply to one side was not in the interest of another.

When a Bosnian fighter of whatever army put an anti-tank mine in the road before a Warrior, the instinct and wish of the commander may have been to remove both, but he could not do so under the terms of the UN mandate which restricted shooting to responsive fire only. For all their Warrior firepower, the British usually had to embark on contorted negotiations to get aid in. Though they hated to do it, and denied it much of the time, their small force had to become brokers in the aid 'market', oiling the links in the supply of food from one side to the other. Often there was no even balance, and the Croats held inordinate power in this game through their control of the only roads into central Bosnia.

Frequently the aid, loaded in UNHCR lorries, never made it out of the warehouses in Croatia. A driver would be killed or a lorry shot up and the UN suits would lose their nerve for a while, or else the Croats along the line at Gornji Vakuf would simply refuse to let anything pass up-country. Sometimes weeks went by with no aid appearing for the British to escort. So they filled the vacuum by mediating between the Croats and Muslims in an attempt to ease the overall situation, becoming the chaperones to every type of exchange on the human meat market: dead bodies, wounded, prisoners, refugees. Alternatively they roared around the countryside in their Warriors trying to chart the progress of the fighting in order to establish who controlled what. It stretched even the ablest of minds. 'Anyone who thinks they know what's going on hasn't been paying attention,' a major remarked dryly at the end of one long day's liaison.

They encouraged the media to accompany them on these tasks as they felt, with the optimism of the time, that public awareness of what was really going on would benefit everybody in Bosnia. The arrangement suited both sides – most of the time. The Brits wanted a high profile; the media wanted to see them in action.

93

Officers associated freely with journalists, who in turn could, if they wished, attend briefings twice daily at a small house outside the gates of the Vitez base.

It was interesting to see the evolution of opinion in the British commanders as the war progressed. Although technically an impartial force, many officers would privately admit to sympathies with the Muslims who were still largely the representatives of a secular ideal, and also were fighting a war against better-equipped forces while crippled by an arms embargo. Later British units, deprived of the opportunity for maverick expression by a revamped chain of UN command with a different political agenda, started spouting the organization's euphemisms that sought to paint every Bosnian side the same shade of guilty grey.

Apparently eased of my fear by the company of friends and a period of hedonistic idling, I began to work again. My dread was like malaria. With a treatment of like-minded spirits and relaxation it went into remission, though the fever returned at lengthening intervals in diluted form. The BiH pushed the Croats away from the edge of Travnik and squeezed them back from positions in the surrounding hills. The front lines, such as they were, proved moody and unpredictable. In quieter moments it was still possible to reach the BiH troops along the main road west to Travnik or east to Zenica. But the fighting in the hills was more ferocious, and as more journalists' cars were shot up so more of them took the opportunity, when available, to ride in the back of a Warrior. You could move through gunbattles without having to think about it, and on a good day get to see the Brits putting some fire down themselves. I stopped marking off in my mind the number of firefights I had watched, and lost count of the number of dead I saw. But some corpses still tore down the barriers of familiarity: the tortured Muslim soldier in Bandol;

the HVO hand whose body had detonated an anti-tank mine, and the one that always stayed in my mind: the catmeat muj.

One day as I loitered in the HVO Vitez headquarters, an excited Croat captain approached me. 'We've just killed four mujahidin near Novi Travnik,' he said. 'Do you want to see?' There was nothing else happening and it seemed peculiar that the dead men, Islamic fundamentalists who had come from abroad to help Bosnia's Muslims, should have died in a Croat village some way from the lines.

I was with Corinne at the time. An American a few years older than me, she combined feminine compassion with a high tolerance for violence and a fine temper. She was later nicknamed 'The Shadow of Death' in Africa for the spooky way in which her presence seemed to herald bloodshed and mayhem. Not surprisingly, her humour was so black it could verge on the infernal. We met at Viktorija's house and had since often worked together. It was a union cemented at the war's altar, and we struck up a loose partnership as road comrades that lasted for nearly a year until her posting to Africa.

We drove off from Vitez to take a look at the slain. By the time we arrived a crowd of villagers had already gathered round the bullet-riddled jeep, which lay tilted in a ditch, skid marks on the tarmac and a trail of oil marking the driver's last moments of frantic flight. The mood of the crowd began to change as we watched. At first they were almost fearful of the bodies. Here, after all, in the middle of their village, was a nightmare come true: three Arabs and an African, proof of the dreaded legions of Allah of which their leaders warned them. They gawped in disbelief. Then some of the younger members stepped forward and began to poke and prod at the bodies through the car's shattered windows. The crowd's silence broke, turning into an angry hubbub of voices. Someone produced a long stick and began to jab at the cadavers. It looked very much like the foreplay to mutilation.

The dead were still sprawled in the car, except the driver, who slumped out of his door. I checked out his papers. He was a Jordanian. There was a bloodied sketch map with him showing the demarcation of the lines, the roads, and some minefields, but the route to reach Travnik went straight through the Croat village in a line of blue. Whoever had marked out the map for them had as good as handed out a death warrant. They had simply driven into the Croat zone, panicked on realizing their mistake, scrambled a U-turn, firing as they did so, and died in a hail of return fire. There was one Croat casualty: an old man having a crap had been hit in the head by a ricochet; hardly dignified, but at least he went out like Elvis.

Then it happened. An HVO trooper stretched through one of the windows to pull a body upright for a better look. The corpse seemed to loll up almost of its own accord, a black African with the side plate of his skull missing. The head tilted gently over the edge of shattered glass, there was a slow squelch and the man's brain fell intact onto the road like a shelled egg. As the crowd went quiet for an appalled few seconds a kitten ran out of nowhere and seized the slippery lump of grey. There was a kind of collective groan from everyone there, and the kitten was kicked away by the HVO.

'Man, the guy sure came a long way to end up as Kit-e-Kat,' Corinne remarked as we drove off, giggling horribly at the awfulness of what we had seen. Emotions are so contorted in war. There are labels which brand sentiments according to shade rather than detail, words like 'afraid', 'revolted', 'shocked'. Most of the time you do not know how you feel in situations, there is no single word to describe the swirling kaleidoscope, so you come out of it and try to cast whatever feelings you had in the right bin – in this case the one marked 'horrible' – where they stay chattering and jibbering like lunatics in secure units, imprisoned until the night's darkness paroles them into your dreams.

Then the war rolled right into Stara Bila like an ugly wind, wrenching open the doors on the UN's power, exposing the emptiness inside for all to see. It arrived on the wheels of a Bosnian civilian aid convoy, named with prophetic irony the 'Convoy of Joy'. The convoy, some 450 trucks, had been organized by the mayor of Tuzla to alleviate the food shortages crippling his northern town, and had loaded up with supplies in Split at a time when the fighting in central Bosnia was still at low ebb. Most of the drivers, though not all, were Muslim. Ignoring UN warnings, the convoy began to roll slowly up through Hercegovina northwards. Doubtless there was a lot of money at stake. Black marketeering had always been big in Yugoslavia, and the war had accelerated its development to the point where every town had its gangs of mafia getting rich on the suffering of others. Often these men were the same ones controlling the fighters, so civil authorities and the police either bought in on the scams or became isolated and ineffectual.

However, Tuzla was always a little different. It was the least damaged of Bosnia's large government-held towns, still more integrated than anywhere except Sarajevo. Although sometimes shelled, it was not broken by a front line. There were mafia in the authorities' hierarchy, but the town remained under a civil control which still retained a high degree of integrity, almost devolved from Sarajevo. Whatever the cut the drivers were to receive on reaching Tuzla, and it would not have been small, the Convoy of Joy's main aim was to relieve the plight of the hungry.

The British commanding officer in Vitez could not stop the

convoy from entering central Bosnia. Since it was not a UN operation, it was outside his jurisdiction. He could, however, advise the convoy leader that he was about to enter a war zone where the codes of normal human conduct had vanished in the wake of the fighting in Travnik. He did so at Prozor, dealing with a Bosnian already so drunk as to be barely coherent. The convoy proceeded regardless. The Croat drivers assured the HVO that much of the aid was for Croat civilians in the north, and this together with hefty pay-offs of money and supplies helped the vanguard of the convoy to drive safely through to the strip of Muslim territory between Gornji Vakuf and Novi Travnik. Here the trouble started.

The advance trucks were entering a zone filled with Croat refugees displaced by the recent fighting with the Muslims. Almost the entire Croat population of Travnik had fled their homes, with thousands escaping through the Serb lines on Mount Vlašić, and others swelling the population of what was by now the Vitez pocket. Cut off from other Croat areas, and afraid for their own future in a zone where commodities were already strained by the overload of refugees, these people were charged with hatred. Though the HVO command in Hercegovina had ordered that the convoy be allowed safe passage, its authority had little or no effect in Vitez. A British Warrior ferried in the senior HVO commander who blanched at the angry Croat mobs and failed to get any guarantee from local units.

It was nearly dark when the first small group of trucks neared Novi Travnik, the scene of the initial fighting in the Lašva Valley, and now divided by a front, to be met by a mêlée of barricades, enraged civilians, Warriors, and HVO troops. The atmosphere was like the prelude to a riot, a charged pressure cooker of mass-hysteric sentiment releasing itself in squalls of rage. Under the eyes of the British troops several unarmed Muslim drivers were pulled from their vehicles, beaten and shot. What could the British do? Under their rules of engagement they could not attack the HVO, who were in any case caught up in crowds of Croat civilians. For a time it seemed as though the mob might turn on the UN troops themselves. We were already getting spat at and punched and, for those who could understand the language, there was talk of killing 'all the foreigners'.

After intense negotiation and what appeared to be a promise by local HVO commanders to keep their people under control, the next vehicles from the convoy, which had been held over-night behind Muslim lines, took their chance the following day, this time with Warriors picketing the roads. The situation was repeated: trucks halted by mobs; looting and robbing accom-panied by bursts of gunfire. I saw one driver punched and kicked repeatedly by civilians and soldiers before being swung onto the prongs of a pitchfork thrust by a woman. Worse followed. Not fifty metres from Viktorija's house a truck was waved down by an HVO soldier. The driver slowed, produced his documents and waved them out of the window at the soldier. Unhurriedly the soldier lifted his Kalashnikov with one arm and fired into the driver's head at point-blank range. The window on the opposite side of the cab blew out in a spray of brains and the truck lurched across the road, crashing into a telegraph post. The gunman walked away. I ran up and peered in the cab. The body was slumped across the seat. His head looked like the pale and empty skin of a squashed baked potato, only with hair. Bits of his brain lay on the seat like jellied semolina. Men, women and children jostled aboard the truck and began to take sacks of flour from the back. They dispersed as more gunfire rattled around us.

Down the road a Warrior did open fire, cutting down two HVO as they prepared to attack another truck. The Croats dressed the bodies in suits, claimed they were innocent bystanders murdered by the British, and invited a TV crew to film the cadavers. I got to know the father of one of the men quite well. He is still trying to get financial compensation out of the UN, though he later admitted that his son had been in uniform that day.

A lone man ran down the road past Viktorija's house in a state of helpless fear. He was a Muslim driver who had miraculously escaped from his truck alive. 'Help me, help me,' he cried. We took him to the small UN press house outside the gates of the base. He sat under an apple tree with his head in his hands while a British captain and a colour sergeant actually argued about the man's fate. The key to his survival lay in getting safe passage through the UN camp to the tiny Muslim hamlet on the other side. Yet under UN rules no Bosnian civilians were allowed into their bases. It never looked as if the British soldiers would kick the Muslim out into the street again, yet what seemed like an obvious course of action – providing an armed escort to take the man down the road through the base to the other side – took a long time to discuss, and even longer to implement. It made your blood pound to see two 'peacekeepers' arguing about a man's life.

Unarmed people were getting murdered before the eyes of a British force which had the firepower and equipment to take the whole valley in a matter of hours if it wished, yet could only watch, like bovine commuters in a London tube who shuffle past a gang of skinheads kicking a hapless individual on the platform. It was not the soldiers' fault, and ultimately the troops who saw what had happened must have faced much more personal disillusion than me. The blame lay with the organization that put them in that situation – the UN. Thank God it was not me in a Warrior that day, battling the instinct to crush the barricades and those upon them with its tracks, while instead having to look on as innocent men were bestially murdered.

By night the situation calmed. The majority of the convoy remained behind Muslim lines as news of their comrades' fate reached them. Those trucks that had crossed ended up in a nearby quarry where their supplies were more systematically unloaded by the HVO. When the lorries were finally empty the quarry was abandoned. Later, lying in one of the cabs, a human finger was found stuck to a piece of soap – the only remaining vestige of the unfortunate drivers.

That night Viktorija's capacious cellars were filled with sacks of grain and flour taken from the captured trucks by a procession of wheelbarrow-pushing locals. A group of journalists and I got very drunk on the floor above. Really drunk. Boorishly and expansively arseholed. Viktorija walked in. In common with many Bosnians she was very tall, but her face in profile was less typically Yugoslav, more like a woman in an ancient Greek mosaic: a handsome forehead, Illyrian stepped nose and proud chin. She had been born in Zenica where her family still remained. In her late thirties, she was very much a city woman, an outsider to the village mentality around her. Until only days before she had been happy to talk her way through the Muslim lines in order to visit her mother and sisters in Zenica, ignoring the locals' talk of mujahidin and other fundamentalists. Tonight was different. The lines had solidified. She had not liked what she had seen going on in the road outside her home, but she was deeply afraid for her own future and the stolen foodstocks were an insurance against what she feared could be an indeterminate siege. It was unclear whether Bosnian government forces would come rolling down the road in retaliation for what had happened.

Viktorija's entry halted our slurred debate. She looked almost unhinged with stress, and pushed her long arms back against the walls of the room in an unconscious parody of crucifixion, pressing her head against the cool of the plaster.

101

'I will never surrender my home to them,' she declared to her dumbstruck audience. 'If I have to leave it I shall burn it first. I would rather torch what is mine than have the Muslims take it.' There were tears in her eyes and her brown skin had gone very pale. We shuffled awkwardly and in silence like schoolboys, and to my eternal discredit, as one who spoke the language and had a good rapport with her, I looked at the floor, hoping the situation would somehow diffuse without my involvement. I had just been saying loud and brutish things of the HVO. Yet here was as much a reality of Bosnian Croat people as the murderers outside: a desperate yet open-minded woman, brought up among Muslims, struggling with the new rules war had thrust upon her, her husband an HVO conscript, afraid and trapped in a valley through no choice of his own.

You could take sides in Bosnia easily enough if you wished, but it never allowed you complete peace of mind.

6

I got my 'break' as a war correspondent at the expense of a mutilated girl, one dead prisoner, probably two, and a wounded journalist. It may have been the carte blanche I needed, and wanted, to stay in Bosnia indefinitely, but the irony of the cost in human suffering has not been wasted on me. Not that I feel bad about it; if an opportunity lands in your lap you do not waste time questioning its origins. I was trying to close down on my sentiments like the French photographer had advised. Walk on looking ahead. Don't look back, don't look down, don't look inwards. You will fall eventually, one way or another, but with those rules at least you will be up there for a bit longer.

The summer-climax sun was so bright it had drained the sky of colour, stonewashing the Bosnian hills into a flat limewash haze. I took a ride in a battered Renault, accompanying two young French photographers through the hills north-east of Travnik. It was a bit of a stupid idea, a kind of 'Search and Be

Destroyed' trip, but I had begun to resent the anaesthetic quality of travelling in a British Warrior. You had to share the terror of those around you sometimes to justify your intrusion upon their suffering; and anyway, there was a limit to how much you could freebase on the war so far behind Chobham armour. Also I was low on cash. Fifty Deutschmarks a photo, a hundred if it included dead or fighting, was barely sustaining me and allowed me little chance to sit around.

A firefight was in progress between one burned village and another, so we stopped behind cover at a bend in the road and began the discussion among ourselves that usually precedes the moment you project yourself into a fight. Cold-bloodedly you talk things through, weigh it all up and intellectualize, before agreeing that the best solution, at least the only one that will allow you peace of mind at that moment, is to blunder lemming-like into the maelstrom and hope you don't get killed, wounded or unhinged.

We were reprieved, temporarily, by the grumbling sound of a Warrior, which trundled obliviously past the action and approached our position. When you know nothing of what lies ahead, you snatch at any piece of information, whoever it comes from, in the hope it will give you even a tiny bit of protection. So I waved the Warrior down and asked what they had seen.

The NCO who came out of the turret sucked his teeth. 'Oh, just one group of Johnnies having pop at t'other,' he enlightened us in a Yorkshire accent. I tried not to roll my eyes and was about to ask if he could be more specific when he spoke again. ''Ere,' he said, as though about to give us a tip for a race. 'One of you lot's been wounded near Vitez.' Immediately we gathered closer around him. If you become inured to the suffering of others, and most war correspondents do, this never seems to include the pain of your own casualties. A war reporter gets hit and bam, everyone busts a gut to get them out, the driest and most cynical usually leading the charge. 'Ours.'

'Sounds like a mine,' the man added. 'Badly injured. Patrick something or other.' My mind flashed to the only Patrick among us, an experienced and erudite writer for a British broadsheet. We had got trashed together on a couple of occasions, and I had drunk deeply from the cup of his wisdom and advice. The Warrior ground off elsewhere as we tore back towards Vitez, the gunbattle forgotten.

A mere hour earlier we had driven out across the Muslim-Croat front line at the western edge of the Vitez pocket. It had been silent, an invisible point in a hamlet marked only by an increase in the damage to the buildings on either side. Now, turning the corner for the long dash back down this road, we saw a log barricade and mines ahead. As we slammed on the brakes gunfire erupted around us, whacking into the tarmac and verges beside the car. Booting open the doors we rolled out, slithering on our bellies across the grass to the cover of the nearest wall, minds the usual whirling pool of surprise and confusion. BiH troops from the 17th Krajina Brigade, a famed refugee unit, had begun an attack seconds earlier, fighting the HVO through the houses around us, and we had driven into the middle of it. Greeted with the inevitable wave of a Kalashnikov in the face, we adopted a nonchalance we didn't feel and offered cigarettes. The gun barrels pointed our way were soon dropped.

In the chaotic scramble of shooting, running soldiers, ricochets and shouts, two HVO troops were dragged from a house right in front of us and spread-eagled against a wall. Perhaps it was our presence that saved them at that moment, for though the Krajina troops were generally better disciplined and more humane than other units, prisoners were routinely shot by all sides. The two men were forced to kneel while a tall red-haired soldier stripped them of their webbing and ammunition pouches, taking one set, with a handsome bone-handled knife attached, for himself. Its previous owner began to cry. The HVO were both very young, battle-shocked and uncertain of their fate. It was only later that I discovered the real reason for this particular man's fear.

When I gave him a cigarette he calmed down and began to talk. 'We did not want to fight our Muslim brothers,' he said trembling. 'The war was forced upon us and we had to join the HVO.' I swallowed this and the ramble of the same nature that followed. He was nineteen, and seemed like one of the many victims who had ended up in combat unwittingly. He said that his parents lived in Vitez and asked me, the tears beginning again, if I could let his mother know that he had been captured but was alive. With the acquiescence of the BiH troops I took his address. The armija fighters seemed quite indifferent to their two prisoners at that moment. There was no trace of the malice you might have expected under the circumstances. The pair were led away as the fighting escalated.

Unable to reach our car let alone continue the journey because of the concentration of fire, we stayed with the Krajina soldiers. They were a product of the war with whom it was easy to empathize: most of them young men whose only church was rock'n'roll and miniskirts, but who had been purged by the Serbs from their western Bosnian homeland because their names identified their ancestors as converts to Islam. Many were former inmates of Serb concentration camps, notorious centres of murder and abuse, who had been dumped across the front line at Turbe like sectarian garbage. I had seen these crossings several times: shattered-looking civilians plodding along the road, their worldly goods, if they were lucky, jammed into a plastic bag. On occasion the Serbs would fire around them as they went over the line, a passing send-off of fear. In Travnik they would find temporary accommodation in either the gymnasium or the schoolhouse, where they packed onto floorspace already contested by other refugees.

The 17th Krajina Brigade had been formed early in the war the previous year by Mehmet Alagić and Fikret Ćuskić, both former JNA officers who happened to be Muslim and whose homes lay in the Krajina. It was a small refugee army, fighting to return home, and the 17th's recruiters found no shortage of volunteers among the families of dispossessed jammed into the refugee centres. They were men with little to lose and everything to gain. Bosnians are terrible snobs, and very parochial in their loyalties. Sarajevo citizens were the ultimate snobs, regarding the rest of the world as populated largely by peasants and *papci*. However, the trait was also present in village and small-town communities, and even the inhabitants of the lowliest hamlet knew secretly that everyone across the valley was their social inferior, regardless of their religious denomination. So the Krajina troops, for whom the central Bosnian war was an inconvenient distraction from their real desire to fight the Serbs and regain their homes, became the ultimate military snobs of central Bosnia, scorning both the local Muslims and the Croats as hinterland idiots fighting among themselves at the expense of the effort against the Serbs. 'We are fighting one set of oafs for another here,' one soldier explained.

The gunbattle lasted for six hours. Teams of troops rushed forward, then back in disarray, then forward again, against a continuum of RPG exchanges and bullets. The scene became increasingly surreal. At some point a group of soldiers found a calf in a shed, which they slaughtered, skinned and began to barbecue in the lee of a stone wall. They made an improvised table out of a broken door, resting it upon two chairs, and asked us to eat with them. Someone produced bottles of unlabelled šljivovica and we were quickly drunk. A burst of HVO machine-gun fire cut branches from the tree above us which landed on the table in a salad of splintered wood and leaves, and the BiH diners kept interrupting their eating to return fire from the corner of the building, or to shout orders to the flanking troops locked in battle.

At first I thought the red-haired soldier was offering me a succulent morsel of veal. Then I noticed the lobe. A human ear lay in his palm. It was pink, delicate and feminine. He looked shocked: he had just discovered it while searching through the contents of his newly acquired ammunition pouch. The conversation faltered slightly. The bone-handled knife with which we now sliced our meat had been used with equal relish elsewhere. Small wonder the prisoner had cried, knowing the impact such a discovery might have on his life. Two men were sent back to 'deal' with him. They walked past us nonchalantly, out of it for the easy price of the trigger pull. Bang bang bye bye.

Eventually the fighting subsided, more through a will of its own than positive advantage to either side. A BiH trooper slalomed across the road, rolling the log and a mine out of the way; we ran to our car, skidding fast through the front lines, untouched. What could I tell the boy's parents? 'Hi, yeah your kid was fine to start with, but then they found a Muslim girl's ear in his pocket. So he got topped'? I tore up the address and left it fluttering in the road behind us.

In Stara Bila I found Patrick alive and in better shape than I had feared. A claymore mine had sprayed shrapnel into a leg and arm. He was very lucky. Accompanying a British patrol he had got out of the Warrior to witness a front-line liaison between the UN troops and the HVO, the last in a file of men walking up a path towards the Croats. The first British soldier noticed the claymore tucked in foliage at the edge of the track; not difficult as for some reason it was painted blue. Word of it passed back down the line of men to Patrick. There seemed little danger as they were there to talk with the HVO. But some panicking kid in a trench clicked the switch anyway. A second earlier and Patrick would have been torn to pieces. As it was, he had walked to the edge of the weapon's arc, and so lived. He was leaving to recuperate, and he asked if I could cover for his paper until someone else arrived. I told him of the day's events, and he suggested I write about it.

I did not know how to type, so wrote the story in biro on scrap paper, dictating it down a UN satphone to the paper in London which ran it uncut. The photographs I had taken that day were useless. Take away the sound, motion and atmosphere from a scene of fighting, transpose an image on to a two-dimensional surface, and you have to have something really special to communicate even a trace of the madness you witnessed. My shots were clumsy and empty: blurred figures running with guns; even the firing looked cardboard, meaningless. I had been there, I knew the reality. Friends there knew it. They were all wise enough to know what might lie behind a fuzzy shot of a soldier running. But people who had never been to war? Their understanding of combat was the Hollywood version, in which you watch one man fire and the other man fall, a tandem you hardly ever see in war, and if you do the chances are it happens too quickly to get on film.

When a photograph does capture 'the moment' in war, whatever it is, it leaves all the other mediums of reportage so far behind as to make them almost irrelevant: a single punch to the consciousness that will not go away until you close your eyes or look at something else. Yet I was not a good photographer, and was too often frustrated by my inability to capture on film the essence of what I was witnessing. Words, though open to different interpretations by different people, at least allowed me greater opportunity to explain what was happening, if only to myself.

Patrick left and I freelanced for his paper until another staff man turned up. Then someone else, leaving for a break, asked if I could cover for another British broadsheet. Happy with the liberty this new medium gave me I agreed, beginning a relationship that was eventually to develop into regular pay. It was not the fulfilment of a professional ambition, more a personal one. Although I had done the photojournalism course in London, journalism in itself had never really interested me – I saw it only as a passport to war. Well, that was what I now had, and I could not be too cynical about it. Anyway, it was an undeniable buzz at first: wow, they published my story in the newspaper.

The main problem was that I neither knew if I could write, nor what was expected of me. Were there stock questions I was supposed to ask? Was there a formula to be followed? How did you fit all the details together into a story? In the absence of knowledge I resolved to carry on like a photographer, only writing about what I saw instead of taking pictures. With a few notable exceptions, print journalists in Yugoslavia hamstrung themselves with a work ethic so empty and meaningless that its only benefit was one of physical security. It went like this: 'There is no need for writers to go to the front as it offers no width of perspective, is worthlessly dangerous and repetitive. Better that they put their energies into speaking to figures of authority a little way behind the line, who will afford a broader understanding of what is going on.'

All participants lie in war. It is natural. Some often, some all the time: UN spokesmen, Croats, Serbs, Muslims, the lot. Truth is a weapon more than a casualty. Used to persuade people of one thing or another, it becomes propaganda. The more authoritative a figure, the bigger the lies; the more credible his position, the better the lies. Why waste time listening to an officer in a head-quarters crank out the party line when you could see the reality of a situation for yourself in the dirty bunkers up the way? That others chose not to go to the scene of fighting was understandable. It was dangerous and frightening. On one level there was no match between death and 600 words on page fourteen. If you went, then you went for yourself. If you did not that was fine too; and, ironically, editors were probably happier with lies from names their readers recognized as power figures, than with real talk which they wrote off as 'colour'. Colour? At the front it was always laid out before you in black and white. No room for pretence and posture in the dying places, only an awful purity; the fear of death which democratizes the emotions, the struggle for survival which distils the life-force into a concentrate. Basic humanity. No colour there.

The changes this new job brought me were slow to show themselves. Deadline pressures dictated some of my movement, and I spent more time with journalists than Bosnians. Sometimes, it seemed the more I wrote the more distanced I became from the war, packaging it out to faceless men in a London office like the middleman in a business deal, handling the goods without consuming. But, then, that was the deal I had chosen, and there were consolations. As I was not paid much I was still largely left alone to do what I wanted. The paper had a 'news' gathering operation set up in Sarajevo, so I was allowed to wander around while someone else copped the heat of fact gathering.

Primarily, though, writing suddenly gave me a sense of purpose. I had found the war to be as unjust as it was brutal. There was no equal guilt. There was right and wrong. I still believed that if you showed enough people something that was flagrantly evil, they would react to try to stop it. I was a child of British culture. I had been an officer in the British army. I had no problem with the concept of killing when killing was due, but I thought the nation of my home had some kind of moral integrity. I was not purely sentimental in my idealism. Less than two years before I had been part of a force sent to the Gulf to take Kuwait out of the hands of one tyrant and return it to those of its original dictators. I knew that most foreign policy was governed by raw pragmatism. Yet if you laid aside values like compassion and justice, was there not still a need to stop the war in Bosnia? Was there not a necessity, on every level, for Europe to challenge and counter the dark forces of nationalism, intolerance and state murder?

Gone was my wandering impartiality. I was for air strikes, for NATO intervention, for arming and training the Muslims. I believed something fundamental was at stake in the war. I found an ideal, and with it new enemies: the dreary, cynical, flaccid suits in whose pudgy fingers lolled the reins of Europe's power. I was one of the 'do something brigade', the words Douglas Hurd used to describe and dismiss the growing numbers of people wanting interdictory action in Bosnia. When you are faced with a prophetic abscess in Europe, something which if ignored will have far-reaching consequences for the future of all who live there, is not 'doing something' the whole point? It was no contest of course. We lost. They won. The hollow men usually do.

Paradoxically though, crossing the front lines in Bosnia could be like walking through a mirror into a perfectly symmetrical opposite world. Leave the final positions of one side, pass the line of debris and damage into a new zone where everyone looked the same, spoke the same language and increasingly had the same opinions but with different buzz words. Few fighters spoke of Muslims, Croats and Serbs any more, it was all Turks, Ustaša and Četniks, a clumsy force-fit parody of previous conflicts that never quite squeezed into the new reality. Moments of human sanity seemed so incongruous that when they occurred, the war could look like a terrible game.

Turbe was the door to the second half of the war. A battered snake of houses at the foot of Mount Vlašić, it would usually only open one way, inwards, to disgorge refugees from the Krajina. Crossing the Muslim–Croat front lines was one matter for foreigners: if they were quiet it was manageable. Crossing the Muslim–Serb lines was something else: impossible, except in a very few Checkpoint Charlie-type areas including a road to Sarajevo. Sometimes the scene of fierce fighting, Turbe was also the trade point for body exchanges, black marketeering, and a waste-chute the Serbs used to dispose of those they continued to purge from their territory: Muslims and Croats. It was a no-go crossing point for journalists.

So when Beba asked if I would like to go across to the Serb side with him, I thought he was joking. He was a liaison officer in the government army, a Muslim. We were standing together on a crest of ground overlooking the Serb lines. A ceasefire had been organized so that the Serbs could collect some of their dead from a failed attack of the previous week. Under the terms of this deal, Beba and four of his men, wearing purple sashes over their smocks, tuned in to the Serb net on their motorolas, and stood up above the trenches at the foot of Mount Vlašić. The Serbs came out of their lines and began searching through the scrub for their dead, responding to the shouts of Beba and his men.

'No, left a bit, left a bit, are you blind? Yeah, there, see him?' they would call out. There looked to be about a dozen corpses, but the Serbs only managed to retrieve four. The rest lay in a minefield, and were abandoned to the earth.

'Now I'm going to meet them,' Beba said to me, 'do you want to come?'

I was stunned for a minute. Muslim soldiers talking to the Serbs on radios or across trenchlines happened all the time, but to actually cross into their zone was something I had not heard of. Of course I agreed. We crammed together, a six-pack of unarmed men in a dented civilian car, and began the drive out through Turbe, past the war's scabby detritus of rubble and shredded metal to the point where the film seemed to reverse, and we crossed the 'line'. Driving on for a mile or two, past Serb soldiers who stood sullenly by the roadside, we reached a lone building outside which sat a group of Serb officers and men.

'Stay in the car, don't look around, and don't say or do anything until we call you over,' said Beba as he and his boys disentangled themselves from the vehicle. Two minutes later he reappeared and invited me out. It was not a moment to ask questions that may have stilted the scene, more a time to be as invisible as possible and watch what unfolded. I quickly said hello to the Serbs, sat slightly to the rear of the group, and listened.

'We are still missing nine from that attack,' the Serb officer said. 'We can see six in the gully among the mines, are you sure you haven't got the other three?'

'There are seven in the gully, one is almost hidden behind a rock. We definitely don't have anybody prisoner from that night. You know what happened, the guys never even made it as far as our lines.'

'Yeah, I know.' The Serb sounded tired. He and Beba talked like two friends discussing an issue at work; there was neither malice nor coldness. It appeared that nearly all of the fighters knew one another from before the war, having either been to school together, served in the same JNA unit, or got drunk together.

'What about the five of our guys missing from last Thursday?' Beba said. 'We heard some were taken alive.'

114

'No. We've got the three from the previous week you know about, no-one else. You know how the line is there. If I hear anything I'll let you know.'

'Same channel same time?'

'Same channel same time. Fuck it, let's have a drink.'

The conversation changed, and the men began to talk about mutual friends. How was Huso? Huso was wounded. Shit. Mladen? He left Bosnia last month, yeah, with his family, got out to Novi Sad. Lucky bastard. Beba's brother had been badly wounded a few days before, shot in the head by a Serb sniper at Turbe. The news of it seemed genuinely to upset the Serb officer.

'I am so sorry,' he said, shaking his head.

'*I mene,*' – and me – replied Beba.

What defined these two groups? Race? They were the same race. Culture? They were all Tito-era children. Religion? No man present had the first clue about the tenets of his own faith, be it Orthodox or Islam. They were southern Slav brothers, pitted in conflict by the rising phoenix of long-dead banners raised by men whose only wish was power, *vlast*, and in so doing had created a self-perpetuating cycle of fear and death that grew in Bosnia, feeding off its own evil like a malignant tumour. Rendezvous such as these were not avenues in which to see division and hatred. The war was about polarity and separation.

I was silent for the journey back. It was often easier to understand a world of Četniks, Turks and Ustaša than this.

7

Nikola was having a barbecue. It was to be a great event, a gastronomic extravaganza of slain livestock, Travnik cheese and šljivovica. It exceeded everyone's wildest expectations, though for reasons different from those originally anticipated. He was the head of a small Croat family in Stara Bila. Two of his three daughters had already left Bosnia and were living as refugees in Split. The youngest, Nikolna, was six years old, a beautiful, angelic-faced child who had remained with her parents. They had often agonized over whether to try to get her out, but as the lines solidified around the pocket it seemed better to have her stay at home, even though the Muslim positions were just across the meadow.

Like many families, he and his wife Ljuba had rented out part of their house to journalists. The foreigners who stayed in Stara Bila for any length of time transcended the position of mere tenants, becoming something between patriarchal guests and family. Foreigners were big assets. They paid in Deutschmarks, and brought in food, cigarettes and generators. Yet in return they were overwhelmed with hospitality of such charm it plastered over the deal's seams. Blash and Wayne were just concluding a long stay with Nikola before heading back to Split and the world. They were a TV crew, a double act combining Zagreb savoir faire with South London savvy. They had become close friends of mine, and in turn lavished upon me the logistics I often lacked as a lone entity: whisky, smoke and music.

The barbecue was to be held in honour of their leaving. It was time for me to leave for a while too. The previous day, while I was smoking lazily on my back, eyes closed, in the sunshine near Viktorija's house, a small Croat boy had thrown an empty plastic jerrycan from a window on to the concrete patio below. He only wanted to fill it with water but as it hit the ground beside me it made a loud, explosive *doomdoom*. It felt like my back muscles alone propelled me upwards in fright.

'You fucker bastard,' I screamed at the kid, on my feet now and gripped by an overpowering rage. For a moment I wanted to punch him. What the fuck was he trying to do? Making a noise like that. He was about six years old, and looked terrified. I calmed down. It was definitely time to go. I had left England thinking that I would be away for eight weeks. That was over five months ago.

I had gone to see Wayne and Blash. They said I could ride out with them, and Nikola asked me to his barbecue. I could hear the pig squealing in the yard as he cut its throat, the protracted gurgling shriek that always preceded a good party in Stara Bila.

I never liked the lane where Nikola lived. Like the Bosnians, I was getting a bit snotty on the top floor at Viktorija's, where the third-storey view seemed to dominate more than just the valley. The other half of the village was without doubt the

117

carrot-crunchers' end of town, not that you could ever tell them that. Viktorija knew it, and I knew it. It was our understanding. 'Them' and 'us'. On several occasions locals she disliked came to the house to ask a favour. As soon as they left she would call me over conspiratorially, grimace at the departing individual, gesture accusingly at the other side of the village, wink, then flip her hand dismissively. '*Papci*,' we would say quietly to one another, nodding wisely. The world was full of them, and the nothern avenue in Stara Bila seemed to have a surplus requirement of fascist brutes.

Besides, you always had the uneasy feeling of being watched as you walked down the other lane. The BiH looked right over you. They could make out the colour of your eyes with a good scope. As well as the war, the road seemed to have attracted a bad power of its own. Nikola's son, a young man in the HVO, died mysteriously in the shower one day; my friend Alex, the Canadian journalist, was found there half-conscious in a vegetable patch, one leg multiply broken. He had got very drunk the night before and fallen off a balcony. Somehow it would never have happened at Viktorija's. Later in the same lane I saw an old man sniped in the leg as he checked his goat. So it was a zone where even washing, getting trashed or checking the livestock took on added menace.

But I had friends there, and it was the venue of the party – which began well. Blash, Wayne and I got stoned inside while Ljuba laid the table in the yard and Nikola threw the first chops on the fire. By dusk we were raising toasts to all and sundry. '*Živjeli* Wayne, *živjeli* Blash, *živjeli* Antonio,' Nikola would start, '*moji stari, stari prijatelji*': my dear, dear friends. 'And long live Nikola, and long live Ljuba,' we would reply, again and again, each time whacking back another glass of slivo. Šljivovica was a national institution in Bosnia, a clear brandy made out of plums, the cell-popping tonic for every occasion; the catalyst of happiness, the balm to sorrow, a cure to boredom, the fuel to aggression, even the excuse for murder. You could see God through a haze of slivo out there, even if it was the other guy who manned the bar.

Within a short time we were all off our heads. Then the Croat helicopter came in. Though not infrequent it was always a novelty, an unseen presence in the dark night sky, a shapeless whockathrob of rotorblades – often pursued by Muslim tracer fire – which dropped ammunition and supplies to the HVO and took away the wounded or officers to receive orders in Hercegovina. It had a small landing pad covered from shellfire by a knoll near the quarry. In order to reach it without too much exposure the pilot had to come in high over the pocket, then corkscrew sharply down to land.

Either the pilot was a new one this night or the mist disorientated him, for he got it wrong and flew in low and slow, close above Nikola's roof. We gaped at its fleeting shadow from the Bacchanalian chaos of our table. 'Nellicopter,' we slurred at one another, grinning like idiots.

And then there was bedlam. The BiH opened up at the chopper from the hill barely two hundred metres away. These were no selective probes, but thunderous peals of machine-gunfire. The HVO fired back from beside and behind us. Caught in the middle and itching for an excuse, the British soldiers in their camp sangars, just beyond the end of the garden, started firing in both directions. Nikola's yard became the epicentre of a three-way shootout and, not to be outdone, he lurched to his feet, pulled out a Luger and started blasting away at the muzzle flashes in the darkness. A catherine-wheel of flying food and glasses ignited as we threw ourselves away from the table, Wayne wrestling Nikola to the ground shouting the only word he knew in Bosnian, '*Ne*, *ne, ne.*' It was all you needed when it really came down to it.

'Fuckin' 'ell,' Wayne drawled at me behind the cover of the shed, 'thought the fuckin' Brits would have us there . . .'

The helicopter had banked away, drawing the fire with it. The party resumed, if anything with an accelerated thirst. Bosnian barbecues: the world is never the same again.

Next morning, heads battered and sorry, we loaded up the armoured Chevrolet and said goodbye. Nikola and Ljuba were suffering. Once again they were wondering about the future of Nikolna. If there was a chance for her to leave for Split then it was now, with us. Neither parent could make up their mind. Ljuba leant down and asked Nikolna what she wanted to do. Six years old, and confronted with such a choice. Leave your parents, and you may never see them again. No coming back until the war ended. You do not know how long that will be. The little girl looked very serious, and gazed from one parent to the other. 'I'll go to Split,' she said. There was something very solemn and dignified in her eyes.

Squashed between an edit pack and camera gear she sat on my knee for the ride out, crying softly. She had not been in a car since the war started, and was made uneasy by its motion. Shortly she stopped crying, and puked over my legs. It was a long eight hours to Split, and the sun beat down mercilessly.

I returned home to a small, hardcore group of friends – a talented, incestuous band of West London hedonists with leanings towards self-destruction. Though all a few years older than me, they had drawn me quickly into their circle, treating me with almost parental respect – a new tribe whose company I fell back into whenever I came home from the war.

Alex was a ball of energy contained in a roguish exterior, an engine of ideas that were usually realized, whichever side of the law they fell. His beautiful honey-blonde wife, Lela, tempered his excesses with an often intuitive insight and gentleness. We were exceptionally close, perhaps recognizing some shared essence in one another as good friends sometimes do, and she became like a sister to me.

There were three other primary players. Shimmy, puckishly cynical, was the couple's jaded spiritual shadow. Stella was one of the most striking women in West London, an actress with a gymnast's body, cropped black hair and laser-blue eyes. Then there was Leon. Leon could have stepped out of the frame of one of his own cartoons. Tall and thin, he had the drawn face of a weary Judge Dredd, dragging a wounded sense of integrity out of his black ink world and into Portobello's streets and cafés. He was an old friend whose dry humour, sense of calm and imagination I deeply valued. We had sealed our bond with a lot of drug taking.

There were other faces at the edge of this band, but none I knew as well as these five. Inevitably there had been a black side to the turned-on liberalism and open-mindedness that characterized our easygoing philosophy: marriages down the pan before partners had turned thirty, furious rows, while the frequent drug use that bonded us began to grow around our feet like nightshade, sending curling shoots past our ankles unnoticed, at least by me, at that time. Yet ultimately we had always had each other and our dealings with one another were marked by forgiveness and compassion. We had had a good time, kicking the days faster and faster, oblivious to the first darkenings on the horizon behind us.

It was they who had gathered with me for my final evening in London to see me off to war months before. Though my plan to go to Bosnia had encountered a lot of opposition, it had their full support. War? They saw it as a potentially extraordinary new experience, and I had felt like a messenger who should go forth on their behalf as well as my own to bring back word from the new frontier.

'Well, Ant,' Alex had told me that night, standing in the centre of the room and raising a glass like the master of ceremonies, 'I think it is a fucking mad idea, but all power to you. Whatever you learn out there will be amazing, regardless.'

We had hung out, drunk a bit, got a little stoned, then someone produced some gear and the hubbub of conversation quietened a little as the focus of attention followed the path of a strip of silver foil and smoker around the room.

It was not a big deal to me then. Smack was an excess I felt I could sample once for the knowledge, then maybe again, but I never imagined it becoming a habit. Whenever I had shared it in their company it seemed eminently manageable, an enjoyable numbing of the senses that made me relaxed and garrulous. I never awoke the morning after a session with the urge to do it again, and felt that addiction must be something to do with character more than exposure to the drug.

We chased the dragon. It was more of a shared experience than booting up. There were friends who preferred the needle, but it seemed like an unnecessary commitment to most of us, a handing over of control.

We had spoken about addiction several times, dismissing its threat to us on each occasion. 'It's all to do with personality,' Alex would say, 'a question of whether or not you have an addictive nature. And you and I, Ant, are definitely going to be OK. We can take it or leave it.' I would nod and grin at him knowingly, knowing nothing.

I remember that final send-off well. I had liked the way I felt, cool and distant on the threshold of such a great adventure; I had liked the way that the ghosts of my friends' farewells still flickered in the dawn light of departure, liked the last hit in the kitchen from an unwrapped smoker, the final shot of deserved Dutch courage, liked the final ride in my girlfriend's car to South London where I transferred my rucksack into the Moldova-bound friends' Skoda, liked the final kiss.

If only coming back had been as good.

At first, seeing everyone again had been a delight, and all the familiar traits of life at home were novel luxuries. My friends in London were eager to know 'what war was like', and I was happy to tell them what I had seen. That bit was easy. More difficult was the task of explaining that I felt something was at stake in Bosnia; that I had found an unexpected sense of idealism out there, a feeling that the war was a burning issue; that fundamental concepts like multi-ethnicity and religious co-existence were again threatened in Europe by the tyrannical intolerance of nationalism.

However tuned in my friends, we were all consumerist children of the Sixties with an appetite for quick kicks without complications. They wanted to feed their senses – as I would have done in their position – by hearing of the blood and violence without the complexity of it all. Sixty years earlier perhaps they all would have volunteered for an International Brigade and gone over to fight in Spain. That they did not now was the result of being a product of a different age, a different society. We did not have the sense of idealism, awareness and conviction of our forefathers. It was not our fault, but it was, I guess, ultimately to our detriment.

My mother and sister were excited at the way things had turned out. They had both been into the idea of the Bosnia venture in the first place. With her family history my mother had been all too familiar with the desire of men to go to war for war's sake, if no other, and now not only had I returned alive but she had read stories that I had written in the newspapers. She thought it was cool. I guess it was.

But after little more than a week I began to feel uneasy and disconsolate. The sensation was clumsy and unformed, but it left me moody, disembodied and restless. Once a fortnight had passed I felt conscious of being unhappy. It was like stepping off a speeding train. My senses cartwheeled hopelessly in the vacuum like a forgotten satellite, and I started to feel very alone.

How do you begin to transpose one experience into the 'normality' of another? How can you even expect those at home to understand? Should you even want them to? Why start pushing the damage you shoulder through choice onto the lives of those close to you at home?

My relationship with my girlfriend needed urgent confrontation of some sort, but I felt remote from my feelings and unsure of what I should do. I was sure I still loved her. But my overriding urge was to get back to Bosnia and I could not square that with any other commitment. Rather than face the conflict of interest I chose to duck it and hope that everything would somehow muddle its way through for the best. We had a couple of rows, stirred around the pieces, sorted nothing out. I preferred silence and solitude to company and communication. It was the beginning of the end for us, though we hung on to the rags of our relationship for a long time before finally letting go.

I spoke to a couple of editors. They were interested in taking more stories from me. I kicked around for another week or so, then packed up my rucksack and headed back to Bosnia.

GODS

Soldiers in wartime are among the most superstitious people in the world, every one of them augur to their own fortunes. Invariably each individual carries some charm or other with him into action, or goes through a complicated private ritual, hoping to slip past the reaper unnoticed. Units have 'lucky' fighters, bestowed with more benevolent power than mascots alone – at least until they get killed and the mantle slides onto another's shoulders – while death can escalate the memory of even the most unremarkable man to an altogether different realm, like a living ghost. Overlaying all this are the natural portents: stars and storms. I even met a Muslim commander who insisted that the clarity of the previous night's crescent moon prophesied the coming of Kali Yuga; a time of vengeance and retribution. He was so into the whole vibe he would go into firefights unarmed, encouraging his men forward with spiritual exhortations. In Tito's time maybe he would have been a political cadre, attached to a unit to keep them politically straight. But in Bosnia communism had died with the Marshal, and perhaps after all it was Kali who stepped forward to take over from where brotherhood and unity left off.

I was no different. In spite of a natural cynicism, which I fought dearly to hold onto during the war, I became little more than an existentialist hypocrite touting my values of chaos and futility on one hand, laden down with talismans and superstitious awe on the other – back-up should my cover get blown.

In one pocket I always carried a whirling blue and red shell from the Indian Ocean. Shimmy had given it to me, telling me that fishermen called it the eye of Shiva, and that it bestowed great power upon the bearer. In another pocket I carried a bullet that had been pulled out of Adrian Carton De Wiart in France during the First World War. In my jacket I had a small silver chiming ball from Nepal given to me by a lover. Around my neck on a leather thong were two Buddhist charms from Thailand and Indonesia. I never carried a cross, but I guess the ultimate fallback position lay in a teenage death's-head tattoo on my shoulder.

Now the war is over, my war charms lie abandoned in my bedroom, leaving me with death on my shoulder and a monkey on my back. Peace seems to allow so little space for belief in destiny, fate, God or ghosts. That could just be the smack talking, but even discounting the iced-down state of my senses and intuition, London seems a wasteland of spiritless order, the unvarying rhythm of its days somehow denying the possibility of any other dimension.

Looking back from this perspective it is too easy to mock the war's superstitions, to write them off as no more than manifestations of fear. Unless I had been there, I would be the first to deny them any credence. But there were some very, very heavy vibes going down during the war that I would be hard-pushed to explain rationally: twilight zones where your five senses counted *for nothing but a sixth kicked in like a motor, sending your skin shivering over your flesh and presentiment squirting into your bones. Animals were especially attuned to it: when NATO finally embarked on a series of extensive air strikes in 1995, one of the first wave of bombs to fall on the Serbs above Sarajevo was heralded by a howling chorus from the city's dogs that began well in advance of the jets' nocturnal arrival. The dog story came as no surprise to me for the city was a crucible of sensation. There were times in 1993, once I had adapted to the capital's rhythms, when I swear I could feel incoming on my skin minutes before the whistle of the first shell. The trouble was that it was not a conscious re-action, so I never knew how far I could rely on it, or if it would fool me into making the wrong move either by its presence or absence.*

The question of destiny still has me confused, though. To accept it as a concept seems like a big cop-out to me, the final surrender of your own power. That said, my war had too many coincidences, full circles and déjà-vu experiences to discount the hand of fate completely.

Even the way my grandmother's words on the day of Tito's death came back to me, words that had meant so little at the time, sticks in my mind as something more than a little strange. The timing was too perfect . . .

The heat bounced around the hotel's small roof garden shimmering into a straitjacket that pinned me to the edge of the waist-high wall overlooking Marrakesh's Djemaa el Fna. I lolled across it, gazing down on the stage before me, entranced by the entertainment the square afforded. Jugglers, snake-charmers, beggars, street-urchins, fortune-tellers and acrobats formed small cornerstones for the rippling streams of Moroccans weaving through them like tendrils of river weed. But I did not want to go down there myself. I had tried that on several occasions, each ending in a fury. It was the summer of 1991, just after the Gulf War. Feelings still ran high against the West in much of the Islamic world, and Foreign Offices throughout Europe had recommended their nationals avoid North Africa and the Middle East. In the dearth of pale-skinned travellers those that chose to venture there became the focus of attention for every hawker with something to offer. In three weeks of travelling not a daylight hour had passed without my feeling as if every conversation with a Moroccan would end in an exhausting battle to avoid buying something I did not want. Perhaps if I had owned a carpet warehouse, a chain of antique shops, or been a henchman of Howard Marks I might have a different opinion of the place. It was exhausting. If there had been a few other foreigners to commiserate with, it might have been more bearable, but there were not. Rather than call it quits, however, I set myself a month-long target, growing more bad tempered and unhappy each day.

The only relief had been a murder in an Atlas mountain town. Eight years before three Italians, two men and a woman, had scored a sizeable amount of dope off a local dealer there who had immediately tipped off the police. The Italians were busted and sent down for seven years. A week before I had arrived a wild-eyed bearded man had entered the town, sought out the dealer and asked to buy some dope. The dealer had grinned away obsequiously and produced a brick or two, doubtless with the same jail stint in mind. According to his young nephew, who witnessed and survived the whole thing, the bearded man then produced a pistol, said 'You don't remember me, do you?' and drilled the dealer with four rounds before making good his escape. Eight years is a long time to bear a grudge, unless, I guess, you spend most of them in a Moroccan prison. The killing was still the talk of the bazaar when I arrived, and amused me immensely. I saw it as a symbol of fittingly just resistance on behalf of all beleaguered

128

travellers. Yet it was a tiny glimmer in the overall grind. Even in Essaouirira, a place I had been assured had lost none of its spirituality since Jimmy Hendrix wrote 'Castles in the Sand' there in the late Sixties, I found only dead dogs and oil on the beach. The one person who had not immediately tried to trap me into a buy was a fisherman who had found me wandering alone with my thoughts miles from the coastal town. He engaged me in polite conversation without any obvious ulterior motive. I was intrigued by the thick, semicircular scars that coated his legs, arms and torso. 'Er, shark attack?' I finally asked. 'Bad acid,' he replied simply, making chopping gestures across himself, then asked if I would like to score. Enough was enough so I headed back to Marrakech on my way out.

Now, for the first time, I was happy. No trader could touch me up here: there was a big doorman downstairs to see to that. It did not stop them from trying, though. Even four storeys below the occasional merchant would spot my burned red face staring over the wall and offer up some silk, a hubbly bubbly or prayer mat. I responded crassly to each offer by sticking them a finger. Then I spotted a small buzz of activity in the square, a cluster of people pursuing two Europeans heading towards the hotel. As they neared I could make out their details. The first was a girl of exceptional beauty, visible even at that distance. She must have been close to six foot, moving fast with the swivel-hipped arm-swinging assurance of the very beautiful, cutting a swathe through the crowd like a female Moses. Travel books warn female travellers in Muslim countries to dress modestly in order to avoid offending local customs. She was wearing denim hot pants that barely covered the tops of her thighs, and an off-the-shoulder T-shirt. Behind her hurried a shorter person, a broad-shouldered bearded man. She was probably taking a lot of verbal abuse but no-one dared touch her. Instead they thronged around him,

129

grabbing his arm and pulling at his clothes. An orange dealer squared up to him, proffering a basket of shining fruit; the next second the whole thing exploded in cartwheeling coloured globes as the man strode forward, the sound of swearing carrying up to the roof garden. I laughed happily as they disappeared from view below me. It was good to see someone else getting it for a change.

A few minutes later they appeared in the doorway, pulled up a couple of chairs and lowered their heads onto the table. 'Having fun?' I asked and offered the man the rag end of a joint. He looked as though he needed it. He was sweating profusely, great beads of moisture rolling down his face soaking his beard, plastering his long hair against his scalp. The girl smiled gracefully. I joined them and the conversation opened up with the ease of pressurized minority groups. They were Serbs from Belgrade. The first Yugoslavs I had ever met, their story had me leaning forward attentively to catch every word.

They had been living together in a squat in the Serb capital. Dan said it was a nice squat, Micki said it was revolting. Somehow the authorities tracked Dan down and presented him with call-up papers. He had already done his military service in what was then the JNA, the Yugoslav People's Army, but was still on the reservists' list. A crisis was growing in their country, they told me. A state called Croatia was making a bid for independence and war was imminent. Dan had turned up at a barracks as requested, hoping that he was required only to confirm his continued availability for service. He was presented with a gun and uniform and told he would soon be going to a city named Vukovar. He ditched the gun that night, picked up Micki and all the cash he had, and legged it out of Europe to Morocco. 'I'm not going back till it's over,' he told me angrily. 'If Croati people want their land they can have it. I don't want to die for it.' He warned of an approaching conflagration, of a war that would last for years *rather than days, of thousands dead and the end of Yugoslavia.*

I thought he must be exaggerating. He was hot-tempered and perhaps had overreacted. War in Europe? It was not possible. Where was Croatia anyway? I had hardly heard of it. We smoked some more dope, changed the subject and bitched about Morocco. Dan went inside to get a shirt as the sun lowered and the temperature dropped. There was a small silence when he left us. Micki broke it. 'He's right you know,' she said, turning to me with eyes of absolute certainty, 'there will be a big war. I love Yugoslavia. But it is finished.' I shrugged with empty incomprehension. Then across the space of ten years my grandmother's words floated back to me and the hair rose on the back of my neck. It had begun.

At that stage I felt fairly desperate to find another conflict, above all because of the vacuum left in me by the one I had just attended. The Gulf War had been one of the greatest anticlimaxes of my life. I had been about to leave the army when Saddam Hussein invaded Kuwait. My regiment was not among the brigades first sent out to Saudi Arabia, and though I had mentioned to my commanding officer that I would extend my time in the army if there was any chance of going to the Gulf, I held little optimism. However, two days before I was due to be a civilian, I got a call from the Light Division depot. Fresh battalions, though not Light Division troops, were being sent out. They were short of officers. In Winchester I signed on for the duration of the war, should it actually happen. A doctor at the medical centre warned me that there was not enough time to stagger the vaccinations I needed to be given over the required period of days. He gave me the lot there and then in each arm, a head-spinning mix that included anthrax and bubonic plague. Immediately afterwards I drove to my mother's house to say goodbye and threw up as soon as I reached the front door. 'I'm off,' I told her grinning, then sent another jet into the herbaceous border. She did not look very impressed. Doubtless her father, leaving by that same front door to join his squadron when the Second World War began, made a rather more dignified farewell. There is not as much room for grace and poise in these chemical times.

Days later I was in Saudi Arabia, only to wait tedious weeks in the desert, with the strange new culture of the Scottish regiment to which I had been attached wearing at my nerves, before we lumbered confused into Iraq. The enemy surrendered en masse. I could not believe it. I had waited five years for this moment. I was pumped up in anticipation of chemical armageddon only to be greeted by a Mexican wave of Iraqi hands. I had left the beloved Light Division and come a very long way for a war that did not happen, not to me anyway. The closest I got to shooting anybody was a moment when I considered killing one of our own sergeants in a fit of rage at his ineptitude. I was furious.

'Anthony.' My company commander took me aside as our troops rounded up the last desultory group of Iraqi prisoners from one position. 'Do you think anyone would really have noticed if we hadn't turned up?' I ground my teeth and rolled my eyes. Now he asks me, I thought, and stretched three syllables into a moody 'No', then gave him a grin to let him know it was all right. He was a fellow cynic and did not miss much. On returning to England I was immediately sent on terminal leave, crewing a boat across the Med with three friends, before travelling on alone through Spain and into Morocco to mull things over and decide what to do next.

The army had not been a replica of school. In many ways I loved it more than I could have believed, and the tribe I chose to leave, the Light Division, had instilled me with great pride. It had valued me as an individual and given me space. It had a specific and unique style to its inner workings which I admired. My tour of Ireland and time afterwards training soldiers at the depot are some of the happiest memories of my life. I regretted having to say goodbye to the gallery of professional rogues among the NCOs and ranks, and to some of the officers whom I had grown to love as brothers. I shall probably not find that depth of communication and understanding again.

That said, I had not been a very good officer. Though I was always able to look after myself, loved soldiering, was fit and could shoot straight, I often found the responsibility of command irksome and unfamiliar. I did not like telling others how to conduct themselves, and I did not like being told what to do. My slowly developing self-confidence was a raft too easily overturned by any setback. Had I stayed on then maybe with maturity the army would have got value for money from all that it had invested in me. None the less, I remained as intrigued by war as I ever had been. The end of the conflict in the Gulf, however, signalled to me only that it would be many more years before another war. It was definitely time to get out.

Back in London after Morocco I fell into deep despair. It started slowly, my dark moods multiplying in strength and frequency on the fertile mental field left by the sudden change in my life. I would be the last to admit that the army had institutionalized me, as my sense of freedom is something I have always valued and guarded jealously. Yet, robbed of the focus the army provided, the happiness I had once enjoyed in my own company suddenly went, replaced over a period of weeks by the rushing white noise of depression. I was not into smack then, and alcohol seemed the only tonic that could blunt the black dog's teeth. So I began to drink heavily. It became an effort even to draw the curtains of my room in a Shepherd's Bush flat each morning. After a while I left them closed and sat hunched inside the darkness, alone with thoughts of suicide.

It is like addiction, and as hard to explain. Nothing made sense. I could not track the path of this mood and thought I must be going insane, a feeling which was confirmed when I was sent by a GP to the psychiatric wing of a Wandsworth hospital for assessment. I sat in a room for an hour while a wild-eyed woman thumped her head against the wall beside me and a shuffling old man repeatedly put coffee cups upside down into a machine, howling in a low monotone each time the scalding water shot over his hands. Finally I was called into an office where a tired-looking young man asked me what was wrong. I told him I had an almost overwhelming urge to blow my brains out. He checked my address, told me I could not be helped in Wandsworth, and suggested I try Kensington. I staggered out like one of George Romero's zombies, and lurched into a small clinic off Ladbroke Grove in much the same state a few days later. It seemed such a pointless and hateful exercise. I felt beyond help and close to death.

I had never had psychotherapy before and regarded the thought of it with great suspicion. I saw it as an admission of vulnerability, and it was a signal of how damaged my pride had become, how fucked up I felt, that I agreed to it at all. Yet if I had not found that clinic, whose staff reacted as soon as I walked in the door, then I might not have been around for much longer. It did not bring easy answers. At first it was just a matter of keeping things together enough to make sure I made my weekly appointment with the French psychotherapist who was handling my case. The prospect of sitting before a stranger for an hour at a time, talking, was not one I found appealing, but she was happy to let my uncomfortable silences extend to the point where I was embarrassed into saying something.

A lot of the time I did not know what to talk about, or if I did then I did not wish to talk about it. There was no magical cure, but as the weeks went by I found myself more able to put a few black childhood memories in context and the very fact of having to meet someone for a weekly appointment, a neutral presence in my life whom I grew to trust, in itself gave me a sort of lifeline. My mind seemed to clear, I stopped drinking and started to run again. Running was something I had found in the army, something that seemed to repay whatever energy I expended on it. I ran all over West London, pounding the tarmac beneath my feet for miles and miles, pumping the endorphins into my blood. The white noise faded. It was replaced by a revamped urge to go to war. And now there was a proper war to go to, a war in Europe.

By the time I started to pull out of the pit into which I had fallen, the conflict had slipped out of Croatia and into Bosnia. Spring 1992: roadblocks were going up as the masks rolled down over the faces of Serb death squads; propaganda machines pumped out filth and vitriol against a backdrop of localized murder and massacre that was to grow into an enormous wave of 'ethnic cleansing', that empty euphemism for purging and pogroms that should be put in the same bin as 'friendly fire' and 'collateral damage'. Sarajevo was encircled and besieged and the United Nations sucked reluctantly into the war.

I still felt too stunned by what had just happened to me to entertain immediate plans of getting there but put my energies, such as they were, into doing a postgraduate course in photojournalism at the London College of Printing in the Elephant and Castle. Of course I was not a graduate, but there was a lot of mileage to be had out of saying you were a Gulf War veteran in London that year and I was allowed in. I had no clue about journalism, nor much enthusiasm for it, but figured that if I could learn how to use a camera then I may be able to get an employer to send me to Bosnia. It did not happen that way, but at least the course gave me enough knowledge to pass myself off as a freelancer once I got to the war.

Deep down I was aware at the time that many of my motivations were fairly dark. On one level my sense of despair had been dispelled by therapy, yet on another it had not been replaced by either the desire for a future or the concept of one. I felt more aware of who I was, but that in itself – dominated as it was by sensations of fragmentation and isolation – filled me with no great hope, and in many ways only fuelled an appetite for destruction. I wanted to throw myself into a war, hoping for either a metamorphosis or an exit. I wanted to reach a human extreme in order to cleanse myself of my sense of fear, and saw war as the ultimate frontier of human experience.

Hindsight gives you a strange wisdom. In some ways we all get what we want. I have so few regrets, even now.

8

An old man, you could define him as Muslim if you chose to accept the terms of the war, lay on a couch in the living room of his family home, a flat in one of the many apartment blocks in Vareš, an ugly mining town north-west of Sarajevo. He had had a stroke and was unable to walk, talk or feed himself. Yet he could see and hear, and his mind was clear. The day's light was fading and his daughters and their children were gathered around him. They must have been fearful, for their lives were under threat from the strangers that had entered their home town only a few days previously. There was a knock at the door. An HVO soldier entered the apartment. It was not difficult for him. He had a gun and they did not. He was part of the town's new authority and they were part of the powerless minority. I do not know if the soldier was drunk or sober. He looked around the people in the room and his gaze settled on the old man's youngest daughter, a

137

woman in her late twenties. The man forced the rest of the family out of their flat at gunpoint. They knew he could kill them if they did not acquiesce. It had already happened to others. Besides, they were '*Balije*', the derogative term for Muslims. The old man could move only his head. Once the others had gone, scuffling fearfully down the dimly lit concrete stairwell, he raped the daughter while her father lay motionless on the couch. Then the soldier departed. Shortly afterwards the daughter also left the flat. I saw her on the street outside, collapsing into the arms of neighbours, barely coherent with sobbing. Sometime later a small group of UN soldiers entered the flat and carried the old man away. It was not a dignified sight. His paralysed body sagged awkwardly between the four soldiers, whose concentration was distracted by the air of threat around them. He was dead the next morning. His body lay wrapped in a blanket on a stretcher by a woodpile. There were many names for what had happened in his flat. Some people called it 'ethnic cleansing'.

Evil: if I had encountered it before then it was so well disguised that I saw it as something else – an old woman walking alone down a track crying; a distant plume of smoke from a village in the hills; dead-eyed soldiers stepping down a road in silence – banal details of its hidden tread. Even the killings I had seen so far seemed no more than the brutish product of the war's ratio-nale: men did bad things – it was in their nature. Words like 'wicked' and 'evil' had a mediaeval ring to them, a throwback to superstition and the histrionics of the pulpit. I have no personal God and mostly feel in no position to judge individual actions as either 'good' or 'evil'. Yet I am certain that what I witnessed at times in Vareš was more than mere wrongdoing.

The history of Bosnia's war may be written as a collage of

survivors' accounts, UN statements, NATO briefings and witness impressions, with supposition filling the gaps. Over a three-week period in the autumn of 1993, the fate of Vareš opened before me like a perverted fairytale. The cast included the Muslim folk of a forest village; a murderous pilgrim rogue and his band of killers in the valley below; a Serb warrior who had the skull of an imam mounted on his jeep; and the embattled forces of good, represented by a company of Swedish troops.

It was the only story that I saw from start to finish, a perfect small-scale replica of the war's strategy as a whole, and a spotlight on the character of those pulling its strings. As a journalist, I was able to see the mechanical detail behind euphemisms like 'ethnic cleansing'. As an individual, I saw much more than rape and murder alone.

By late summer there were no longer any active fronts between the Croats and Serbs, except for a few areas in northern Bosnia where the HVO had remained loyal to the government army. Though the trench systems and bunkers remained intact, the lines were almost entirely porous, and had the status of quasi-borders. In some Croat areas, most notably Kiseljak, the Croats even rented military equipment from the Serbs to fight the Muslims. The co-operation in other regions, like Žepče to the west, was so entwined that Serb units actively bolstered Croat positions with troops and gave them artillery support in assaults upon the BiH. There was little real trust between the two circumstantial allies, but they were the pawns of distant political agreements between Zagreb and Belgrade to divide Bosnia between Serbia and Croatia at the expense of the Muslims.

The majority of Vareš's population was Croat, and so it lay relatively untouched. It was an old mining town, with twin lines of buildings – most of them modern, ugly and sprinkled with red dust from the pit works – that stretched along a small river valley enclosed on either side by forested hills. It had succeeded in riding out the pressures of the Muslim–Croat war without succumbing to the conflict itself. Though the town and the surrounding swathe of land were controlled militarily by a local HVO unit, the Bobovać Brigade, it still had a significant Muslim population, a Muslim mayoress and tolerated the presence of BiH troops in the surrounding villages who wished to visit their families. Separated from other Croat areas by Muslim territory to the north, south and west, Vareš fronted Serb-held ground to the east. It had become rich on the war, an autonomous statelet that was a door to blackmarket trade with the Serbs on one side and the Muslims on the other. So although a little sluttish in its ambivalent loyalties, the town was nevertheless still at peace and integrated.

This in itself made it an enemy of the extremist nationalist politics spreading from Hercegovina. Vareš and its environs represented an unwelcome blip of Croat-dominated multi-ethnic neutrality, a bit of gristle to the knives that sought to carve up Bosnia along lines of religious ancestry. In the eyes of Croatian hardliners its population needed to be radicalized, purged of Muslim elements, and its lackadaisical HVO force utilized in the fight elsewhere. The Serbs were entirely sympathetic to this idea as it fitted perfectly with their war aims. However, they had their own agenda, which revealed itself later.

Towards the end of October, Ivica Rajić, a notorious HVO hardliner, left his base in Kiseljak with a posse of extremist Catholic fighters, including members of 'The Pilgrims', a local death squad. They liaised with Serb officers before travelling through Serb lines and entering Vareš, where they took over command of the Bobovać Brigade. This stage was simple. The next step was to polarize a population of more than 25,000 people, and purge the town and its territory of Muslims.

***

I knew I had missed some action while away in London. The BiH had taken most of Gornji Vakuf and Bugojno to the west, defeating the HVO in urban fighting. They had also massacred the Croat population in the village of Uzdol, in the hills to the east of Gornji Vakuf. In England I had watched the news footage of the Croat bodies with fury. I did not want to believe the Muslims had done this. It confused my loyalties and I knew it would jeopardize the war effort of the side I believed to be the victim. Whether it was a planned atrocity or the result of troops running amok in the wake of battle I never found out. Much later an insider told me that it had been ordered as revenge for the massacre of Muslims at Ahmići. Predictably, it provoked a knee-jerk reaction from British UN troops in central Bosnia. 'They can all go and fuck themselves now as far as I am concerned,' I was told by a captain who had witnessed the scene of the massacre. 'Happy fucking Christmas to the lot of them: I'll be at home eating turkey; they can slaughter each other to their hearts' content.'

Can you ever grade atrocity? Not if you are the victim, living out your last moments in terror and pain. The rules of war are complex and contradictory. Is dropping fire from aircraft on to civilians in Dresden more acceptable than cutting their throats with a knife in Bosnia? Apparently so. And what happens when you kill by accident, as was the case when an allied missile hit a Baghdad bunker during the Gulf War? That is OK too – unless, again, you are one of the casualties.

I believe any man, given the right pressures, could kill an innocent in cold blood. In accepting the reality of war rather than the ideal, however, I believe there are categories of atrocity. If fighters lose their heads and murder civilians or prisoners they are certainly guilty. But if a state uses atrocity as a tactic to polarize

141

the population, like Serbia and latterly Croatia did in Bosnia, then it is guilty of a greater crime. In my mind, cold-bloodedness and the culpability of the state are the keys to apportioning guilt. Yes, Muslim troops did kill civilians and prisoners on occasion, but their actions were dwarfed by the scale of the crimes of their opponents. In the absence of a deep-rooted nationalism, their mentality was largely more humane, and their government's strategy opposed to massacre.

Back at Viktorija's I brooded on these thoughts.

Then, during an evening briefing for journalists given by a British major in Vitez, the word 'Vareš' appeared like a dull black pearl among the general sludge of war detail. There were confused reports of a Croatian attack on a nearby Muslim village named Stupni Do, the major told us, and a subsequent BiH advance. The UN were being prevented from moving into the area, and information was scarce. In itself word of a localized attack in one region or another would have been of little significance, but since Vareš held an unusual status as a zone of Croat–Muslim détente, the news triggered surprise.

Corinne and I decided to go to Vareš the next day, accompanying Kurt, an American journalist I had first met in Sarajevo. Bespectacled and intense, Kurt had that rare, shining light that you seldom find in men, a quality which translates into apparently fathomless energy and drive. A tough man, his clarity of thought was like a flint's edge. He had come to journalism late in life, and fast assumed the high priest's mantle in the media's coverage of the conflict in Bosnia. I often thought it a shame that politics, administration and business had taken up so many years of his life. For an army had missed out there. With all that focus, clinical detachment and subliminal anger, he would have made a fine killer.

We left Vitez with a fiery Scot named Sean and two Croats,

Zoran and Boris. The rich mix of nationalities may have sounded like the beginning of a bad joke, but it worked. Between us there was a chemistry that seemed to allow us to skate through many of the obstacles ahead. This was essential. Travelling alone, I had sometimes found the strength and freedom to go places that I could not have reached in company. Bosnian soldiers on checkpoints were often more easily charmed by an individual who could take time to hang out, smoke and talk with them than by a crowd of flak-jacketed foreigners with expensive cars and equipment, whose personality was neutralized by their need to communicate through an interpreter. Moreover, the arrogant, the easily intimidated, the ignorantly bold and the overly afraid were bad travelling partners, guaranteed to shackle your freedom by the limitations of their nature. But when alone you carried all the weight of your fears. And there was no other voice to act as a sounding board to help evolve the decisions on which your life could depend.

This time, however, I could not have wanted for better company. Riding in two battered Land-Rovers, not one of us was a newcomer who had to be looked after and watched: everybody 'knew' the war, everybody was prepared to expose themselves to high risk, yet no-one was crazed. Not by the standards of the region anyway.

After a back-breaking journey tearing north-eastwards for hours along rutted tracks and pitted tarmac we arrived at Dabravina, a Muslim village at the start of the Vareš valley and the final point before HVO-held territory. There were two shattered-looking villagers from Stupni Do there, a BiH soldier and a young woman. They spoke of a massacre, of masked men entering their village the previous day, of slaughter and burning. Both had managed to escape into the forest, leaving the sound of screaming and gunfire behind them, lying in cover from which they saw their village torched and the bodies of the slain thrown into the conflagration until night fell and they fled southwards to government territory.

We wasted little time with them. Deep shock was setting in and their stories became more confused as each minute passed. Screwed-up behaviour. Push someone to relive the most traumatic experience of their life, then throw them away like a squeezed lemon because they stop making sense.

Used.

Forgotten.

Next.

Dwell on it too much and you might stop and never start again.

Dabravina itself afforded us no clue as to what lay ahead. Other than the two survivors there was little indication of action by either side. There were hardly any Muslim soldiers there, and no sound of shelling or gunfire, just an eerie silence from the valley before us. We drove on, the hillsides rising steeply on either side of the road, the forest clustering darkly around it. There was no front line of any description, just a threatening emptiness. Each minute we expected to be stopped by Croat fighters, or to see mines laid on the narrow road. It seemed inconceivable that we could travel to Vareš unmolested if a massacre had taken place near by. The survivors' stories had ignited a feeling of anger and curiosity within us which pumped our sense of momentum. We wanted to see for ourselves what had happened. We needed to for professional reasons, but as always we really wanted to see it ourselves, to allow our feelings to focus on the reality rather than on the second-hand medium of another's account.

Just before the final bend that led to the town we saw a small group of frightened civilians cowering beneath the guns of HVO troops in a farmyard. If we stopped we would surely be allowed no further so we raced past them and on to the edge of

Vareš. There, inevitably, a handful of HVO blocked the road, standing nonchalantly around a string of anti-tank mines. Beyond them were two stationary, white-painted APCs, a cluster of blue helmets and gun barrels sticking out of the hatches like a half-eaten bunch of grapes. The men inside might have been UN but they were playing by a completely different set of rules. They were Swedes; in terms of individual intelligence, integrity and single-mindedness I was to find them among the most impressive soldiers I had ever encountered. In Vareš their moment had come.

A large figure disengaged himself from a turret and clambered down to speak to us. The HVO seemed strangely relaxed and we talked them into letting us pass with surprising ease.

'Hello,' the large Swedish soldier began, his Nordic green battledress jangling with grenades, binoculars and radio equipment. 'My name is Major Daniel Ekberg. Who are you? Journalists? Good, very good.'

I was tempted to laugh in the face of such urbanity and had to turn away and bite a finger. We introduced ourselves and the major began his story. If he and his men had been either of another nationality or familiar with the UN's do-nothing policy in Bosnia, we might have been confronted by the usual stale set of self-justifying phraseology and inaction. However, the Swedes had only just arrived. Together with his APCs, Major Ekberg had driven through the night to reach his advance troops at their new base in Vareš only forty-eight hours earlier. With almost comical timing these soldiers were experiencing their first days in ex-Yugoslavia pitched into a town that was in the middle of mayhem. They were Swedes. They saw something was wrong. They wanted to put it right.

The comedy ended when he told us of the recent events in the town. Croatian extremists from Kakanj and Kiseljak had arrived in Vareš and taken over control of the local HVO. The situation was very tense: up to two hundred Muslim men had been rounded up by the Croat troops and locked into a pair of buildings. Shots had been heard from inside one but the Swedes were barred from entering by the HVO. The Muslim quarter was being terrorized at night: rape, pillage, shooting. 'The bad things really happen when it gets dark,' he explained. Heavily outnumbered, the Swedes were trapped in the town by Croat checkpoints at either end. They had been shot at and had grenades thrown at their vehicles. There was no directive from the UN command advising how best to deal with the situation and no reinforcements.

The previous day Ekberg's men had seen Stupni Do begin to burn in the hills to the south-east. They could hear gunfire and explosions, and managed to get their APCs within a kilometre of the village before being blocked by HVO and mines. The major told us that even at that distance, and in spite of the noise of firing, his men could hear the screaming.

He invited us to accompany him to the centre of the town. The streets were deserted except for loitering groups of HVO, and these men were very different from those we had encountered at the first checkpoint. Mean and confident, they either eyeballed the Swedes while tapping their rifles or skidded up and down the high street in cars bristling with weaponry and bizarre headgear. Bandannas were for the more passé among them. Some of these fighters were into German helmets or black sombreros: the fashion accessories of intimidation.

We alighted from our Land-Rovers in a small square outside the main school building where the HVO were holding the majority of the Muslim prisoners. There was a tense stand-off in progress between Swedish soldiers and the HVO. Nothing was said, but there was some very heavy communication going on in the staring. One of the HVO commanders, a fat man draped in bandoliers, walked up to me. 'I know you from Gornji Vakuf,' he said affably and smiled. 'How are you?'

'I'm fine,' I replied, rather embarrassed to meet such an acquaintance while the Swedish major was only a few metres away. 'What's happening?'

'These UN fuckers have turned up and are behaving like it's their town. It's not. It's ours. And if they try anything there will be much blood shed. Their blood. Oh, and tell that cameraman to stop filming or I will kill him.' I looked round. A BBC crew had turned up.

The major, who had had no sleep for two days, seemed curiously rejuvenated by the presence of the TV camera and suddenly announced a plan that left us open-mouthed with its audacity.

'It is time now to enter the school building,' he said simply and walked over to brief his men. APCs were deployed at either end of the street, blocking it off to the HVO. Swedish troops with anti-tank weapons dismounted from their vehicles and took up position on street corners. In the centre of the square a group of a dozen troops was assembled to enter the improvised prison. I admired the major's spirit but the idea was madness. Somehow he believed that the HVO would back down in the face of the media, and if they did not then at least the world would know that in Vareš Swedish troops were trying to right a wrong.

The HVO had no intention of backing down to anyone. They held a clear military advantage, and files of their fighters peeled off into the surrounding slopes and the buildings overlooking the square. It was like watching the prelude to a Western gunfight. All it needed was a soundtrack by Morricone and some drifting tumbleweed before the sheriff and his men bit the dust.

I walked with Kurt to the side of a deep culvert that ran down the edge of the square. 'If I survive the first two seconds that's where I'm taking cover,' he said, echoing my thoughts.

I felt fine. It was bizarre, to feel unafraid standing in the square with a group of UN troops who probably would all be dead within minutes of what was to follow. Yet since my attack of dread in Travnik fear seemed to come and go from me as it wished, usually unrelated to the situation about me. Some days even the distant chatter of a Kalashnikov would send a chill into my stomach, on other occasions I felt completely detached. To be forewarned of it was to be forearmed, and I learned to wrestle the fear when it struck. To be frightened of being afraid was the worst thing and once I had discovered – through the advice Gilles had passed on to me – that fear was natural in war, I accepted its arrival like an unwelcome guest. Tolerate it, adapt around it. It will go. But this day I was phlegmatic and removed.

The BBC spoiled it. Their correspondent, a wise and responsible man, saw the imminent death of his crew and ordered them into their vehicle and away. As he walked to join them, Major Ekberg strode over to him.

'Where are you going at this moment?' he asked. 'We are about to enter the school.'

'Major,' the BBC man replied with quiet precision, 'I think that this is an unnecessary confrontation and that if it is carried through everybody will be killed, so I am leaving with my crew.'

The major's face fell. 'But we cannot do this without the TV camera here. It is important.'

'I'm sorry, Major, but I am leaving.'

I could not believe my ears. In the major I saw a man who was taking the relationship between the media and the military to new frontiers. Not only did he want us in on the action, the action was dependent on our presence. It was fantastic. I felt almost angry with the BBC. With their departure the major deflated like a pricked balloon. The Swedes were forced into a humiliating backdown. The troops remounted their APCs which then left the scene. Within minutes there was not a Norseman to be seen in the square. From the houses around us the HVO began to reappear, and with them the fat commander from Gornji Vakuf. He swaggered up to us with the smug look of victory in his eyes. He raised a set of keys in one hand, dropped them, then caught them with the other hand as they were inches from the ground.

'That close,' he said.

We needed the permission of Ivica Rajić himself to reach Stupni Do. It seemed unlikely that he would grant it but we had to try anyway, for without it the roads to the hills were as blocked to us as they were to the Swedes. We found him the next day in the headquarters of the Bobovać Brigade, a large hotel chalet beyond the northern edge of the town. He was a fat, squash-faced villain with porcine features and a large pot belly over which a rosary lay, the cross sliding first one way then the other across his gut as he moved.

Kurt questioned Rajić artfully, emphasizing our 'understanding' of the need to imprison Muslim males in Vareš, and our 'empathy' with the necessity of the HVO's 'pre-emptive military operation' at Stupni Do. It was a good mind-game to watch: can the journalist persuade the murderer to trade power and allow him to the scene of crime? Rajić insisted that the village was a major BiH position that the Muslims had been using as a platform for an attack on Vareš. He and his men had fought a battle there and won. There was no massacre, only an HVO victory. We nodded in assent. Sure. Christian brothers, no problem. After much brandy, much coffee and dozens of cigarettes, the discourse drew to its decisive moment.

'We need your permission to go to Stupni Do to show the world that the massacre allegations are a lie,' Kurt said. Rajić paused for a moment, then called over another officer, Krešimir Božić, the newly appointed commander of the Bobovać Brigade. A tall, bearded man, he approached Rajić deferentially.

'Get these people a guide and an escort to take them up to Stupni Do,' Rajić ordered. As he said the words I thought that perhaps his account of events was true. Why should he allow us into the village if there had been a massacre? Yet when I saw Božić's reaction I knew I was wrong. He looked stunned and repeated the order back to Rajić, who nodded. Božić's head dropped in disbelief, his shoulders slumped and he stared at the ground, then walked away slowly. And so the mind-game concluded. We thought we had won. It took me a long time to realize that Rajić was the victor.

Our two HVO escorts were far from happy with their task. They talked too much. We rode with them up a winding mountain track high into the mist-laden forests. At the edge of a small grass plateau we found a tiny hamlet of three houses, smoking and stinking of burned flesh. A few woodsmen sat on the grass cradling weapons, their peasant faces deeply burnished by the sun. These had been Croat homes, they told us, torched by the Muslims. The proof of their lies lay in small domestic details: a child's carving of a crescent and star on a dog's kennel; a small Bosnian lily crunched in the dust.

Beneath the plateau, cupped in a fold on the valley's slope, lay Stupni Do. I had never seen such a concentration of destruction. Almost every house was blasted flat, collapsed inwards and smouldering, the remaining walls barely waist-high. We argued for a minute with our two HVO guides who wouldn't let us go into the devastated village. Then in the distance came the throb of APC engines. The first Swedish patrol, strengthened by reinforcements from Tuzla, had succeeded in getting through the HVO checkpoints and was approaching through the trees. Our guides disappeared into the mist and we ran down the track into Stupni Do.

Ahead of us a small group of Croat civil-defence men scrambled frantically down grass slopes out of the village and back into the valley. They were middle aged and wore blue serge uniforms. I guess they had been tasked to 'clear up' the scene. With the arrival of the Swedes they puffed and floundered away in panic. Like Božić's crestfallen expression, it was a powerful indication of guilt.

Even so, I had nothing in my experience to prepare me for what lay there.

Stupni Do – a whirlpool black and white transparency that sucked the colour out of your mind and eyes. The village blown to rubble-strewn shreds. Livestock roasted in the charcoal stalls of their stables. Humans smashed and burned. Not a sign of life. Even a child's rabbit crushed like a bloody white cloth in the dust. The raised houses like crematorium where the dead spat and crackled beneath the heat of torched masonry. Swedish soldiers standing mute with shock. A captain shaking with rage: 'This is fucking shit, this is worse than fucking shit, this is . . .' The words just gagged to a choke in the back of his throat. There were no words to describe this. A body no bigger than a black carrier bag cocktail-sticked by white tibia. Another half fried. Its head smashed in. Face-down. A child. And what do you say? Fuck fuck fuck fuck and Jesus fucking Christ. It's not enough and the rage comes in like a hurricane and then you want them dead, the people who did this, you want the scum erased for this. You could do it yourself there and then at that moment, blast every one of them forward in a pink spray. And walk away to find some more.

And there was something more than what you saw, smelled and felt inside. The atmosphere. It chainsawed through your senses and squirmed glass over your body; shut your eyes and you could still hear the screaming. For whatever had been sucked out of that place, something else had been pumped in. An open scar in the ether; pleading chokes scabbing the edges. Some empty black infinity inside that spat and laughed. Ever had a bad hallucination? You've seen nothing. Nothing.

Only one room in that place was untouched by flame. It was no more than a stone-floored shed, tacked to the wall of a burned house at the far end of the village. The light was fading fast grey-black and the Swedes had gone and the mist came rolling in tendril waves down through the forest into the ruins and I knew that whatever it was that made me want to run up the track back to the Land-Rovers and out of it had nothing to do with the threat of the HVO coming back. The six of us were alone. Then Kurt staggered backwards out of that room he'd found, cursing and shocked, so I walked in.

For a moment I could see nothing in the smoky gloom. My torch began to flicker, dimmed and died. I beat it back into life on my thigh and looked again. Three women looked back at me.

They were kneeling in a small box-shaped pit sunk into the stone floor, huddled together in fear, their arms and hands entwined in support. Normally the hole would have been used to store grain and covered with the wooden trapdoor that now lay upright on its hinges behind their backs. It would have been the ideal place to hide. Close the lid and the pit would be nearly invisible. There would have been just enough room for three people to lie beneath it. What gave them away? I wondered. A cough? A sob?

Two of the women were in their twenties, the third was an old lady. Someone had shot her in the mouth and her shattered dentures cascaded with her own teeth down her front like mashed melon pips. One girl had been shot repeatedly in the chest. It was difficult to tell whether the other had had her throat cut or been shot; a great gash of blood crescented her neck. The expression on their faces had survived the damage. It was so clear. A time-valve that opened directly on to those last moments. So you saw what they saw. I hope beyond hope that I never see it again.

In the recess of the shed something moved. It was a cow. The only survivor in Stupni Do. Someone had pulled a large plastic barrel over its head. The neck of the barrel fitted tightly around that of the beast, whose horns impaled the sides, keeping it locked in place. It must have taken a great amount of time and energy to bring the cow to this state: unable to see or eat.

So that was how we spent our last few minutes in the dusk at Stupni Do. Fighting the impulse that wanted our legs to kick us out of that place as fast and far away as possible, wrestling in a shed with a cow and a plastic barrel watched by three murdered women. Pulling and shouting and cursing and grunting with a torch that barely worked and a pathetic penknife because we wanted the cow to live. We wanted the cow to be able to see and eat again. We wanted that more than anything.

We had seen many more bodies than those in that village. We had seen worse mutilation. It was not the dead that affected us. It was what else still lay in the place. The presence. Corinne seemed the only one of us to be wholly unaffected. I hope she left her cameras outside her room that night because, given what they must have filtered off before it reached her consciousness, they were surely crackling with possession.

Stupni Do was transformed the next day. Its secret out, the HVO checkpoints in the forest all but disappeared and the village was swamped by UN soldiers, EU monitors, war crimes investigators and journalists. Even then it preserved something of the previous day's evil. I think they finally discovered sixty bodies or so. More must have been burned to powder-ash in the houses. A British brigadier, chief of staff to the UN in Bosnia and conditioned to restraint and reserve, came out of the shed in fury having seen the three women.

'In thirty years of soldiering I have never seen the like of what I have seen here,' he declared before television cameras. 'We know who did this, Krešimir Božić and the Bobovać Brigade and they are scum.' It was good to see a man like him so angry. If his fury managed to shatter the self-control of an officer of so many years standing, then my own reaction was more understandable. Whatever your character or the degree of your self-possession you could not escape it: a terrible deed had been committed there. Its legacy remained and would affect you deeply.

Yet we were outsiders. For Bosnians who had lost family or friends in such a way, whether it was Stupni Do or Uzdol, the hunger for retribution would be all the stronger and less easily assuaged. What we had seen that day was just the tiniest fraction of what was going on in the surrounding hills and forests. The key to our reaction lay not in feeling anger, but in the understanding it brought of how easily such atrocities provoked a response in kind. To see the vision in those three women's eyes was to see your understanding of humanity banished to a barren wilderness of darkness and howling. If you did not feel that way, then you were already there.

Once the cameras had got in to Stupni Do and the news hit the radio, rumour became reality. It confirmed the worst fears of the

Muslims in Vareš and, crucially, of the indigenous Croats there. They were tarred with the brush of guilt by religious association with the killers as well as by the British brigadier's misplaced condemnation of Božić and his Bobovać Brigade. BiH units gathered to the north and south to move on the town and the Vareš HVO found themselves deployed against the Muslims more through fear of their vengeance than through idealism.

For four days Rajić and his men remained in Vareš, the Swedes were left alone and the UN command did nothing. In Kakanj, to the south, we visited Nehru Ganić, a BiH operations commander for the troops mustering to push north. A former JNA officer in his thirties, he had talked to me during fighting in Zavidovići and I had been impressed by his intelligence and open-mindedness. As someone directly involved with Vareš, he was well-placed to fill in many of the gaps in the story.

When Rajić and his men had first arrived in the town a fortnight before, the BiH command had negotiated desperately with the existing HVO officers in Vareš in an attempt to preserve the détente. Ganić himself had met the Bobovać Brigade commander near the demarcation line between Muslim- and Croat-controlled areas. Then, four days before the massacre at Stupni Do, some of Rajić's fighters moved into a Croat village west of Vareš, Kopljara, and shot five Muslim men who were on their way to collect water. Next they took over command of the Bobovać Brigade, putting Božić in charge, and dialogue between the BiH and HVO ceased. The BiH forces took Kopljara in a morning attack two days later. I went there. The houses were looted but mostly intact and there were three fresh graves marked with crosses dug by the BiH for the HVO killed in action.

Stupidly, I was still puzzled by Rajić's decision to have allowed us into Stupni Do.

'It is possible that he believed most of the dead had been

155

burned to ashes when they were thrown into the houses,' Ganić
replied, 'and that you would see nothing that contradicted his
version of events. But it is more likely he wanted the publicity. It
fits his aim. Watch what happens to Vareš now. After Stupni Do
it can never be the same again, whatever the outcome of the next
few days.'

So we returned to Vareš. The once-deserted high street was
unrecognizable, though the stand-off between the Swedes and the
HVO had resumed. About two hundred Muslims, mostly
women and children, were huddled behind a pair of Swedish
APCs positioned at the edge of the pavement. Rajić had intensified the terror in the Muslim quarter, and these people, though
miserable and afraid, felt better sleeping hunched on the cold
tarmac behind Swedish armour than in their own homes. Many
told stories of rape and murder. One old woman, rocking back
and forth with tears, spoke of how her two sons had been dragged
from their house by Rajić's men the previous day and killed
before her eyes.

More refugees arrived every hour. Some came in cars driven
by Vareš HVO. It was the B-side to Bosnia's story: local Croat
fighters weeping as they escorted their Muslim friends to the
only place they knew could ensure their security, the Swedish
APCs.

'My only hope is to escape,' one of the Bobovać troops told
me as he helped three Muslim neighbours out of his car, hugging
them and crying. 'These bandits and criminals from Kiseljak have
ruined our town for all of us. What can I do now? I do not think
we can hold out against the Muslim forces that are pushing us in
the hills since the massacre so I cannot stay, but where can I go?'
He was in his twenties, another young cat whose life was being
destroyed by ancient forces. There were many of them, Croat
fighters unafraid to help Muslims, to shed tears for them in

the face of Rajić's men who still screeched up and down the road in cars upping the ante of fear, or leered knowingly from across the street. The Vareš Croats were to become as much the victims of what was happening as the Muslims, and for them fate held a particularly cruel hand in store.

As darkness fell a young woman staggered weeping up the street and collapsed into the arms of those sheltering behind the Swedes. Friends managed somehow to extract the story of what had happened to her – the rape – and told the Swedes that her paralysed father still lay in the apartment block. We went with a Swedish patrol to find him, carrying him back to the other Muslims for his final night of life. The idea of some things is enough to jam your mind, let alone seeing the reality. If you read about it in the newspaper you may not feel it, you may fall for the empty sterility of the phrase 'ethnic cleansing' without ever understanding what it really was: persuasion through terror. Many people outside Bosnia went further than falling for it. After the war had finished one of the columnists who wrote about Bosnia without ever having been there offered the opinion that 'ethnic cleansing' was a good idea as it led to the definition of peaceful borders similar to those between Britain and Scotland. He seemed very pleased with this comparison. Perhaps if he had his youngest child raped beside his death bed, he would have a different view.

Vareš became a ghost-town overnight. The only HVO that remained were the three dead men, killed in action in the hills, who were left lying in the hospital in their bloodied uniforms. Rajić and his killers, the Bobovac Brigade, and 20,000 Croat civilians disappeared. Squeezed by advancing government troops on two fronts, their fear of retribution translated into a flight through Serb lines to the east, then, with notable exceptions, on to Kiseljak further south. If Rajić had expected Serb units to come in and bolster his forces his hopes were dashed. The Serbs had other ideas, which involved the Bobovać Brigade. As for the Muslims, they had fled en masse to the sanctuary of the Swedes' camp at the northern edge of town.

Except for a few snipers left in the high ground, Vareš seemed to us totally deserted, its heavy silence broken only by the crackle of flames from an apartment block torched by the retreating HVO. Then a pair of arms reached through one of the smoking windows and pulled out a line of washing. We stared up in disbelief. A man looked out.

'Hey,' we called. 'What are you doing?'

Some minutes later he appeared at the door: a handsome man in his forties wearing an immaculate blue pin-stripe suit and a pair of winklepickers, and carrying a guitar.

'I thought I'd hang out the washing before I left,' he said. 'I'm a Serb and I'm not too sure where I should go.'

Other than an unnatural shine in his eyes, there was nothing to indicate he was insane. As the windows shattered with heat and the ground floor began to collapse inwards in fiery cascades he lit a cigarette and wandered away up the empty high street, guitar on hip like a lonesome cowboy.

The Swedes broke in to the two improvised prisons to find the Muslims beaten and humiliated but otherwise unharmed. Those in the schoolhouse had to remain there because of the snipers on the valley slopes. A lone woman ran ducking through the alleys towards the building, the Croat wife of one of the prisoners. Her husband watched her progress, hope and fear running through his eyes in a concourse of emotion, blowing out into a spasm of tears as she made it.

It took the BiH troops a further twenty-four hours, moving on foot across the hills, to reach the town, and the first reconnaissance unit to arrive was, ironically, a Croat one made up of Catholic troops loyal to the government. 'I am from Vareš,' one of them told me, 'and my brother in the HVO has fled with Rajić. I believe in multi-ethnic Bosnia, not the fascism of Rajić and Herceg-Bosna.' I had heard the refrain a million times now and rather than admire the speaker's idealism I began to wonder at how he would deal with the inevitable disillusion ahead.

Following quickly behind these men were files of fighters from the 7th Muslim Brigade. Some saw this unit as a disciplined, religious force, others regarded it as a rabble of thugs and Islamic extremists. The brigade was in fact a hybrid of the two images, and their entry to Vareš took the level of Balkan bizarreness to new heights. Behind the vanguard banner of a green crescent they embarked on a rolling spree of looting that progressed northwards with their advance through the town. Amid a crescendo of 'happy fire' that lasted for hours some officers harangued their men for drinking captured alcohol, explaining that it was *haram*, forbidden. Others joined in the drunkenness with thirsty abandon. One of the first stores to be broken into was a women's hat shop and as each soldier passed he grabbed an item and jammed it on his head, adding a touch of Ladies' Day at Ascot to the unruly 'liberation': wide brims, no brims, flower posies, felt, cotton and straw, the 7th Muslim Brigade had never looked so good.

The Swedes' sense of fairness was offended by the looting and, though once more outnumbered, they patrolled the town like armoured traffic cops. Whenever they saw a car being commandeered the soldiers would jump fearlessly from their APCs, point their rifles at the driver and ask, 'Is it yours?'

More often than not the incredulous Muslim troops stumbled out of the vehicles shamefaced with embarrassment. Yet as their numbers increased and the looting became more frantic they were less open to dissuasion and more inclined to confrontation. One group challenged by the Swedes hot-wired a Zastava regardless, crammed inside, lit the petrol tank, then tore off down the high street like a comet before crashing into the kerb and spilling out of the car giggling, seconds before it was enveloped in flame. Inside a department store about thirty other fighters ran amok, tearing goods from the shelves and hangers until a Swedish colonel stopped his APC by the doorway. Together with two men he leapt onto the tarmac, chambering a round as he did so, and ordered the Muslims out. There was a tense moment of pushing and shoving; a Muslim fired a burst into the air; another cried, 'Allah allows.' But they left, thirty faced down by three. Even Kurt was impressed. 'Hey, there goes another kind of cat,' he said of the colonel as he remounted his APC.

'It's useless of course,' the colonel told me afterwards with earnest deliberation. 'I need a brigade of UN troops here to stop the looting. But we must do what we can in the meantime.' Again I had to restrain my laughter. Looting was de rigueur in Bosnia. I had long since ceased to regard it as an issue. What was the colonel going to do? Hold everything in store until the Croat owners returned?

In the hospital there was another stand-off in progress. It epitomized the complexities, the hollow idealism and pointlessness of the war more than any other incident that day. Some Swedes had entered the abandoned building in the morning and taken possession of the three dead HVO troops left there. One of the dead was then recognized by a Muslim soldier as a childhood friend from the same village. The soldier was overcome with grief and demanded that the Swedes hand over the body so that he could take it home to the village for burial. The Swedes refused. They had orders to hold on to the corpses until an exchange could be made at a later date. A bitter argument followed before the

Muslim fighter was led away by his comrades, leaving the body to the Swedes.

The Swedes' crash course in Balkan politics ended three days later two miles east of Vareš outside a village named Dastansko. It marked the forward edge of the Serb lines and was the gateway through which Rajić had piped the Croat exodus. The Bobovać Brigade, however, had not been allowed to pass through. Rajić and the Serbs halted them at Dastansko, where they were ordered to hold the Serb segment of line against the advancing government troops. There was an ugly dispute and Rajić and his men shot several HVO soldiers dead in a quarry to enforce his authority. Munitioned and fed by the Serbs, the Bobovać, some of whose soldiers had been weeping for the fate of their Muslim friends only a day before, were turned to face the Muslim army.

The Swedes pushed out into no man's land to speak to these troops. They found them dejected and miserable. Then a group of Četnik irregulars arrived in the village led by Vlaško, a bearded maniac dressed in black leather, a variety of pistols strapped across his chest. He had a splint on his leg from an earlier wound and relied on his black jeep for transport. The skull on the bonnet he claimed to be that of an imam he had killed. For whatever reason Vlaško decided to take hostage three Swedish soldiers he had found on the road. His men had two truck-mounted anti-aircraft guns and some mortars, which they began to fire at the BiH positions on the ridgeline at the same moment as the Swedes sent a small group of APCs through these lines to negotiate.

The vehicles were led by a new Swedish colonel, a tall stern-faced man whose gravity was lent an edge of spookiness by the tinted circular glasses he wore. He was a hawk whose outspoken views on what needed to be done in Bosnia eventually upset the UN and led to his removal from the theatre. Our first meeting was brief. For a few minutes he paused on the track beside us, calling in some air cover, until incoming mortarfire started hitting the slope to his near flank. He looked at us with grumpy apology and shut the door of his APC in our faces. You could hear the pump of sound from the Serb mortars a quarter of a minute before the rounds blew in. You could fit a lot of thought into that time: thirteen seconds of looking cool, two seconds to sprawl on the ground. Corinne and I crouched down beside the colonel's APC every time the mortars fired, laughing helplessly, our dialogue reduced to 'Oh Shit' and 'Fuck', while Kurt stood in the roadway, thumbs hooked into his trousers, as the rounds bloomed in brown dust on the meadow behind him.

'You two are beginning to make me shaky,' he said dryly as we giggled up at him. I stopped laughing. His coolness annoyed me. It was an average day for me. Normality: not afflicted by fear but still unsure that I would make it through without being hit. I knew Kurt's mood. More or less. Somedays you could be sure, almost, that it would not happen to you. But it was still irritating to see others in that ethereal cocoon when you were hugging the dirt. I would have felt a lot better if he had been hit in the arse by a fragment of shrapnel. Nothing too heavy, just a reallocation of dignity.

The colonel and his vehicles advanced on to meet Vlaško, who had just been hit in the leg by a ricochet and was furious. As the firefight gathered momentum, Vlaško raved at the Swedish officer unintelligibly. In a moment of decisive insight, the colonel snatched one of the pistols from the Serb's chest, offering up his own in exchange before the man had time to react. Some men intuitively understood the Yugoslav mentality: Vlaško was placated and intrigued by the gesture. He released the three

162

hostages and the Swedes returned hurriedly westwards as the fighting picked up.

The Bobovać Brigade spent the rest of the Muslim–Croat war in Dastansko, which became the scene of heavy fighting. Perhaps by the time it all finished some of them remembered how they had cried while carrying their Muslim friends to safety in Vareš. But I doubt it.

9

Central Bosnia, Winter 1993

'Don't shoot, don't shoot,' the three soldiers cried out to their comrades as they staggered up the rain-sodden slope towards the Muslim lines at the edge of Novi Travnik. The BiH troops scrambled out of their bunkers among the trees, stumbling down the narrow trenches to take up their positions on the knoll of ground overlooking the Croat-held houses little more than a hundred yards below them. These were confused moments, though once in place it took the fighters only seconds to understand the full horror unfolding before their eyes.

The men approaching them were their own, captured days earlier during a dawn infiltration of the Muslim lines by the HVO. Now, forced back across no man's land, the prisoners lurched unnaturally up the hillside. Their hands were strapped to their waists. Improvised claymore mines were attached to their chests, linked to the Croat houses by coils of wire that unravelled slowly with each step of their robotic progress. The human bombs were returning home.

As the distance narrowed an officer shouted at his men to shoot them. They refused. Two of the prisoners were from Novi Travnik itself, pre-war friends of those in the trench. The third man was from the same unit. The Muslim troops argued frantically among themselves. Some of the soldiers ran back from the lip of the trench to their bunkers. The officer was screaming at the three men to halt. They kept on walking. As they neared the edge of the trench he too fell back. There were three individual explosions, so close together as to roll into one protracted thunderous roar that bounced echoes between the cold black hills. Blood, shrapnel and tissue sprayed through the trees.

For a few seconds there was silence. A couple of soldiers and the officer peered cautiously over the edge of the trench. In the shredded, ankle-high scrub before them they could make out three pairs of legs. It was all that was left of their friends.

Though short of ammunition the Muslims' rifle barrels were smoking with heat by the time they finished blazing their empty rage away. The limbs of their men lay before them, tantalizingly close but dangerously out of reach. It was several days before they managed to negotiate a ceasefire and British UN troops came in to remove them.

The winter seemed to pull more than just the heat out of the central Bosnian war. In summer sometimes the pressure of the storms had paralysed my mind for hours at a time as the black cumuli trailed like slugs over the hills around me, dragging me down into torpor and lethargy. Yet the winter brought its own gluing constraints. Though the cold lifted my energy, the mists and blizzards that accompanied it often reduced visibility to zero, blocking the ragged roads with heavy drifts so that even a journey of the shortest length became an unequal ordeal of mind and machine over the elements. Petty crime, by which I mean armed hold-ups and robbery rather than murder, grew uncontrollably as the gang hierarchy controlling the pocket turned on foreigners and each other to acquire precious resources like fuel and cash. Outside my room one day two Italian journalists were relieved of their car, cash and possessions at gunpoint. With foolhardy optimism they went to the military police in Vitez to report the loss. Sitting there in uniform was one of the men who had held them up. He punched a journalist hard in the face before he had time to say a word. By nightfall it was often safer to remain in the house.

There was no running water at Viktorija's and after a while I gave up trying to heat a saucepan of water over the woodstove and wash my hair. The room was freezing, the temperature outside so cold that if I did not reach for a towel quick enough sometimes my hair would form icicles around my shoulders. It was easier not to bother. I grew a beard and at night slept – my breath a heavy vapour – in the clothes I wore during the day, and even then the chill crept through to my bones. My skin started to smell different. Dried sweat, woodsmoke, cigarettes and brandy: the smell of the winter war.

I was fine. I had money. I could eat and I could leave. I could savour discomfort as an experience rather than be overwhelmed by it. But in the cold shells of their houses, in the crowded refugee centres, in the concrete cells of their flats, the Bosnians suffered. Many spent hours each day in search of food, standing in frozen queues beside aid distribution centres, sometimes tramping for miles on foot through the white wasteland to carry sacks of flour back on their shoulders, often expending more energy than they could gain; a sick form of negative equity, getting weak trying to get strong.

'No-one is actually starving,' I heard a TV correspondent, belly warm and full with food, bray dismissively to some British officers. 'There is so much hype attached to the supply of food here but no-one is close to dying of hunger.' Bosnians were humiliated, depressed, cold, hungry, frightened, even hopeless, despairing. In the remote eastern enclaves children were having their shrapnel-shattered limbs amputated with woodsaws operated by surgeons who used brandy as an anaesthetic and were paid two Deutschmarks a week. On both sides of the line people had their lives broken every day by bullets and shells. But no-one was actually starving.

The lines around the Vitez pocket had scarcely moved since the end of the summer. Ironically, the Muslim commanders needed the Croats there. Without Vitez there was no guarantee that their Croat counterparts in Hercegovina would allow food supplies passage up-country. If Muslim forces overwhelmed the enclave it would sever their bargaining power in feeding their own people, who had been totally surrounded since the start of the war with the Croats. However that did not preclude breaking the power of the HVO around Vitez through a war of attrition. Both sides sought to kill as many of their enemy as possible with little other game plan in mind. Strategy and taking prisoners ceased while the tactics modified themselves to the simplicity of meatgrinders.

The Bosnians applied their ingenuity to new ends, and in the absence of conventional weapon supplies crafted the most innocuous items into killing devices. Fire-extinguishers were transformed into heavy, short-distance mortar rounds known as 'Babies'; television sets were eviscerated then packed with explosives and nails, the resulting 'TV Bombs' laid at the flanks of positions and wired; Coke cans were converted to hand grenades with such frequency that the UN made it conditional for their

167

troops to crush them after drinking as their rubbish tips were being raided to supply the HVO: recycled consumerism flicking back on destroy.

The BiH had pioneered the first death-as-life weapon form south of Vitez late that autumn, filling the packs of two mules with explosives and rigging them to detonation cords before slapping them off towards the HVO trenches. In true Bosnian style the animals, reluctant *šehids*, began to graze in no-man's-land and after a while wandered back to the Muslim trenches. You did not even have to be there to get the grim joke.

Designing explosive devices became the rage. For the Croats there was no shortage of the chemicals themselves. At the edge of Vitez lay one of the biggest explosives factories in ex-Yugoslavia. Held by the HVO, its decaying stockpiles required only the most rudimentary engineering knowledge to be converted into individual weapons. The Croats got so carried away in the mood of the moment that they converted the whole complex into an enormous bomb, linking up the storage pits with detonators and wire, and threatening to blow the lot if the Muslims launched a major attack on the town. Even had it not all gone up at once, most of the Lašva Valley would have disappeared under a mushroom cloud. In other wars, in other nations, perhaps you could have laughed off the threat as self-dramatization. But the whole psyche of the Bosnian war was blown through with suicide. You sneered at your peril.

It added a peculiar edge to life at Viktorija's. The explosives factory was only a kilometre or two away. From my room I could see its chimney, striped red and white in warning. A few weeks earlier a Croat sniper had climbed up to the top and shot an aid worker who was leaving Stari Vitez in a Land-Rover. He had used a Barrat .50 calibre sniper rifle to do it. The bullet passed through the back door of the Rover, through the rear of the cab, through the back plate of the aid man's flak jacket, through his chest, through the front plate, before lodging in the dashboard. It was murder, but what a weapon, what a shot. It was hard not to be impressed sometimes. For a while that was all the significance the chimney had in my mind. Now, with the news of the Croat valley-bomb, it assumed new distinction, and I sometimes wondered at my choice of top-floor room. It was like getting paranoid about the nuclear threat in the early Eighties. But funnier.

Darko scored the first spectacular explosives success. He was in his late twenties, a Croat, one of the many hard young men whose physical courage and mental unscrupulousness had promoted them to the status of quasi-cult heroes. He led a group of fighters, The Jokers, a like-minded bunch of men whose killing abilities had bloomed without constraint in the borderless scope of the conflict. Heavily implicated in the massacre at Ahmići as well as countless other atrocities, he and his men were labelled as war criminals by the BiH.

Describing his pre-war profession as 'businessman', he had acquired a fuel-hungry white Mercedes in which he used to drive ostentatiously between missions, carrying with him a teenage moll and an inner circle of gun-toting henchmen. He was married, sometimes beat his wife, and once presented a silver Colt .45 to a senior British officer as a present. Loud taste and brutish-ness: it was the HVO's purest psy-profile.

'There are better shots, but there are no better killers,' his deputy, Misha, said of him. Yet Darko exuded a hypnotic charisma common among many of those who have found their vocation in killing. Without doubt he was bad, but he was also intelligent, charming and quick-witted. 'Anthony,' he said to me on one of the last occasions I saw him, 'I've killed so many

Muslims now I'm having difficulty getting to sleep at night.' He searched my eyes for a reaction and when he found none roared with laughter, slapped my leg and got me a drink. On another occasion he had held court to some journalists while seated beneath an enormous swastika. After a time a photographer, thinking the opportunity was too good to miss, asked timorously if he could take a picture. Darko leaned forward, eyes twinkling mischievously. 'You don't get it, do you?' The photographer did not get it at all, and withered on the spot.

He was not a fascist, though some of the more stupid of his men believed in a pure-race Bosnian Croat state. Darko was one of many in Bosnia who had tapped into their own darkness and found there bountiful power. The meek and humane were the war's losers. The vanguard of those quick or bad enough to get with the new agenda reaped immense profits in terms of personal power and prestige. For certain, the driving forces behind the war were geared to nationalism. But many of the individuals prepared to serve these causes were simply murderous opportunists. On each side there were gangs of men whose ability and appetite for killing was used by the authorities regardless of their religious denomination. There were even Muslim killers working among Serb death squads. And Juka Prazina, the one-time hero defender of Sarajevo, served for a time with the HVO in Mostar fighting the government army, before ending up dead in a car in Belgium. It did not undermine the war's overall ideology. It was just a part of the syndrome of evil that so often transcended revitalized religious identities.

At first, though, I felt uncomfortable whenever in Darko's company. I could not equate what he did with who he was. It was another of the war's anomalies that took me a while to work out: you did not have to like what someone did to like them, or at least find them interesting. If you stuck to the values of home, it only hamstrung your ability to see the war clearly and understand the mentality of those fighting it. But if you prostituted those values, your wisdom multiplied. What that knowledge ultimately brought you is hard to say, but at least it accelerated you beyond the trite hypocrisy of so much of the media.

In the small pond of the Lašva Valley, Darko was a big fish and there was no legitimate body to stop his excesses. He entertained journalists more out of a combination of amusement and self-aggrandizement than anything else. His tours of the front line became something of an institution. With scant regard for his own safety he would call out to his Muslim adversaries, many of whom he knew personally, as he fired both pistol and Heckler-Koch simultaneously, seemingly impervious to the angry crackle of return fire.

Then one day he and his men booby-trapped one of their own trenchlines with copious quantities of buried explosive. They provoked a firefight with the Muslim troops opposite before making a deceptive withdrawal. The Muslims stormed across into the empty Croat trench. When enough had entered one of Darko's men, safe in a reserve position, clicked the switch, spreading their adversaries in a dust purée across the hillside. Darko made sure it was all captured on video. Vitez may have been remote, but it was well up to scratch with screen war, and the plan was a relative victory when weighed against some of the Croat defeats of the summer and autumn.

So it was perhaps inevitable that the Lašva mind-set should turn to the possibilities of employing human prisoners as weapon systems. I do not know if the Muslim prisoners were captured with the aim of being used in such a way. Five men were taken initially. One was quickly released by the HVO as his wife was Croat and living in the HVO-held zone of Novi Travnik. After two days of captivity the other four were taken to the gymnasium, then the headquarters of the HVO in the town. They were individually escorted to the restaurant area, where about thirty Croat troops were drinking; and kicked, punched and beaten with baseball bats before being locked in two rooms. One of the men was beaten so badly he could not walk. It saved his life. About two hours later a small group of HVO called the prisoners out of the rooms. The most injured man was left lying on the floor. He was handed back in a prisoner exchange forty days later, and filled in many of the story's blanks for me.

The next time the three Muslims were seen was when their own troops watched them staggering across no man's land. In the small community of the valley it was a very public war crime. The Croats even admitted it. They could do little else. How else do you explain three pairs of legs in no man's land, two of which still had hands attached to the hips with wire?

For a long time it did not disturb me. After Stupni Do I seemed to accept most of the brutality of the war without question. It was a playground where the worst and most fantastic excesses of the human mind were acted out; and since the autumn's events in Vareš I seemed more remote than ever from emotion. What earthed my sentiments once more was meeting the relatives of the three dead soldiers. They were poor people, as you might have expected. You seldom found the sons of the rich dying out there.

The baker gave me cakes, and cried softly in his bare apartment. He had lost a brother, a soldier, to Serb shellfire. He had come to terms with this death. But the way the Croats killed his son? Vengeance did not cross his mind, he told me. He was still too full of the pain at the realization of the fear his twenty-one-year-old boy must have felt in his last minutes. Alive he was nearly 200 lbs. They buried 33 lbs, including the coffin.

Then there was the widowed mother whose eldest son was killed three days after her husband was blown apart. She wept noiselessly, with great dignity. 'I have no use for anger or revenge. I lost everything in this war. I have only poverty and six children to feed: justice will bring me nothing.'

The three brothers – all soldiers – of the third man murdered had already lost fourteen members of their family in the war. They were articulate and measured. 'If it is a question of revenge then Bosnia shall have war until the end of the world,' the youngest told me.

You feel like shit sometimes. I would have understood, expected, even wanted these people to thirst for revenge. My sympathies with the Croats were at an all-time low, in spite of the likes of Viktorija. If Stupni Do and the terrorization of the Muslims in Vareš were cold-blooded acts of realpolitik, then the killing of the three Muslim prisoners in Novi Travnik had required such perverse premeditation that it was a crime on a similar scale.

I could rage at massacre, yet I could not help but like the company of people such as Darko, who was capable of carrying out almost any act of killing. I could admire the skill of the shot that killed an aid worker and feel little about the horror-killing of three prisoners. Until I spoke to their families: then I felt enraged again.

Love hate, war peace, life death, crime and justice: to say my mind was stretched by trying to figure it all out would be an understatement. I tried to cling on to the values I learned in peace-time and during an affluent childhood; I could dumb-mouth them to anyone who asked, but behind it all I and others shared the turmoil of an inverted morality. War: don't believe the hype:

it could be heaven as well as hell. Some people snatched themselves back from its mental tumult, got on with their lives and kept their perspective. If you want to call people heroes then these are your candidates. Others died: they are your victims. Too many like me, threw themselves into the waves and never looked back until the undertow kicked in.

10

For all the joviality of their nickname, the Fish-Head Gang were confident bandit killers who on occasion even hijacked UN military vehicles with the same apparent ease with which they robbed or murdered civilians. They had come to light late in the spring of 1993, the lawless guardians to the long, narrow ravine leading from Gornji Vakuf northwards to Vitez. Their first raids were comparatively tentative affairs, and journalists were the victims. At a particular corner in the gorge, where the ground to the right of the gravel track was bordered by a river and ruined fish farm, armed men in a ragged array of uniforms without insignias would leap in front of solitary vehicles, drag out the occupants, take from them everything, even their shoes, before forcing them to walk barefoot back to Gornji Vakuf.

They quickly became meaner. In June they had held up some Italian aid vehicles and taken the crews to a deserted area before instructing the frightened men to run for it. Three of the five

Italians had been shot dead as they legged it, the two survivors escaping through the thick woodland only by chance.

Bosnian civilians were also targeted as the gang, named by the media after their fish-farm haunt, became more ready to shed blood. At the end of the summer I had seen a bullet-riddled Jugo slewed at the gorge corner, three bodies inside. By that stage both the British and Dutch UN troops had lost vehicles and equipment at gunpoint to the bandits. Unarmed travellers needed a Warrior escort to negotiate the gorge. Even then the robbers were not above trying to filter civilian vehicles out of the convoy.

In late autumn they suddenly disappeared. Corinne and I were travelling from Vitez to Split for a break. We had first checked in with a British ops room to ask if there had been any recent reports of Fish-Head activity. They assured us that they had not been active for weeks, and must have disbanded.

'Oh, I'm getting a real bad feeling about this gorge,' Corinne announced encouragingly as we entered the mouth of the ten-mile-long ravine in a clapped-out Land-Rover, flak jackets, cameras, luggage and clothes piled in a tempting gateau behind us. She said it as though she had just bought a new pair of shoes and was having second thoughts about their style.

'What kind of bad feeling?' I said sulkily. I was tired. I wanted to be in Split, have a bath, drink good wine and eat seafood, catch a couple of days' rest then a Hercules to Sarajevo. The fear of the Fish-Heads was gnawing at the back of my mind and I objected to the way my concerns were accentuated by Corinne publicizing her own.

'Well, you know, a baaad fucking feeling, that's all.'

'Listen,' I began, trying to quell my own fear, 'the Fish-Heads haven't been seen for weeks. There's shitloads of UN traffic coming up this route. The gang are under pressure from the BiH after the last UN patrol got whacked and must have fucked off into the mountains. Don't worry about it, OK?'

'OK.'

Five minutes later, as the gorge narrowed around us, casting the road ahead into deep shadow: 'So, Anthony, what happens if we round the corner by the fish farm and there's a whole lot of raggedy guys with guns in the road?'

'Just drive through fast, no drama.'

'What happens if they've got RPGs?'

'Maybe stop?'

'Mines in the road?'

'Stop.'

'There's no fucking way we can do a U-turn in this shit-heap. It goes about forty tops . . .'

'Corinne,' I implored, 'don't fucking worry about it. There's fuck all we can do and we're not turning back. It'll be OK, forget it, all right?'

'I got a real bad feeling about this gorge, that's all, OK?'

'OK.'

After half an hour or so of mounting tension, alone on the desolate road, we neared the crucial fish farm bend. I had already started a reassuring grin at Corinne when I saw them: ten men or so; all armed; ragged uniforms; no insignia; RPGs; mines in the road.

'Shit. Stop.'

'Stop? Shit.'

We ground to a halt before the necklace of anti-tank mines. The men clustered quickly about the vehicle, one of them wrenching my door open before I had time to reach the handle. He pushed himself into the cab, gun up. Corinne, a non-smoker, flipped a Marlboro into her mouth with the expertise of an habitué before offering the man the packet. I was carrying a letter to a BiH commander in Gornji Vakuf from a soldier in Travnik, and flicked it out of my pocket into the man's face.

'Hi, you know this guy? Can you give him the letter?'

The bandit took in the letter, the cigarettes, Corinne, and our gear in one eye-swivelling stare. He seemed surprised by something, we never knew what, and paused for a second, then turned back and called out an order to his men. One of them pulled the mines from the road.

'You go, you go now,' he spat, waving us forward with quick, aggressive stabs.

We drove away. My knees were shaking. Corinne looked pale.

'Cool?'

'Cool.'

'Cool.'

In Gornji Vakuf we drove into the periphery of a gunbattle and were stuck in the broken town for a long while. Corinne had been passenger in a Rover that had detonated an anti-tank mine there the previous year. Her face gashed, she had crawled out of the car and taken pictures as the BiH, themselves under fire from HVO positions, rescued the other wounded occupants. But this day, having survived the Fish-Heads untouched, we knew that to walk on water all we needed was a pond, and the humming of the bullets was as inconsequential as that of houseflies. We reached Split six hours later, long, long after we had begun to laugh hysterically over our luck. As we were sitting in a hotel bar, a shaken TV crew walked in. They had been travelling the same route an hour behind us. The Fish-Heads had robbed them of everything, forcing them to kneel along a ditch while gun barrels were laid at the back of their heads as an added intimidation.

Cool? The word came nowhere near.

✻   ✻   ✻

I needed another break in London, but before I left I travelled back to Sarajevo. The city broke my euphoric sense of invulnerability before it had time to recede of its own volition. Bosnia's war was really a multitude of separate conflicts, each of a different nature: the war between Serbs and Muslims, Muslims and Croats, Mostar and the south, Tuzla and the north, the eastern enclaves and Bihać in the west; town, village and city: the same sound but infinitely different styles. Sarajevo's war also retained an identity of its own, though it sent its vibrations rippling through the rest of the state with the force of an evil crystal.

Yet I felt very cynical towards some of the media in the city. Too many simply walked into the basement of the Holiday Inn each day, drove out in an armoured car to a UN headquarters, grabbed a few details, filled them in with the words of 'real people' acquired for them by their local fixers, and then returned to their sanctuary to file their heartfelt vitriol with scarcely a hair out of place. It had an inordinate media prestige as the Bosnian capital, which distracted journalists from much of what was happening elsewhere.

'Sarajevo', even the name had a sexy roll to it once you dropped the emphasis on the vowels until the final 'o'. However, returning to it now after many months away, I was stunned and angered by the changes that had overtaken those I had left there. Momčilo, Petar and Yelena, their friends and neighbours; all were paler, thinner, jumpier, more afraid than when I had last seen them at the end of the spring. Their faces had the look you see in the dying; the skin a waxy grey and the eyes way back in the head, circled by darkening rings. Had I stayed with them, perhaps I would not have noticed these changes, but after so long an interval they appeared as shocking evidence of the war's erosion. Only the gunfire in the empty street outside seemed as fat, energetic and full of malice as before. If the siege had gone on until every last living thing was dead I expect the sound would still have been there, echoing through the emptiness like a stuck record, immortalized by its own malignant power.

I had brought little for them with me; some batteries for Petar's torch; coffee for Yelena; cigarettes and grass for Momćilo; pitiful supplies from the outside world. Once the ritual hugging and kissing had been performed we talked for seven hours straight. Who was dead, who was wounded, who was in the army, who had escaped; in another place in another time it would have been like a long-absent godparent being filled in on family developments. In the time I had been away everything and nothing had changed. As before friends squeezed into the flat, the cigarette smoke reaching previously unknown levels of density, and in the background the coffee grinder crunched away in Yelena's hands like a piece of industrial machinery. Misha dropped round with his wife Natasha – his teenage daughter Ozanna had recently been wounded by shrapnel but she was OK, she was doing fine; Mira came upstairs with Bratso; Endre arrived with his neighbour Mirela; even Sandra paid us a visit, stepping shyly into the flat on the finest pair of legs in central Sarajevo. Serbs, Croats, Muslims: there were none in that room. Just Sarajevo Bosnians.

Nothing I can say, nothing I can write, can convey to you the sense of purity in those moments, the fading soul of multi-ethnic Bosnia, battered but still so alive. By the winter of 1993 it did not have long left. That ideal of co-existence was something I had lost touch with in central Bosnia. In Vitez the cleaving of communities was so fast and ugly you were presented with fait accompli partition before there was time to do more than watch the foulness of the way it was done. Sarajevo reached into my mind again and pulled what was really at stake in the war out for me to face. Secularism or nationalism: which side of the line do you stand?

Momćilo took me aside as the conversation rose into a

symphony of different voices and the grappa bottle emptied. His eyebrows flicked up and he grinned, the amusement of the moment suddenly lifting the sadness out of his drawn face.

'No-one knows what will happen to us. There is no end in sight. I'm thinking of getting out.'

'Getting out?' I asked. 'How?'

He told me of his plan to cross the Miljacka River at night. The nearest stretch of the river, and the Vrbanja Bridge across it, were sometimes the scene of 'people trafficking' as well as heavy fighting. Local gang leaders in the army had a tenuous line of communication with the Serb forces on the other side, and worked out deals for cash to get people out under cover of darkness. It was a dangerous option; either side could renege on the agreement halfway through, or a twitchy soldier would fire a shot and the whole thing would fall apart, leaving corpses in the dawn light.

But Momćilo was getting desperate. He had a wife and child still in Croatia, and the conscription gangs in the city were getting harder to dodge. Petar had approved of the idea in principle. It was just a matter of time and contacts. I had no advice to give him. He knew the situation better than me. Inside I hoped he would not try it. I could see him floating dead in the Miljacka while Petar and Yelena were left to fend as best they could without him. We talked for a few minutes more together, honesties between friends, then rejoined the crowd.

Dinner that night was the usual Sarajevo fare of beans, bread, UHT milk and meat-fat, but beneath the flickering candles it had the significance of a Last Supper. I left the next day for Split and on to London, swearing I would return to them soon. Petar asked me to take two pens in a crafted case to his young granddaughter. I was to hand them over with the message 'Be a good pupil'. Yelena told me to tell her daughter not to worry, in spite of it all they were alive, had enough to eat and somewhere to stay. She told me that she was at an age when she thought a lot about her granddaughter, and was missing not being able to see her grow up. Petar laughed and joked that he had forgotten all of his family in London, and would save his wishes for a better time.

These were brave, brave people. Beside their wisdom my own clumsy grapplings to understand the war were pitiful. I felt shamed by my inability to help them, and shamed by my nation, which had assisted Bosnia's war by its ostrich-headed foreign policy.

I felt close to tears when I said goodbye, and tried to tell them that they meant more to me than almost anything in my life.

Momčilo gave me a final wink before I walked out of the door. It was the last time I ever saw him. He hooked up with some sort of deal a fortnight or so later, splashing through the Miljacka at night during a snowstorm. The plan went awry on the other side. Rumour filtered back across the lines that he had been beaten and incarcerated by the Serbs. Then that he had been press-ganged into the Bosnian Serb army where he found himself part of a tank crew besieging the city. Much later, word came back that he had raged at the Serb troops that they were murdering civilians, then refused to soldier and had been taken away and imprisoned. Before I discovered his ultimate fate, I would think of him whenever I found myself saying brutish things about the Bosnian Serb army; my worst dream, that one day on a battlefield I would see his face on the body of a dead soldier, frequently thieved me of sleep. How often that dream must have been shared by Bosnians. How often it must have become reality.

WICKED GAMES

Withdrawal is the kind of thing you like a little warning of. Like going to the front, you need to steel yourself against the potential pain and fear of it all before you cut off and throw yourself in there. The cops busted a middleman, leaving my dealer out of gear. It was the first time that it had ever happened in my transactions with him, and the sudden dearth left me drying out by mid-evening like a stranded fish on a mudbank.

I cannot have had more than four or five hours' sleep in the previous three days and exhaustion was beginning to breach the crumbling drug walls. The sweat was upon me, a pungent sheen smelling of burned rubber that coated my body from head to toe; the inside of my nose felt like I had inhaled caustic acid; my mouth was sore and foul tasting. Worse of all was the soul-ripping depression that slipped in quick on the heels of the drug's last slow paraglide.

I realized that 'the man' would be in a state infinitely worse than mine; the thought of his desperation gave me hope, for I knew that he would go to almost any length to score. I had already rung him three times to know if anything had changed, and there was increasing exasperation in his voice.

'Look, I'll call you if anything moves,' he told me finally. 'If you don't hear by ten you'll have to rough it for the night and call me in the morning.'

I slumped on my bed miserably, smoked a dozen cigarettes, each one viler than the last, and swashed whisky in liberal doses down my throat as I checked my watch every two minutes; somewhere near nightmarish sleep, but not near enough.

By nine-thirty I faced up to the likelihood of nothing coming through, so downed some Neurofen and ran a deep bath to try to get rid of the smell of my own skin. Ever optimistic, I placed my mobile phone in the soap dish as I sank down into the water, letting it swirl over my head as I crunched up in a foetal position to cover as much of my body as possible from the increasing chill of the room.

Then it rang, the gurgling bleep reaching me from the fathoms of the deep. I shot gasping to the surface, water cascading over the sides of the tub.

'Right,' said the voice, 'I've got two for you but you'll have to meet me like now cos I've got to be elsewhere in twenty minutes and if you're not here in fifteen I'll have to go without you.'

Fifteen minutes? Jesus, the journey usually took twenty. I was out of the bath and out of the flat in thirty seconds, water pouring down my hair, back and legs, soaking the T-shirt and jeans I had pulled on.

The car? Where the fuck had I parked the car? I sprinted up and down the London street, arms outstretched in rage and frustration, frantic with fear. Seeing it finally in an alley, I shunted the vehicles parked at either end until I got it out on to the road, and sped northwards in a squeal of rubber.

He was just walking away from our rendezvous as I arrived, having jumped every light along the route. He did not say much, though looked at me a little quizzically as he handed over the gear.

The car ran out of petrol on the way home, chugging to a stand-still in the middle of the road. I pushed it into the kerb and walked to a garage to get some gas. The man behind the counter stared at me doubtfully as I squelched in to pay for the container I'd filled. My hair was still thick with soap and water, and by this stage my clothes stuck sopping to my skin.

'Fuckin' 'ell mate,' he shot at me as I turned to leave, a drip-ping trail following me towards the door. 'Wash and Go don't mean you don't need a towel.'

Wash and go? Wash or go would sum up my choices better these days. Once again, it seems a life or death question, same as it has been for a while now. However much I try to fool myself that a habit is just a disengaged limbo state, the reality is much worse, robbing me of my strength, health and life-force, as well as attracting a whole array of other damaging influences into the situation as its beat gains pace.

Go: I can stay with the habit, leave things to chance and depart one night choking on whisky puke, too drugged to wake up. Sooner or later it's bound to happen. Or worse still, wither away broken by slow years of sickness. I can go for the quick option and end it myself. I've thought about it often enough, usually during sleepless nights when I smoke alone with war ghosts and watch the city lights outside. You can squeeze an awful lot of thought between taking up first pressure on a trigger and putting that extra millimetre's worth of force into your index finger.

Wash: I can take the life option. Try to work my way out of this shit. But to me that hardly looks like a worthwhile choice: the oppressive stagnation of peacetime, growing older, of domestic tragedy and trivial routine. Could I accept what to me seemed the drudgery of everyday existence, the life we endure without so much as a glimpse of an angel's wing. Fuck that. Sometimes I pray for another war just to save me.

The shrink is right: I feel sane as anything in war, the only one there earthed to rational thought and emotion. It is peace I have got the problem with.

Just for the record, though, choices aside, if I bother to try to explain my present state by looking at my past then part of the reason could be my relationship with my father.

It sounds trite, and it is. Dysfunctional families are symptomatic of the times. If everyone with a vaguely screwed-up background ended up going to war and getting a habit, the whole Western world would grind to a halt. But I encountered many Westerners in Bosnia, in many different guises, who came from equally fractured family backgrounds.

My childhood experience did not necessarily lead me directly to the conflict in Bosnia, but it did lay some very strong foundations of resentment within me, sentiments that found a focus in the war, that much I know for sure. And as for internecine struggles, from an early age I was no stranger to those. Admittedly my family conflict was not played out with Kalashnikovs and artillery, though there were times it seemed very close to violence, but all the other tenets of war were there.

It is a tumult of memory. And it was a long time ago.

My mother was the youngest of two daughters. There was no longer enough money to give her the same private education as her sister so she went to a local grammar school. She did not have the fiery temperament of my grandmother but was, like her father, shy and self-possessed, bestowed with good looks and *figure, and was the guardian of a great inner strength and fierce independence. Leaving school at sixteen, she travelled back to her roots in Austria, before returning to London. She met a young British cavalry officer in 1962. They were married the same year. I was born in 1966, four years ahead of my sister.*

I accepted this version of events, and my position as the first-born, as any child would. It took a few more years for another truth to be sharpened up and thrust my way.

I have scarcely any memory of my father before he left us, and I hope that with the passage of time the later recollections can be jettisoned like unwanted ballast down the same dark well as the first six years. One day, while walking the dogs near our large Berkshire house, my mother told me my father had left home, was in love with another woman, and that they were getting divorced. I was six, and at the time this left the shock of discovering that Father Christmas was a myth, though in terms of sorrow the news was still out-distanced by the recent loss of a much-loved terrier killed by a car. You have to keep these things in perspective. I cried primarily out of a realization that my childhood 'happy-ever-after' perception of life could obviously be filed under bullshit alongside Santa Claus. Clearly the world was a place to be regarded with suspicion. Our house was sold, the divorce went through, and my mother, sister, remaining dogs and I moved elsewhere.

Some people tell me now that my father and I were very close. I remember nothing of that.

Soon it felt as though a heavy cloak had been shed: no more night sounds of fighting and tears from downstairs to interrupt my sleep. The three of us were together, living in a chaotic house in the country, accompanied by the menagerie of the animals my mother adored. For a time they were glorious days, rich with the freedom of rural life. My mother loved us unquestioningly, and

187

we her. Then came brutal intrusions from the outside world. Death was the first and worst. Within the space of a few short years my grandfather and aunt were taken by savage, short illnesses. Then cancer killed my grandmother too, closing the doors of the past to my mother. She bore each successive loss with great stoicism. We were a small, close-knit family and these were truly bitter wounds. For me, as a child, each sudden tragedy was cushioned by the belief that death was not the end, that I would see the lost again one day. I would give almost anything to find that faith again now.

School holidays would have been bliss but for the fact that I always had to spend one of the weeks with my father, which I hated. He seemed authoritarian and remote, and his household full of rules and rigidity. There were times to get up, times to eat, times to be seen but not heard, times to be neither seen nor heard, and mention of the past in which he had been married to my mother was forbidden. My sister never had to go through the experience. Strangely, she never saw my father at all. I begrudged her her freedom and often asked him why she did not have to stay too. Usually these questions were met with brush-offs, though my father once told me that it was something I would learn the answer to when I was older, which did little to assuage my curiosity. There was no debate allowed over the length of my stay. It was always a week. When I suggested that it might be better to stay for shorter periods, he informed me that as my father he had rights of access given to him by law and that I should 'toe the line'.

He was big on the line being toed. Furious at the news that I had run away from boarding school, he lectured me again on the necessity of 'toeing'. A couple of days after this scolding I discovered at last why my sister was exempt from my fate.

My father's teenage half-sister was staying with him, and one afternoon, having been requested to do so by the old man, she told me fairly baldly that my sister was not my full sister, and not my father's child. I was ten years old, but wise enough in the ways of the world for the implications of this news not to be wasted on me. Whatever his logic in having me enlightened this way, it back-fired. I had long regarded him as a hostile intruder in my life, and the realization that my mother must have had an affair with someone else during their marriage came as little real surprise. More than this, I saw his attitude as unjust, and the issue became a focus of growing contention between us, particularly as there was no certain answer over my sister's paternity. She may or may not have been his child. It was unproven and to me should not have been a question anyway. He had lived with her for two years during his marriage to my mother and accepted her as his daughter then, knowing there was some doubt over the whole thing. To suddenly reject a child for genetic reasons, real or perceived, seemed a kind of criminal prejudice to me.

Some of his friends agreed with his attitude. There was plenty of innuendo concerning my mother, sister and me – the fallen woman, the bastard offspring and the problem child. I despise those people and their small-minded bigotry.

There followed an incident which completely severed any chance of a real relationship. Shortly before being collected by one of my father's employees to be taken away for another joyous week, I had a hysterical fit at the prospect and threw myself down the stairs. It seemed to have the desired effect at first as my mother promised that she would collect me and take me home if I agreed to spend one night at my father's farm. Stupidly I consented.

The old man was enraged when I met him and he was told of the deal.

'Got a train to catch, Anthony?' He smirked at me the next day as I looked at my watch in anticipation of her arrival. He then had *me driven away in a car by the same employee who had brought me to the house the day before, so that when my mother arrived she was given no option but to leave without me. When I was returned to the farmhouse, I was slapped by my father's wife and forced to listen to his denial that my mother had ever intended to collect me. He explained that she had merely come 'to discuss my schooling'. The phones were then disconnected in the wing in which I stayed so I could not ring home. 'The phones are faulty,' I was told: more transparent lies. This episode was part of a custody battle over which I had no control. Even at that age, however, I was aware that my own feelings were being completely disregarded by my father's abusive and intimidating attitude.*

The following holiday I ran away when the car appeared to collect me. And the holiday after that. My father threatened to take the custody battle to court, then bottled out of the idea. I cannot recall spending another night in his house.

As the years passed we maintained a tenuous and irregular communication, our antipathy developing, the details of individual bones of contention eventually almost irrelevant as our mistrust of one another grew. I remember the last time I saw him. It was in December 1992. I had driven to his farm for one of the triannual ritual lunches, during which we talked only about subjects which would not provoke a fight. This narrowed the field so dramatically that our discussions on these occasions had become almost verbatim replicas of each other, like a tired and meaningless mantra. By this final lunch I had no idea who he was, nor he I. The effort of finding out would have involved so much bloodshed that the only thing we agreed on was this arid détente. I found even these visits objectionable. The bleak, bad childhood experiences stained my memories and I would have preferred to rendezvous anywhere but his home, an option he refused point blank.

But he seemed to blow his own rules that December. We were sitting around the dining-room table, a tense arena that forced us into the same physical space, and the conversation was ballet dancing along well-rehearsed steps. It may even have become a little more risqué than usual and touched on current affairs. His views on the world were underpinned with racism, reactionarism, and anti-Semitism. He was into revisionism not only with history but with his own life too. To talk about something that had happened the day before in another country thus became a potential bomb between us. Yet in other ways he was a very sharp, very intelligent man. With his wife beside him he could be especially formidable, and knew it. Which is probably why I could never get to meet him individually. Alone I could have opened his mind like a steamed mussel.

More than anything, I raged at his defensive reclusiveness. His unwillingness to meet me away from his home was the most visible and unhealthy aspect of this attitude, a wall that I tried again and again to breach. That he adored his new wife and stepchildren I accepted. That he did so at the expense of everything else I did not. I felt that if I could discuss the situation in the open and alone with him it would somehow revolutionize our relationship into some new form of understanding.

It could have been that at this particular lunch we drank too much wine as the meal progressed, but more likely it was just a meltdown of my tolerance of the farcical nature of our relationship. I made some dig at a remark of his that I found particularly offensive. He retaliated. At that stage there was then no real anger on either side, but somehow it unlocked a discussion on attitudes and the past, a previously taboo theatre of battle.

He was still wholly unable to face reality or accept any responsibility for his actions. I became enraged, above all by the confident smirks that crept across his mouth as the debate heated.

191

Within the narrow confines of his household he was so assured of his own superiority.

'I am only sorry I don't believe in God,' I said. 'If I did, I would at least have the satisfaction of knowing that you would burn in hell.'

I do not regret these two sentences which had formed in my mouth without the contrivance of thought. I meant them and still regard them as a reserved understatement. There were plenty more where they came from. They were nothing.

At first he greeted this retort with a supercilious smile, as if it confirmed everything he had ever thought about me. But beneath the tightened mouth edge I knew I had drawn blood. The debate continued, coldly. Neither raised his voice. Neither interrupted the other. It was like a game of chess; the same atmosphere of chilled concentration and stillness, each player allowed time to move, words like knife-rasps instead of the scrape of pieces.

We moved from the dining-room to the drawing-room. My anger was beginning to shake my voice by then, however, and I felt my self-possession straining. My father seemed to wilt suddenly, and sank back into his armchair, leaving his wife to continue the fight. There was a real core of hostility between us too. I felt she had no right to pass judgment on my family or on me.

Sharing the lunch and the argument was her son, who at that time was, I suppose, in his early twenties. His presence inhibited me from really attacking her. But when my stepmother suddenly labelled my mother an adulteress, my restraint broke. I was not prepared for such an insult from people who were effectively outsiders in our family and my rage was not far from homicidal. I remember the air chilling around my face and my body twitching with fury as I struggled to contain it. I stared into the fireplace for a long time, trying to regain my composure. Then I looked at my father to see his reaction. He sat there, completely powerless, unhappy but too morally weak to lift a finger to stop it.

His wife walked out of the room and I walked out of the house to my car. My father followed me. I turned to him.

'You could have stopped that at any stage,' I said calmly. 'But you just let it go. You know the truths of the past, yet you deny them to your own son.'

He shrugged helplessly. I think now that that shrug affected me more deeply than anything else that day. He was suffering too and was not so out of touch as to be unaware of it. But he was so imprisoned by his inability to communicate, and so totally subdued by his archaic view of the world that he had surrendered all power of self-responsibility. It was pathetic to see my own father in such a state and I would not wish it on anyone.

'I will never come here again,' I added. 'I will see you at any time you want alone, anywhere but this place, but I shall never come here again.'

Predictably, he refused and we never met again.

However, when he heard second-hand of my plan to go to Bosnia, he went as far as to ring my mother to implore her to dissuade me from going. But by the end of the war I was alive and he was dead. Sometimes now it feels like I killed him.

11

Airports: they were like decompression chambers where I sought to balance my mind for a coming immersion, either into war or out to peace. I always seemed to float off into narcissistic death dreams somewhere between customs and the tarmac. Would I die? Did I want to die? Or, if outgoing, why was I alive? Did I want to live?

In Zagreb the March sunshine still bore a winter shade of grey, and as I waited in the departure lounge my thoughts were particularly focused. The war in central Bosnia had ended overnight. The fighting between Croats and Muslims had ceased. A distant peace accord signed in Washington had ended the conflict in the last week of February 1994 after intensive American pressure on the authorities in Zagreb had pulled the rug of Croatian military support from under the nationalists in Hercegovina. I was stunned by the news. My goldfish-bowl war, the halcyon torment whereby the living and dying had pirouetted around me within the pocket's intimate confines, was over. It was not all finished, for the war with the Serbs still remained. But in Vitez the war had been on my doorstep, a presence that permeated my every day. That time was gone. It felt like the end of an affair, private sadness soothed by a wash of sensual blue nostalgia.

There had been an underhand warning of peace from a British officer about four days before it actually happened, but I had ignored it. The Coldstream Guards were in Vitez. They had endured the bitter winter, the feckless loyalty of the media and the grinding bestiality of the conflict around them with tremendous panache. Their commanding officer was a tall, erudite character, regarded with fierce loyalty and respect by his men, who in turn were looked on by the local Bosnians with little short of adulation. Like every good battalion it valued its eccentrics. The Bosnians liked eccentricity, and the Guards were over-endowed with their quotient of it.

Initially they had appeared more cautious than their predecessors, and for a time I had been suspicious of this new regiment. But my responsibility was only to myself. I did not have the lives of men in my hands at a time when the UN's directives had collapsed in a way not seen even during the previous summer. In time I grew to understand the constraints on their operations and esteemed the dry insight given to me in any dialogue with officers or guardsmen. Soon, just as had happened with other British units, they lost their shyness over pulling triggers and blazed back happily whenever the opportunity allowed, usually at the HVO, which made it even better.

Their colonel was always approachable and direct. He was confident in his opinion and trusted me enough to tell me his personal views on the war, though too often I found our communication dictated by professional necessity whereby I ended up asking him questions to which we both already knew the answer, but which I needed to hear anyway to quote him on. As the war around the valley stalemated into a wretched cycle of killing and counter-killing my questions and his replies became more predictable. I had never seen the war get so ugly. Neither side bothered to take prisoners any more and village garrisons were slaughtered first by one side then the other. Viktorija was dropping so many tranquillizers it often became hard to hold a conversation with her. Her mother and sisters were still in Zenica, a bastion of Muslim territory, incommunicado now for weeks. Milan was doing at least three days out of seven on the line. Their goodbyes became too painful to watch as the graves on the hillsides spilt out of their yards like brown scars.

The Croat authority in the pocket began to collapse, with vicious gang fights erupting as various groups vied for control of black market trade. First Jute, the Vitez godfather, was shot in the stomach and paralysed, then Darko too got his come-uppance. He had angered many Croat commanders with his growing entrepreneurial powerbase and arrogance. One day his white Mercedes was riddled with automatic fire from a rival Croat gang at the edge of Vitez. Darko managed to get out, firing, but was hit three times in the chest and stomach. Seriously ill, he was evacuated by helicopter to a hospital in Split. Two weeks later he discharged himself and disappeared. Meanwhile in Vitez his teenage lover turned up face-down in the Lašva River. Someone had shot her in the head.

At the end of a discussion in February, the Coldstream colonel suddenly added that if the dialogue between Croat and Muslim commanders over the preceding few days had been anything to go by, the war could be over by the end of the month.

'What do you mean?' I asked, incredulous.

'Well, all sorts of commanders seem to have been talking to each other, men that usually never communicate . . .' He tailed off mysteriously. I thought that the colonel had lost the plot, and did not bother pressing him further on the subject. In my mind it was inconceivable that the war could end. Neither side was yet in a strong enough military position to push the other to compromise, though for all their advantages the Croats were doing disastrously against the Muslims who, backs to the wall, were fighting with a conviction the original aggressors lacked.

Four days later the fighting stopped, and I listened to a crackling voice on the World Service announcing details of the Washington peace accord. It was a sharp indication of my cynicism that I had a source whom I trusted, valued and liked, yet whenever he told me something important I thought he was bullshitting me.

Little changed in the first days of peace. The killing stopped but both sides continued to regard each other with distrust across the trenches. The BiH, who had never wanted a war with the Croats in the first place, were ironically largely more able to forgive. The Croats in Bosnia believed they had been sold out by Zagreb and looked upon the new peace agreement as a shotgun marriage of expediency. Officially their dream of Herceg-Bosna was dead. The two sides were to be joined in federation, confederated in turn to Croatia. Cosmetic changes were quickly made to the command structures of both the HVO and BiH forces in the interest of preserving the ceasefire. Most of the more notorious officers were shifted aside, temporarily, as the scapegoats for peace. Yet despite the official line, the nationalists among them held their ugly dreams as close to their hearts as ever.

The details of the Washington accord apart, the most poignant day of the new peace came when the Guards decided to have their regimental band play in celebration before a crowd of schoolchildren in Vitez. It was a well-intentioned gesture but as soon as the bass drum thumped out the first beat every child in the hall dived panic-stricken for cover. Different interpretations, different sounds: I knew the feeling. Nothing would be the same again.

Hordes of new journalists descended on Vitez to savour the peace development. I felt angry and bitter. Peace? It was a hideous thought. Then someone stole my passport. It was a good excuse to leave for a while.

I did not have enough money to buy a ticket home but walked out of a freezing rainstorm into the Zagreb office of Croatia Airlines through a sense of jaded optimism. A woman there gave me a ticket for half price because she said my story amused her. Even in a society gripped by officialdom spontaneity broke through when you least expected it.

Sitting in the departure lounge at the airport, waiting for my flight for London to be called, I turned over the memories of the last months of winter in central Bosnia like precious artefacts; gently and with the fascination of a dedicated collector. Drinking coffee, smoking and dreaming, I barely noticed the milling crowd of passengers before me. Then a face detached itself from the anonymous mass, and walked purposefully, limping slightly, to the table at which I sat.

He wore an expensive brown leather jacket and aviator shades. Pulling out a cane chair, he sat down, draping an arm nonchalantly over the backrest, moving fairly easily for a man recently shot three times.

'You're a long way from Vitez,' Darko commented conspiratorially, smiling louchely and leaning forward. 'Or should I say now "federal" Vitez.'

He ordered coffee and lit a Marlboro, pausing to flick a piece of imagined ash from the sleeve of his jacket. The last time I had seen him was in the grime-blasted urban destruction of the line at the edge of Stari Vitez, decked out in bandoliers and chest webbing, grenade-laden, pistol on hip, assault rifle like a toy in his large hands. Even in the soulless plastic confines of the airport he had not lost any of his presence, and his aura seemed to buzz around the table like a swarm of hornets.

The war with the Muslims had given him power, freedom and prestige. While it continued he had been a hero to some, criminal to others. The sudden retreat of the violent tide in the Lašva Valley afforded him no such ambivalence. He was under more threat from peace than rival gangs and posed an attractive fall guy for the sins of more influential figures.

We talked for a time about shared acquaintances, and his views on the future of central Bosnia were shot through with resentment. 'The same men who believed in Herceg-Bosna and encouraged us to fight now turn their backs on us to deal with the Americans,' he said. 'War is strange. This talk of peace and I become the political enemy of even my own side.'

The Tannoy announced the last call for my flight, and I stood up to leave. He rose, extended his hand, grinned again complicitly and shrugged. 'Well . . . see you in Australia.'

I wrote the story of our meeting. It was too good to miss in the context of those days. There was one change in my copy. I swapped 'Australia' for 'Brazil'. Maybe he was lying and, anyway, anyone who really wanted him could have tracked him down, but he had always looked after me on the line and that carried more weight in my judgment than his barbarous killings of people I had not seen. So I was not prepared to give anyone who was after him, and there were plenty, including war crimes investigators, the first clue to where he had gone. It would have seemed disloyal. From another perspective I guess that could mean that I was colluding in something, and flawed in my perception. I can live with it.

Darko is almost certainly dead now anyway, so it hardly matters any more.

12

I had seen so many funerals in Bosnia that after a while they all began to merge into the same amorphous blob of bare earth, tears and shovel scrapes in my memory. I had to reach back and try to recall the shape of the wooden marker or dress of the holyman to define whose dead were being buried. As a foreigner of alien faith and unknown to the mourners I always stood a little apart, hoping my detachment would allow them some privacy.

This funeral was much the same. The service was Catholic, much of it in Latin; the church was modern and ugly and a plain coffin was lowered into the grave, at one moment tilting awkwardly and bumping the soft earth sides. The mourners stood in two groups, to the left and right of the grave, while I was slightly removed near the foot of it. The familiar sound of weeping rose into the air and everyone hung their heads and looked either miserable or at least suitably serious. A few shot me sidelong glances. It happened all the time in Bosnia. People usually wanted to know who you were, and it was more often a look of curiosity rather than hostility. This time, though, it was a little different. The funeral was in England and it was my own father they were putting in the ground.

I had returned to Bosnia, as planned, a little over three weeks after the cessation of hostilities between the Muslims and Croats. The war with the Serbs was still ongoing, and if the front lines were no longer immediate, they were still close. Mount Vlašić was only a few miles west, and a base in central Bosnia allowed me tremendous movement across the length and breadth of 'federation' territory. It was a time when I did consider moving back to Sarajevo, but professional constraints overrode the temptation. The paper I worked for still had its journalist in the capital and I disliked being exposed to the cloying press scene there for more than a couple of days. In central Bosnia I felt more mobile, having acquired a Lada Niva from a friend, hot but no-one was keeping records, and at times more in touch with the war than I would have done within the claustrophobic confines of the capital.

The Muslim–Croat war might have stopped, but central Bosnia seemed empty without it, and the hatred remained. Peering out of my room one spring morning I had seen an old man, his body wrinkled and weak like a tortoise pulled out of its shell, stop his bicycle in the road outside and ask 'Postman Splat' something. Splat had a peasant's build, and though in his forties was a human warthog of sunburned burl. He approached the old man cautiously and they spoke together for about ten seconds before Splat took a mighty swing at him. Splat's beefsteak fist came rocketing through the air from a starting point below his hip. I could hear the smack from my room, a dead sound like the beating of a wet carpet. It caught the old man square in the face and knocked him backwards over the verge into a ditch as his bicycle toppled gracefully into the road. At the edge of the ditch was a three-strand barbed-wire fence, and the old man was strung out on it, head lolling over his shoulders like a broken scarecrow. Splat stepped down into the ditch, spat on his fists, and then laid in with cold deliberation. The old man's head snapped first one way and then the other. It was like watching a seal being clubbed on the Bering Straits.

I ran down, but by the time I got to the drive the old man had fallen off the wire and lay unconscious at the bottom of the ditch. Splat walked up to me, his face florid and sweating with exertion, piggy little eyes absolutely blank. 'What the fuck was that about? Who is he?' I asked, assuming I was on the edge of interfering with a family feud.

Splat shrugged indifferently. 'I don't know, fuck your mother. Some Muslim,' as if that explained it all. What had happened was simple enough. The old man was from Travnik, and under the terms of the peace had crossed the line on his bicycle to try to find some food to buy in the Croat area, which was always better stocked than the Muslim zones. Not wishing to go into Vitez itself, he had stopped and asked Splat if he knew a nearby store. Splat realized he was Muslim, and worked him over for no other reason. The old man's breath came out of his broken mouth like a baby's rattle. One of his eyes was in danger of falling out.

Splat had lost a son fighting Muslims a year earlier.

The hatred could be applied as much to the Croats' own as to Muslims. In Kiseljak four young Croats who had left at the beginning of the war were beaten almost to death with crowbars when they returned to their homes. Their crime? To have disagreed with the sectarian war policies of Herceg-Bosna. Then one night Viktorija made the mistake of having two Muslim friends from

Travnik come to dinner. It was a bold move, considering the atmosphere of the moment, but Viktorija's sense of liberalism had survived the war. She had seen her family in Zenica again, and flourished in the new peace, her skin and eyes lighting up with vitality. The Muslim couple came, stayed, and left unmolested. An hour after their departure someone threw a hand grenade at the foot of Viktorija's stairwell. It gave the walls a light patter of shrapnel scars and no-one was hurt. The message came through by proxy the next day: 'No more Muslims in Stara Bila.'

My own experience of the brutishness was of a more domestic nature, and came when a neighbour shot the puppy I had got as company. The dog had taken one of his chickens, and the man appeared with his Kalashnikov while I was elsewhere and blew the puppy away in Viktorija's drive. Lost in rage I traded a bottle of beer for a grenade, got hold of some wire, and planned booby-trapping dogkiller's outside latrine one night. It was a good plan: as soon as he opened the door the wire would pull the pin and he would be blown to hell before there was time to drop his trousers.

Unfortunately a Croat friend, no stranger himself to killing, talked me down, pointing out that someone else may use the bog before the dogkiller. 'You British are funny,' he said smiling. 'All the time I see English soldiers looking after stray dogs. There are many reasons to kill people in Bosnia. A reason is an easy thing to find. But not over dead dogs.'

So I stored my plan away, like a christening present that I was still too young for, hoping that fate would allow me another opportunity to inflict upon dogkiller casual and extreme malice.

Yet there were pegs of sanity for me that spring. A new British regiment, the Anglians, arrived in Vitez to take over from the Coldstreams. My relationship with the British army was relaxed, though a little one-sided. I had nothing to offer. They supplied me with fuel and detailed information. Their press office was still up and running, by this time operated by an Air Corps major and Light Division captain, men of exceptional intelligence and humour, the long-awaited products of the military's realization that it needed more than simply a mouth to deal with journalists. As by now I was often the only journalist in central Bosnia they indulged my company long after the daily briefings were over, and expanded the often empty details of the UN's situation reports with insight and background. If I saw less of the real war that spring then at least I understood more of the UN's situation, not that it gave me any cause for optimism. The great post-war Charter body could not decide if the troops it sent to Bosnia were part of a trucking company or a fighting force, and was prepared to go to almost any length to preserving inaction at the expense of lives.

In dealing with the British army I had the advantages of knowing how their command hierarchy worked and how soldiers thought. My loyalties, if really put to the test, would probably have lain more with these troops than with the media, with the obvious exception of personal friends. It is a tribal thing. Yet I had no identity crisis over the issue: I was definitely out of the army, and I felt my agenda to be relatively disengaged from both military and media camps. This position allowed me to be very cynical; from the outside it would have been easy to ridicule the rigidity of a system I had left. But if I saw Anglo-Saxon xeno-phobia, ignorance or stupidity, it was always at a level higher than the commanders I grew to know.

Except for action in the unreachable eastern enclave of Goražde and a series of wasteful localized assaults, the war with the Serbs all but stagnated throughout the spring and early summer of 1994. The Bosnians used the time to reorganize and rearm. They were still hobbled by the arms embargo, but the peace agreement with the Croats gave them access to weapon supplies smuggled in to the Dalmatian coast, albeit stocks for which they had to pay exorbitant sums to their former enemies. Their new sense of structure and purpose put them at odds with the interests of journalists, for the Bosnians' strongest card was their status as victims, and reports of a revitalized Muslim army was detrimental to it. In the previous year access to the front had at times been difficult, but the nature of life in Stara Bila meant that most of the details of the Muslim–Croat war were right under the feet of anyone living there. Now, however, reaching the action became more difficult and I had to rely on personal contacts to get anywhere near the fronts at all.

Yet I did not have long to wait for major drama, though the form it took was not what I expected. Returning to Vitez from a successful, if rare, trip along the Posavina lines in northern Bosnia, I found a letter waiting for me. It was from my mother and had reached the UN base where I collected it with happy curiosity. The letter warned me that my father, whom I had not seen for nearly two years, was terminally ill with cancer of the spine. It was thought that he had only two years to live.

For whatever reason, probably because he did not want my sympathy, he had not wanted me to know of his sickness. But other members of his family, thinking this judgment through, had passed the news on to my mother.

I was surprised, and for a while was unsure about how I felt. Because of the bad blood between us I was far from being over-whelmed by sadness. Yet I did feel sympathy, for his pain, his loss of mobility and for the shock he must have felt at suddenly having to face the sure tread of his coming death.

I also felt all the old anger, but this news forced me into a position of compromise.

In Bosnia, the letter in hand, I ran memories of our relationship through my mind again and again. Entwined with them were my thoughts on death and the war. I had come to Bosnia partially as an adventure. But after a while I got into the infinite death trip. I was not unhappy. Quite the opposite. I was delighted with most of what the war had offered me: chicks, kicks, cash and chaos; teenage punk dreams turned real and wreathed in gunsmoke. It was an environment to which I had adapted better than most, and I could really get off on it. I could leer and posture as much as anyone else, roll my shoulders and swagger through stories of megadeath, murder and mayhem; and I could get angry about the poignant tragedy of it all. But what did it amount to? Everything I had seen and experienced confirmed my views about the pointlessness of existence, the basic brutality of human life and the godlessness of the universe. But however oblivious to my own death I became, I saw no reason to allow my fellow man to suffer unnecessarily. Retaining a sense of compassion seemed the only inner victory I could possibly achieve against either the madness of the Bosnian conflict or my father. With this logic I thought that it would be kinder to my father to lay down our fight. The nature of his illness meant that he could no longer leave his home anyway. To stick to my promise never to return to his farm seemed small minded under the circumstances. Whatever had passed between us, he was unavoidably my father and I his son. I did not believe that he could shut that out completely and be in peace at the prospect of his death without seeing me again. So I wrote to him, suggesting that we forget our disagreements and that I visit him at his home.

As I thought he still had two years to live and would need some time to consider his reply, I did not rush back to England. But there was no reply. The days stretched into weeks and my cauterized sense of calm changed to puzzlement. Then word came through, again via a chain of proxy messengers, that he required my 'contrition'. I was stunned. What kind of pedantry was this? I was sorry for nothing. To say I was would have been to lie. I was not afraid to lie when necessary, but lying to one's own father on his death bed seemed ridiculous. More than that, though I was prepared to see him, I believed we both had to take responsibility for our actions. My begging forgiveness would allow him to hide behind the denial that had flawed our whole relationship. I could not do it.

Some eight weeks after learning of his illness I drove down to Split en route for England after a three-month stint in Bosnia. I called my paper from a hotel to see if there were any developments in the war elsewhere that might prevent me taking a break. There was mumbled whispering between two people on the other end of the line.

'Er, Anthony,' the man's voice said, 'your aunt rang us three days ago to say that your father has been given the last rites. You should return home as soon as possible.'

The 'last rites' perplexed me. It is a Catholic ritual. Though this was his wife's faith, my father was an Anglican and a lax one at that. If my father was still alive by the time I reached England, I resolved to drive to his farm and see him despite having offered no penitence. This was a matter between him and me. Anything and anybody else were peripheral. I was not sure, and am even less so today, whether the request for 'contrition' was his or his wife's.

I was picked up from Heathrow by my mother, who told me the news as we drove to her house. My father was still alive, but only just. He had converted to the Catholic faith a few days earlier. It got more bizarre. There were two letters waiting for me, one of which was from my father. He had dictated it earlier in the week, and then had it faxed to members of his family. I am not sure why – I can only presume he wanted to make his feelings towards me public and irrevocable. Its contents passed on like the plague. Upon reading it his mother rang to advise me to burn the letter without opening it.

I did not burn his letter but left it unread along with the second, which came from his wife, as I wanted my mind to be clear of unnecessary anger in handling whatever lay ahead. Instead I rang up my father's house. His wife's son answered the phone. He opened the conversation by calling me a coward, accusing me of delaying my return home until my father was too sick to deal with me. It was an aggravating overture, particularly as the situation seemed to have been stage-managed to ensure my absence from proceedings. I did my best to disguise my dislike of my step-brother and told him that I was coming round to see my father. He replied that my father had no wish to see me and asked if I had read his letter, recommending that I did so, and that the best thing I could do was to stay away and send a fax asking for forgiveness. What era did these people exist in? Even allowing for grief and fatigue, their vocabulary sounded like that of eighteenth-century puritans.

I rang my father's doctor, a man I had never met. He was diplomatic and sympathetic. Almost apologetically he told me that he had had no idea that his patient had a son until the previous day. With embarrassment he said that it was 'unclear' whether or not my father had changed his mind about seeing me but that the prevailing opinion of his wife was that I should stay away.

The Catholic priest whom I next called, the man who had undertaken my father's 'conversion', did not know I existed at all. I hope he did not feel too smug about his newly claimed soul. If the convert could not even admit to having a son, his first confession must have been a little short on honesty.

Even at that point, with an additional call by a half-uncle telling me to keep away, I was prepared to go to the farm regardless. I did not care for anyone's advice. It was not their business. However, I could not avoid it: first I had to read the letter.

I opened the envelope slowly. I knew the contents would be unpleasant and approached the words with the reluctant deliberation of a patient entering hospital for an operation, a kind of joyless necessity.

All things considered it could have been worse. The letter involved all the tenets of damnation, dispossession and disinheritance that I might have expected, but couched in fairly erudite terms. It finished by resurrecting the curse that I had used so long before – my father said he would see me where the flames were crackling. So I guess he was not banking on salvation in spite of his eleventh-hour conversion. I read it once more, then threw it in the fire. His wife's letter followed it half a minute later. I had scanned its scrawl only once. What it lacked in style it made up for in invective.

There was nothing I could do. To drive to his house was now pointless. He did not wish to see me. It was irrefutable. The battles that I had had with him were all in vain. Even in the last moments of his life, a time which I would have thought would have opened the gates to magnanimity in his mind, he was trapped behind the walls of his own creation.

In the morning I rang first the doctor and then my stepbrother one last time. My father was still alive, though he could no longer speak. The doctor said that he had reacted strongly to the news of my return to England. My stepbrother told me that he reiterated his wish not to see me. I did send a fax to his farm. In a way I hated myself for doing it. Faxing my dying father seemed ridiculous, incongruous. I did not ask for forgiveness, however, but merely said that the past was forgotten, that he was my father and should go in peace. So I ended up lying after all.

I ran through the country lanes around my mother's cottage. The chill crisp of the dry morning air stroked soothingly over the exposed skin of my face and hands. I felt calm, near to a release even. I had done everything I could. I felt my position was honourable. I had been prepared to compromise; he had not. I like the solitude of running. You are on your own in more ways than one, and your thoughts stream through your brain un-cluttered by the distractions of stillness. When I returned to the cottage my mother walked outside.

'They have just rung,' she said. 'He's dead.'

The anger came creeping back like the leak from a dripping water tank, the fall of each individual drop passing almost unnoticed until I realized I was soaked with the emotion. He had failed, but found a petty pyrrhic victory in his efforts to damage me. It was a form of injury. I could not ignore it. It felt like I had been shot under a flag of truce while going in to collect the enemy wounded. The ultimate betrayal. I had been lured along the way by requests for contrition, duped, then blown away from the edge of the grave by his letter and the resurrected curse. In some ways that bit of the whole debacle almost amused me. If he had not done the right thing and allowed peace between us at least he had died malicious and spitting.

For a while I rejected the idea of going to his funeral. Though I claimed it meant nothing to me, I became like a poisonous sea anemone, tendrils of rage ready to sting anyone who brushed past. I even eyed my mother and sister with hostility. I felt that they had let me fight their battles alone and way down the river, leaving me to shamble back unaided from the whole bloody climax. Ironically it was they, the real victims of his smears and inadequacies, who persuaded me to attend. Women have more clarity than men in many issues.

'You were prepared to see him when he was alive,' my mother said to me quietly. 'Whatever happened as he died you should go to the service to show that you were prepared to let it all go between you.' I thought about her words for a long time.

It was my friend Lela's birthday the night before the funeral and, having had a celebratory dinner in a club with Stella, Leon and the crew, we returned to West London and sat up throughout the night getting pinned and talking. Appropriately wasted and composed, I departed early the next morning for Oxfordshire. So I did return to my father's farm, the scene of the wake, and I did see his wife again. The whole occasion passed by in a painless grey blur. It was not, however, the last time I spoke to her.

Two weeks later, a couple of days before I returned to Bosnia, she rang me up, making overtures of peace and saying that she wished to see me. I told her that I wished our lives to continue separately and without future contact. Her voice curdled like sour milk as she replied.

'Right,' she said. 'I hope that what I'm about to tell you will not be too much of a surprise—'

'Go ahead,' I interrupted, 'it's never stopped you before.'

'You are not your mother's eldest child,' she said. 'You have another older sibling, quite big now, so don't be too shocked if they come knocking on the door . . .'

I hung up the phone. I felt deeply sorry for my mother. I had to ask her what the woman had meant, but did so with regret, knowing it would open an old wound. She was surprisingly calm, and told me that as a teenager she had had a child, a baby girl, and been forced by the circumstances of the time to have her adopted. I had no problem with this latest skeleton, and felt only a renewed respect for the woman who had encouraged me to go to the funeral of a man whose moral frailty had damaged her so.

But I was a little rattled by the news, taken aback as much by how strongly I felt affected as by the loss of my assumed position as my mother's first born. You never realize these things until they happen to you.

Sometimes, in the days that first followed the funeral, I could be very open-minded about my father: he was not a bad man, merely weak, and had become confused and lost sight of his values. Most of the time, though, I hated him. He was a selfish and damaging bastard. If I ever saw him again I would not even want to waste time speaking to him. Respect for the dead comes second to respect for the living, and I believe no man's demise exempts him from culpability.

With some trepidation I had wondered whether his death would end the anger inside me, so much of which was responsible for motivating me in war. But I had nothing to fear there. The embers of resentment glowed with a new intensity. And I hadn't lost my frustration at my failure to breach his walls. The sentiment merely hardened and turned upon others. I went back to war wanting to suck deeply on the pain out there and blow it back in the faces of people like my father: the complacent, the smug, the sardonic. I was the damned and disowned son. It was a worthy mantle for the messenger.

13

Western Bosnia, Summer 1994

So I went from the set of one internecine fight to another. The line between peace and conflict was so fuzzed in my mind after my father's death that I passed through it almost without noticing, sliding back through the filters of aircraft and road into Bosnia, to brother murder and sister cruel; finding solace in the knowledge that at least I had a war to go home to.

It was ironic, though perhaps no coincidence, that I travelled to Bihać. The isolated government-held enclave in western Bosnia had one of the strangest records of any region in the fractured state. To the west it faced Croatian Serbs, to the east Bosnian Serbs. Separated from allied areas in every direction by swathes of enemy-held territory, its problems had been compounded in autumn 1993 when a pudgy, grey-haired Muslim politician and businessman, Fikret Abdić, led a breakaway movement to establish an autonomous statelet of his own. Munitioned and equipped by the Serbs, he set up a self-styled 'capital' in Velika Kladuša in the north of the enclave, splitting the power of the beleaguered government 5th Corps based in Bihać to the south. For many months the bitterest fighting in western Bosnia was not between Serb and Muslim forces, but between the autonomist Muslims and their kin who remained loyal to Sarajevo.

It was almost impossible to understand his followers' perception of loyalty. Known as 'Babo' – 'Father' – to his supporters, Abdić's political aims were flagrant treason to the Sarajevo government and Muslim people. One-time head of Agrocomerc, Bosnia's biggest agricultural company, Abdić had once come close to being President of Bosnia, though his record was marred by corruption and embezzlement charges. Abdić's intelligence and business acumen had brought considerable wealth to the people of Velika Kladuša and its environs, and his support rested on this as much as on his shifty charisma and oratorial eloquence. Among simple, rural folk who had never had much contact with distant Sarajevo and the concept of central government, he was something of a god.

Yet, from the beginning of the conflict, Serb purges in other areas had ensured that the enclave was crammed with refugees, who brought with them illuminating tales of terror and mass-murder. Whatever their prewar aspirations, it should have been apparent to even the simplest Muslim peasant, let alone the more educated townspeople, that the survival of not only the Bosnian state but also their people was under threat. To give your loyalty to a devolved opportunist at the expense of that struggle was an act of the utmost stupidity and a betrayal.

It was symbolic of the localized cult traditions and parochial mind-sets in Bosnia that so many joined Abdić. Talking to his autonomist followers was much the same as speaking with cult converts anywhere in the world: a wooden, dead-end dialogue hallmarked by the absence of individual rationale and logic. Puppets of the Serbs, whose officers ended up commanding these autonomist forces, their shortsighted attitude was enough to make even an outsider froth at the mouth. They were of immense propaganda value to their new controllers in the fight to smear the Sarajevo government's legitimacy.

However, arrayed against the autonomists were the forces of a figure who was himself little less than a living legend. General Atif Dudaković was a former artillery colonel in the JNA. He had seen action in the Croatian war on behalf of the Serbs, becoming a commander in the Bosnian government army as soon as the JNA turned on the Muslims in 1992, taking over command of the 5th Corps in mid-1993. A dogmatic man with matching stocky, pugnacious build, 'Dudak' was to become the most famed government commander of the war, his concepts of strategy far in advance of those of his peers. Although totally surrounded until the final months of the conflict, he continually led his troops in ambitious operations against the Serbs, and the enclave held out against tremendous odds.

Often the 5th Corps' isolation proved more of an asset than a hindrance, for the Sarajevo high command was notoriously inept, stifling the initiative of field commanders with a web of bureaucracy and incompetence which bore all the trademarks of Yugoslavia's communist legacy. But Dudak's amputated status allowed him the freedom to command as he wished, and he did so employing a speed and flexibility that repeatedly wrong-footed his enemies.

In many ways his troops were Bosnia's last romantics. Separated from the rest of Bosnian government and HVO-held territory by Serb lines, Bihać had been untouched by the social ramifications of the Muslim–Croat conflict. With a few

216

inevitable exceptions, its fighters seemed to preserve the totem of multi-ethnicity among their ideals. By contrast, in central Bosnia, as well as Hercegovina, much of the Muslims' tolerance had died in the war with the Croats. Although there remained a core of purity, by 1994 it was overshadowed by a twisted form of emergent Islamic sectarianism. This prejudice was akin to the nationalism which had earlier poisoned the mentalities of Serb and Croat fighters, although it had not yet acquired the same intensity.

The 5th Corps troops were divided into local brigades according to their municipality, with the best coming from Bihać itself. The 501 and 502 Brigades were composed of towerblock townies, bright boys with smart commanders who, once removed from the grey confines of their dull apartments, seemed to fight with more flair and panache than their rural comrades.

The 502 Tigrovi, Tigers, took their name after inheriting a special forces commander as their new leader. Hamdu Abdić, no relation to the mutinous businessman, was a wily alleycat whose savvy initiative and cowboy instinct were a world away from the somnambulist mind-set of former Yugoslav army commanders who dominated the command of units elsewhere. He was a pre-war 'businessman', a piratical rogue with an easy grin, who had a strong bond with Dudak. The fermentation of their combined mentalities – the disciplined mind of the artillery officer and that of the urban maverick – produced a depth and intuition unmatched by their foes.

Around the time of my father's death they had conceived a plan to defeat the separatists based in Velika Kladuša which showed more imagination and daring than any other offensive during the war. 'Operation Tiger' came into play when the 5th Corps were at a low ebb, besieged by both Serbs and the Abdić autonomists. In total secrecy, without even a coded warning to

Sarajevo, Dudak and Hamdu faked a coup within Bihać town. Playing the part of a disaffected commander, Hamdu negotiated with Abdić and the Serbs to overthrow Dudaković and usurp the 5th Corps command, then surrender it to the separatists. The Serbs and Abdić were naturally suspicious, but convinced enough to agree to give Hamdu a huge downpayment of cash, the thirty pieces of silver required for his treachery. Since their endgame depended on the success of Hamdu's coup, they also agreed to supply him with weapon and ammunition stocks.

Back in Bihać Hamdu briefed Dudaković on the developments. Piles of fuel-soaked tyres were placed in the streets, and the few foreign aid workers present in the town confined to their houses. On the given word the tyres were ignited, and 5th Corps troops fired bursts into the air all day long. Looking upon Bihać through binoculars from distant hills Serb officers saw a town echoing with gunfire and thick with black smoke from the combat. They reported that the coup had indeed begun. The foreign aid workers, trapped in their houses, radioed Zagreb to say that Bihać had become the centre of heavy fighting. The signals were intercepted by the Serbs, adding credence to the plot. Trusted local journalists filmed 5th Corps troops ripping the insignia from their sleeves. The videotapes were handed across the line to the Serbs that night. By the next morning footage of the mutiny was broadcast on Bosnian Serb television. Sarajevo, in its ignorance, was horrified.

Convinced the 5th Corps were all but finished, Fikret Abdić sent truckloads of weaponry to the mutineers, followed by a group of his senior officers to organize the surrender of Bihać. Dudak's moment had arrived. Abdić's officers were taken prisoner and the weapons and ammunition distributed among the 5th Corps. The Serbs were dumbfounded, and turned angrily upon Abdić, blaming him for the debacle. Severely demoralized,

Abdić's forces collapsed along various sections of the front, and were quickly pushed back to a narrow perimeter of land around Velika Kladuša. A short lull followed, as Abdić negotiated to hold on to his power base, using the UN as an arbiter.

More through luck than judgment, I arrived at this point. In Zagreb I had met two friends, Robbie and Bob. Robbie was a freelance cameraman with a useful contact in Knin, the Croatian Serb capital, who had somehow arranged permission for us to travel through the Serb lines to reach the enclave.

After several hours' drive through various sets of lines, each of us nursing the private fear that one or other group of soldiers would halt us and turn us back, we reached Bihać. It was a pretty town, the old quarter forming an attractive stone kernel that offset the more modern communist architecture of the outlying apartment blocks. Bihać straddled the fish-filled deeps of the Una River; the high ground to the east was softer in its topography than the mountain ranges of central Bosnia, and the atmosphere was lighter, a far cry from the brooding turbulence of Vitez.

For all that they had suffered, the Bosnians there were friendly and open towards foreigners. So often in central Bosnia, and later Sarajevo too, you found yourself labelled a representative of an outside world accused by Bosnians of having abandoned them to their fate. It was always an impossible position to defend, for the Bosnians' accusations were justified even if their anger towards you as an individual was misdirected. Yet in Bihać there was no such angst, and a lot more humour. Strangers were relatively uncommon; journalists a rarity.

'Listen to me,' a 501 fighter said to me soon after our arrival, 'a few weeks ago I heard on the radio all the celebrations in Britain, France and America for the anniversary of D-day, the day you invaded France to rid Europe of fascism. You are a journalist so you know all these things, now tell me: should I hold my breath until your armies come to rid us of fascism once again, or try to do it myself?' He was laughing and his eyes danced mischievously beneath the heavy pelmet of his eyebrows. Yet there was an underlying sincerity to his words.

'Don't hold your breath whatever you do.' I grinned back and shrugged emptily.

Bob, Robbie and I found a guesthouse in the town run by a fat profiteer and his gargantuan wife. It had about fifteen rooms, most of which had been taken over by a Red Cross delegation whose money ensured its survival in these otherwise guestless times; there was electricity for at least six hours a day and running water more often than not. Even the loos worked on occasion. By war standards it was the Ritz.

The three of us needed Dudak's permission to travel with his front-line troops but the general, involved in fruitless negotiation with Abdić and the UN, was hard to track down. For the best part of ten days we idled in the summer heat. Patience is an asset in any war, and I cannot say that mine was stretched in Bihać. There was a saying in Bosnia: 'Do not chase the war; wait, and it shall come to you.' It was here that my deal with the English newspaper gave me an advantage, for my boss in London did not mind if he did not hear from me for days at a time. Though I did not know for sure if Dudak would press his advantage and take Velika Kladuša, it seemed likely; and privately I wished Abdić's negotiations to fail. There were no other journalists in the enclave, and I was happy to wait.

We fished, slept, ate a lot of trout, drank a lot of beer and smoked a lot. We enjoyed half a party with the attractive Red Cross girls before a Bosnian soldier walked in and stole the sound system at gunpoint, and we dined magnificently with a company of French UN troops in Čorolići, north of Bihać. They had five headstones in the garden of their base – a neat row facing France – for the soldiers killed while on UN duty in the enclave. These deaths were but a fraction of the total UN casualties, a toll whose majority the French shouldered with considerable dignity.

Eventually losing patience with the general's continued evasiveness, we raced after his jeep as it returned from a negotiation. The general, who knew Robbie from a previous encounter, seemed amused to see us and made an almost careless appointment to meet us on the front the next day.

We rendezvoused at Johovići. The negotiations had failed. Dudak's men had just captured the village and there was some artillery coming in on a nearby slope. The general cracked open a couple of cases of beer regardless and sat at a table with his commanders, poring over maps and discussing the move forward to Velika Kladuša. At first I was slightly shaken by their laissez-faire attitude to the shelling. Who could be sure that the gun crews would not switch the direction of their fire and begin the logical barrage on the village? As a stranger to a new front it was often easy to worry unnecessarily about the risk. Front lines have their own rhythm and character, much like the tide of the sea in a particular bay. There are, of course, freak waves and squalls, but people of the sea understand its mood just as soldiers become familiar with a particular enemy on a stretch of confrontation line. I had seen it in Vitez and Sarajevo, areas where I had spent enough time unconsciously to pick up the rhythm of the violence. So I took my lead from Dudak and his men and unwound.

The general was in ebullient form, pointing excitedly at the map and issuing curt directives to his officers, his short arms stabbing forward from the shell-like confines of his large French flak jacket. Hamdu lounged beside him like a rangy secretary bird, beer in hand, grunting an affirmation occasionally, sometimes adding a suggestion of his own, shooting disarming smiles at everyone. It was a far cry from the silent deference with which officers in central Bosnia took their orders. The respect for Dudak was not in question, but there was a far greater opportunity for discussion than I had seen elsewhere.

From a ridgeline running to one side of the village, a team of 5th Corps artillery troops fired Chinese rockets at the autonomists in the valley below, while another group prepared a Russian ZIS artillery piece for action. It was made in 1942 and must have seen use in Yugoslavia against the Germans. Properly maintained, it was as accurate and lethal as the new arms. Second World War weaponry was much in evidence in the fighting throughout Bosnia, in spite of the ubiquitous Kalashnikov culture. Mausers, Lugers and Schmeisers were abundant. Once I had even seen Bosnians go into action on the Posavina in a decrepit T-34 tank, another machine of Second World War vintage. Hampered by the arms embargo, they utilized everything they could in the struggle against the Serbs.

Dudak told us that his men would soon take Fikret Abdić's stronghold. The three of us argued about what to do next. We did not know whether the general's words were a bluff or not, and whether it was better to stay with his men or try to slip through the lines and reach Velika Kladuša in anticipation of the 5th Corps attack. We chose to make for the town early the next morning, driving unchallenged through a quiet sector, taking an almost empty road into Abdić's self-styled capital. It was a propitious moment.

The sun beat an unforgiving heat on the town from a cloudless blue sky, cooking the fear of the inhabitants into panicking flight. Velika Kladuša was in chaos. Thousands of civilians choked the road leading west out of the town into Croatian Serb lines. Prevented from leaving by the Serbs at that point, they crowded the softening tarmac in a jammed mêlée of horse-drawn carts, coaches, tractors and cars, each laden in turn with whatever items of luggage they elected to carry with them, sweating and miserable in the heat: tears and fear in the glare of the summer's end. There were a few groups of Abdić's soldiers among them, but most still held the faltering lines to the east, though their time too was limited. Most of the civilians had fled because of Abdić's inflammatory rhetoric about impending doom at the hands of 'Islamic fundamentalists'. Few had any idea of where to go or what to do beyond the hazy notion of escape.

'I don't want my family to live under an Islamic tyranny,' one old man said. 'I don't mind where I go. Anywhere but here.'

Often what was left behind was as poignant as what they chose to take. While dogs and chickens meandered through the scrum of vehicles, a handicapped girl sprawled in a wheelbarrow outside the Red Cross office, lolling frightened and confused like an abandoned rag doll.

Abdić himself still occupied his renovated mediaeval castle headquarters overlooking Velika Kladuša. Protected by his praetorian guard of fighters, among them 'Popeye's Group' – a band of indigenous mercenaries identifiable by their shoulder flash of the pipe-smoking sailor – he was involved in last-ditch negotiations with the UN to try to prevent the 5th Corps from over-running his forces and taking his town. The propaganda that Abdić was pumping out to his people was an exercise in self-promotion: he realized that he was about to lose his capital, and that his only hope of clasping on to a continued power base of sorts was to terrify as many of his followers as possible into fleeing with him, giving him strength through numbers. Some were even forced out of their homes by his men at gunpoint. A week earlier he had had his men hang a captured 5th Corps officer from a construction crane in the centre of the town, where the man had kicked and squiggled high in the air before finally choking. It was another of Bosnia's 'guilt by association' ploys used to rally populations by fear of vengeance rather than idealism. In all, more than 25,000 autonomists were to leave Velika Kladuša ahead of the 5th Corps' push, the majority ending up living in one of Abdić's abandoned Agrocomerc chicken farms near Serb-held Slunj.

We tried to check into the town's one hotel but found the manager and his staff packing their bags and all but ready to leave.

'No, you can't stay here,' he said hurriedly, 'the 5th Corps are only a couple of miles away and if you have any sense you will leave too.'

We travelled up on to the hills outside Velika Kladuša with a group of autonomist troops to see the state of the front. We found deeply fatigued soldiers collapsed in the sun after days of retreat, some suffering the obvious effects of heat exhaustion. One man looked close to death, sprawled by the edge of a track, grey-skinned, eyes rolling and barely conscious, his breath heaving itself in and out of his body in unnatural spasms. He was ignored by the others, who were too tired or too disinterested to help. Isolated farmhouses were going up in flames in the undulating fields, marking the forward edge of Dudak's advance, and at one point there was a lively firefight right beside us, the incoming rounds sending us diving to the earth with familiar abandon. It would have been ironic to be shot by the same troops with whom we had drunk beer the day before. The war inflicted many cruel jokes upon people, and, aware of its twisted hand-outs of fate, I always nurtured the fear that I would get killed by fire from the side with whom I sympathized, the government forces.

The disintegration of the autonomists' fortunes allowed the looters to go to work even at that stage. In the town trucks and lorries manned by fighters loaded up with stolen goods from private businesses and homes, while in other areas the lawless opportunism showed a more brutal cast to its nature. As we walked back from the edge of the front a woman began to scream in a hamlet below us. It was not a scream of rage or grief. It was the rhythmic gasping ululation of pain and fear and desperation that had the hair on our necks rising. We walked on in silence, shooting each other shamed glances through the trees.

There was a tiny five-strong UNHCR team in Velika Kladuša that occupied a house on a slope overlooking the town. Run by Monique, an elegant French lady of considerable style, it was our last resort as a place to stay and we asked for accommodation fully expecting to be refused with a flutter of quotes concerning UN regulations and journalists. To our surprise we were accepted as friends, and offered floor space to sleep on. In the clean, well-ordered confines of the house I was embarrassed to realize how badly we smelled, our sweat-sodden flak jackets and salt-stained clothes emanating a rancid odour which our hosts gracefully ignored.

We ate well that night, the atmosphere around the table charged with the excitement you always find when normality has unravelled and the arrival of war promises the potential of new adventure. It is a heartless and ignorant sensation, for it is not your home and livelihood at stake, but an undeniable buzz nevertheless. There was always the chance of getting killed in the fighting but the status of foreigner in the Bosnian war still offered an immense sense of security, particularly here, where we knew the 5th Corps would treat us well if the town fell to them. I would not have liked to be a journalist found in a zone captured by the Serbs, who regarded the media as agents of their downfall, but that had yet to happen to me, and the sluttish displays of empathy with which you had to charm first one side then the other were usually well within my capabilities.

Though all the signs pointed to the imminent fall of Velika Kladuša, we were still unsure of when it would happen. Sometimes the war moved sluggishly, sometimes at lightning speed, while often the predictable never happened at all. So when peals of machine-gunfire erupted around the house at dawn the next morning it brought us relief from the ache of uncertainty.

The UNHCR house, rather than affording us a ringside position from which to watch the fight, put us for a time at centre-stage.

We went through the inevitable flounder of bashed heads and stumbling as we lurched around the room clumsily waving boots and bullet-proofs in all directions, thick-headed with sleep and surprise, before clattering upstairs to the balcony.

The morning mist still curtained the hills but the ground around us was clear. Rolls of heavy machine-gunfire and the thump of mortars swept their sounds towards us from the south-east, while behind the house autonomist troops fired at infiltrating 5th Corps columns. A handful of women and children ran across the fields towards the centre of town in the dawn light. They were quickly followed by autonomist soldiers, frightened and on the run, abandoning their weapons and tearing off their camouflage smocks as they fled before us. Through the mist came a single booming chorus of 'Allahu Akbar' – God is Greater. The 5th Corps were coming in.

Fighters holding out in a police station made a desperate attempt to halt their advance in the suburb immediately in front of us. As the gunfire around the building increased, two vehicles, a lorry and a car, tried to escape through its back gate. Both were raked with automatic fire as they sped away, red tracers lancing viciously into their unarmoured skins. The lorry careered off the road into a lamp-post, its driver hanging dead out of the shattered windscreen. Puff, another life gone right in front of my eyes. It seemed so inconsequential to me, but somewhere did his mother or lover feel a stab in her stomach, or did they remain wholly unaware that he was gone? The car, though hit repeatedly, fared better, slewing away in a barely controlled squeal of burning rubber. Mortars hit the police station and the sound of the gunfire changed, echoing from the interior as 5th Corps troops poured through the doors and windows to take the fight inside.

Then somehow it all went sour. In a lane to our right another car was riddled with gunfire by the advancing troops. This one was filled with women and children. By the time we reached them the 5th Corps troops had done a good job of bandaging them up but were unable to move them for help due to the continued street fighting. A three-year-old girl, Dina, had been hit in the head and chest. I had heard stories of men taking bullets in the head and living but had never witnessed it. Yet here was a tiny mite of a child who had taken a round smack in the forehead and was still somehow alive. And conscious. The bullet must have lost its impetus or else it would have taken the top of her head off; nevertheless it had passed intact into her skull. Her mother had been shot through the hand and received a lucky graze to her temple. Two other small children had received similar gunshot wounds to their chests and legs.

It was like a cold-water shock that gave us a sudden focus, an aim to do something more than just watch the fighting. Our mental equations were simple: at least two of the children were going to die very soon unless they were taken immediately for treatment. There was a large French UN base outside the town, with good military medical facilities. There was a jeep at the UNHCR house, and Monique was in radio contact with the soldiers at the base. The skeleton for a plan formed in seconds. There was one major flaw in the whole thing, but it took me another few minutes to see it.

I cannot understand the few journalists I have met who insist that, if confronted by casualties, their job is merely to film, photograph, or report without giving aid. Most of those wounded before me in Bosnia had been helped by other Bosnians at once, people who were better aware of the location of the nearest medical post or hospital than I, and more adept through their continued experience of war at dealing first hand with traumatic injuries. Usually there was no need for me to get involved, it would only hinder matters. Yet here was a case where the input of foreigners could be of use. Who were we to stand back and do nothing, justifying inaction by claiming with misplaced arrogance that our job was only to report? What good did reporting ever do in Bosnia anyway? By that stage of the war it was obvious that, despite our initial optimistic presumptions to the contrary, West European powers were prepared to tolerate the mass slaughter and purging of Muslims regardless of the reporting.

It was not sentimentalism that made us ditch our cameras and run back up the track to the UNHCR house carrying the bleeding bodies. It was humanist logic. To do anything else would have been indefensible. Journalist ethics versus human life: I knew where I stood on the issue, though the question came back to haunt me later under particularly ghastly circumstances.

We loaded the wounded on to the back of the jeep. As we did so an autonomist APC moved back up towards the police station, and a particularly fierce gunbattle brewed up, sending us all ducking in a ditch for long seconds. Christophe, one of the UNHCR staff, was behind the wheel of their vehicle and ready to go. Robbie and I jumped in the back and we set off, a limb-tangled sprawl of smeared blood and bandaged bodies, our faces greased with dust and sweat, swollen and bug-eyed like bad-acid victims.

I think it was only then, through the adrenalin wash, that I clicked the flaw in the whole idea. We were driving right towards the police station and the front line. Lines could give you the creeps even when they were quiet, but to cross one in an ongoing fight was madness. Yet it was our only hope to reach the distant French base.

Robbie seemed to realize the problems at the same time as me, and we burbled something to each other about which side to roll out with which wounded if we took fire. I do not know what Christophe was thinking. Maybe he knew the stakes already, or maybe, like us, he had not thought of much else than the need to get the children out. Again, it was not a question of courage. There was no weighing up of aim against risk. It was all a confused blunder and when I realized the real danger it came down, once more, to an absolution of responsibility, simple, rough-worded, fuck-it logic: Shit. Fuck. Here we fucking go. Hope we fucking make it.

I did expect us to get hit but felt fairly resigned to it in the chaos of those moments. And I did not want to be the one to say stop.

As we rounded the crucial bend a front-line gauntlet of fighters, mad-eyed with the hype of action, scuttled behind cover, menacing us with their levelled weapons. We had no choice but to pull in and had a selection of hardware pointed to our temples as they screamed at us. We raised our hands and, on seeing the wounded children, the fighters relaxed a little, though not as much as I would have expected. We had to argue our passage through their lines, sealing the deal with packets of cigarettes before tearing off, ecstatic with relief, to the French.

Minutes later UN sentries waved us through the gates into their base, and medical teams, warned by Monique on the radio, whisked the children into the surgery on stretchers. But our troubles were far from over. The French had no interpreter to

229

hand and asked me to translate for them. Normally I would not have minded, but this time the dialogue was between a wounded mother and a military doctor about her dying child.

'What does he think?' she asked me.

'What do you think?' I asked him.

'She could die at any minute. She is very badly wounded,' he said to me.

'It's very serious, but they are doing what they can,' I lied to her.

They asked me to take the mother, whose name was Irma, outside as they performed a provisional operation on Dina and the two other children, who though seriously wounded were not as bad. I spoke with her for nearly an hour until the doctor re-emerged. She was a young woman in her early twenties. Her husband had been in Germany at the start of the war and had never returned. She had been trying to escape in the car with her daughter, accompanied by two children of a friend, when they were fired upon.

The doctor told us that Dina's chances depended on her immediate evacuation by UN APC to a hospital in Bihać. He said that at present the 5th Corps were not allowing their vehicles to move at all, and that it would be some time before their permission for an evacuation was forthcoming. If it did happen, he added, the two mothers would not be allowed to travel in the APC as they were of combat age and might be fighters. I argued with him for a while. Dina's mother was covered in blood from her head wound, dead-eyed with sadness and shock. She was obviously not a fighter, and besides, should her child die I thought it better for them to be together than separated. The doctor, a major, apologized but said that these were UN regulations and he was unable to change them. I decided not to tell Irma the news. It was uncertain an APC would even get through to us before her daughter died and there was enough for her to worry about in the meantime anyway.

The three children, now on oxygen, were laid out in a row outside the surgery. Somehow, though it seemed to defy all reason, Dina swung in and out of consciousness. Her mother leant over her weeping and pleading.

'What is she saying?' a French colonel asked mindlessly.

'She is telling her daughter not to be afraid, telling her that her mother is here with her, to be brave and hold on. She is imploring her to live, and when she loses consciousness she is beseeching her to smile so that her mother knows she is still alive.' I said it fairly acidly, for the officer was the French CO there; despite UN regulations he could have allowed the women to travel with their wounded children if he had wanted. He was one of those officers who had risen to a position of authority without ever having the confidence to know when to abandon the book.

Three hours after we entered the base an APC did finally arrive. Dina was still alive, and was loaded inside with the other children. The French had patched up her mother's head and hand, but true to their word would not let her travel with her kid to distant Bihać. I told the situation straight, you cannot really soften news like that, and she reacted with remarkable reserve, weeping soundlessly on my shoulder.

I felt very moved. In interpreting you filter off so much of the intensity of the conversation yourself, you cannot help but feel affected. More than this though, I had been unwittingly exposed to the intimacy of the moments shared between a parent and her dying child. It was a deeply personal experience and, though the circumstances were very different, it was one that had been denied to me only a few weeks before. The connotations settled blackly on my mind and cast my mood into moribund depression.

The fighting ended as 5th Corps troops stormed into Abdić's castle. Predictably, 'Babo' had long since fled, surviving to fight another day. As soon as the APC had departed the French colonel slung us, together with Irma and the other unwounded mother, out of the camp. There was little more we could do to help the women, so we bade them an awkward farewell in the road and trudged despondently back into Velika Kladuša, leaving them to their destiny.

It seemed a hollow victory, and however justified the actions of the 5th Corps, the fight had been against their Muslim kin. The three of us drove out of the enclave the same day, passing the abandoned jam of machinery left by those of Abdić's supporters not quick enough to escape the fighting. A few lay dead in their vehicles, caught in the crossfire between Dudak's advancing troops and the retreating autonomists.

Another year was to pass before I discovered, by strange co-incidence, the fate of the dying child and her mother.

Some time later, one evening in a Zagreb bar, a Red Cross girl who had heard of the incident with the wounded children approached me and after a short while congratulated me for the 'courage' we had displayed in rescuing the casualties. The account she had heard told of three journalists who on finding the injured had made a calculated decision to risk all by driving through the active front line to save the children's lives.

She looked good, smelled good; I had just come out of the war and could have done with a fuck.

I thought back to Velika Kladuša, our confusion, the sweat and chaos of those planless, fearful moments, the way the events unfolded more through their own volition than any of our input. For a moment I was tempted to play the clichéd role that was expected of me, at least if I wanted to get screwed – shrug nonchalantly and fulfil her expectations by making some modest quip and asking her about herself.

Somehow, though, that night I just could not be bothered. 'Courage', it is seldom what it seems. The word pisses me off so much that most of the time it is not even worth getting laid for. Besides, I was vaguely curious to see what might happen after her reaction to the real version of events. But she stopped me halfway through the story with a dissatisfied frown and dismissive wave of her hand.

'You really know how to spoil a story,' she said. 'Don't be so gauche and cynical.' She flounced away, her illusions apparently broken, leaving me to smirk and snarl with regret into my whisky.

14

Chechnya, New Year 1995

I was trying to sleep, swinging in and out of half-consciousness, too tired to open my eyes but too tense to let go, my mind cartwheeling through the unsettled twilight between the two zones, numbed by the vodka which, although it enervated my mouth and the ends of my fingers, was not strong enough to override the horror of the previous weeks. Eventually I must have drifted off somehow, though I cannot remember how I awoke.

The dead child arrived in my room without warning, standing listlessly at the end of my bed, the suddenness and severity of his presence chopping me out of sleep with a single blow. A second before I had been alone; now this. He was silent and as I started upright he stared into my eyes with an unwavering gaze that seemed like accusation. Two small severed heads lay on the blood-covered table behind him, their hair black and matted, white eyes rolled upwards.

We looked at each other in that way for an age. There was enough time for me to remember a night many years before. I was about four years old at the time, and was woken in the darkness by the sound of children singing outside my bedroom window. Their words were indistinct but combined to produce a soft chorus that carried to my ears, disembodied and ethereal, and pinned me immobile in the sheets with fear. It was late, even my parents were asleep, and the house, old and isolated at the edge of woodland, was full of the soft sighs of night that, like the cry of bats, you hear as a child but seldom as an adult. It was one of my first memories, a portent that had survived the passage of time, carrying a particular significance to this moment.

I had seen the dead child – or what was left of him – only a few days before. He was a Chechen. A Russian jet had bombed his mountain village home in a botched attempt to destroy a nearby bridge. Five hundred-pound bombs had transformed him, his two sisters and mother into butcher-rack-sized lumps of flesh. The severed heads of the two girls, curiously untouched by the blast, had stared blankly from a ghastly pile of severed limbs. Two other sisters had survived, blood-masked and mangled, tiny children with enormous wounds. Now he had returned to me, his body whole again, strangely illuminated against the dark of the night.

The moment disappeared. I cannot recall how he left. Suddenly I was alone in the room again, fighting to rationalize the visitation, telling myself it was just another bad dream. The window was rattling to shellfire, and signal flares were lighting the night sky outside. The fighting was getting very close. I lit a cigarette and got out of bed, determined to stay awake until the dawn.

The war in Chechnya – it was like nothing I had ever seen before. In terms of the scale of violence, fear and horror, it left anything in my experience so far behind as to make it almost insignificant. You can grade conflicts according to intensity if you desire: low, medium and high. Chechnya blew the bell off the end of the gauge, and revealed an extreme of war to me that I had no conception of. Afterwards my understanding of conflict was never quite the same again.

It was indeed a glimpse from the edge of hell.

I was lying in my bath in England, listening to the radio. It had been three weeks since the Russian forces entered the tiny separatist state of Chechnya, 1,000 miles south-east of Moscow, ostensibly to prevent it ceding from the Russian Federation. I vaguely remembered seeing photographs from the previous summer of wild-looking Chechen fighters, smiling at the camera and cradling Kalashnikovs, together with newspaper reports of 'provocation' and 'rising tension' in the region. Now the radio was telling me that these same fighters had smashed the Russian armoured columns that pushed towards the Presidential Palace of former air force general Dzhokar Dudayev in the Chechen capital, Grozny.

The end of 1994 had passed quietly for me in Bosnia. In early November a localized armija offensive near the town of Kupres had caught the Serbs by surprise and, pushing their advantage, the BiH had taken the town and handed it over to the Croats as a symbolic gesture of support for the new federal alliance. It was a turning point in the fortunes of the government army, for although still hobbled by the arms embargo, and with many more debacles before them, it was the first time that they had ever succeeded in recapturing from the Serbs and holding a town of any significance. From a hilltop above Kupres I had watched their subsequent push along a plateau. It had been an amputated way to watch a battle, removed and safe while below you men fought and died.

The offensive had ground to a halt with the onset of winter, and the first snows brought with them a ceasefire throughout the state which was to hold, more or less, until the arrival of spring the following year. It was a good time to leave Bosnia, and the new war in Chechnya appeared to me then like a potential new horizon. I had been a soldier at the end of the Cold War, and had heard so much about the Russian army. I wanted to see it in action. Returning to London I asked my newspaper if I could go to Grozny and they agreed.

I was soaking in the steam and hot water of the bath a day before my departure, hoping that the war would not have ended by the time I arrived. I still remember that moment of warmth, security and ignorance.

In one of the curious anomalies of war the road through the western side of the Chechen border remained open. Russian and Chechen forces faced each other across a few hundred metres of snow-covered plain, as they had done since the start of the conflict. Though there was occasional fighting, the route connecting the two sides remained viable. I passed through this strange mirror in mid-January. One minute there were Russian armoured personnel carriers and bunkers beside the car, the next there were Chechens: swarthy, bearded fighters touting rocket-propelled grenade launchers and automatic rifles.

As the road cut into Chechnya the landscape opened around me. The mud and soulless squalor of the first town gave way to flat, featureless terrain on either side of our decrepit Skoda. The occasional discordant line of slanting telegraph poles dissected this snowy waste, while ice covered the road beneath us in thick, irregular plates. Abu, the Chechen driver, pointed to fresh cratering and muttered something about planes, winding down his window so that he could hear the sound of any approaching jet. It was a precaution, I was soon to discover, that was of no use whatever. By the time you heard a jet, it was already too late to do anything about it.

Goyty was similar to any one of the score of Chechen villages we had driven through since crossing the border. Six miles south of Grozny, its high street was an expanse of mud, ice and slush between rows of nondescript one-floor brick houses. The light was fading as I arrived there, reducing everything to a single shade of grey. A ragged group of urchins hung around by the main intersection. As a car lurched past, slowing down for the potholes, two of them rushed out, grabbed its bumper, and were dragged off along the ice on their arses, shrieking with delight as their mates hooted and clapped while they waited for the next ride. I guess it was the Chechens' equivalent of subway surfing.

'Chechnya is not a place to die in,' a veteran correspondent had warned me in Moscow. I could see what he meant.

In Goyty there was a handful of journalists with transmitting equipment crammed into a small room in a house. The international press corps seemed to have all but deserted Grozny after the intensity of the initial fighting, but I knew that a group of photographers and a freelance cameraman remained, squatting in a two-storey building in the southern, Chechen-held half of the city. I wanted to find them and to do so needed the advice or aid of these people. However, the atmosphere was awkward: they were deeply fatigued, while shared danger had bonded them, making them tense and suspicious of outsiders. It was a situation that, one way or another, I had experienced many times in Bosnia, but nevertheless it was one I still hated, that of having to force yourself upon others as a stranger.

Then to my relief a familiar face appeared in the room, that of David, the American photographer whom I had met two years before in Bosnia when we had driven together into the fighting in Travnik. It was no real coincidence I suppose. The international loop of journalists who specialize in war is surprisingly small, so that the same individuals seem to be present in even the most far-flung conflicts. He knew where the photographers were staying in Grozny, and despite the onset of night offered me a ride there in a Volga driven by a Chechen.

There were widespread rumours that the Presidential Palace, so long the symbol of the Chechens' resistance in the capital, had fallen that day. David and I left together as the last trace of light dimmed from the sky.

The road was little more than a dark shadow beneath us as we began the journey, headlights turned off so as to avoid attack from the air. I did not really know what to expect of the fighting, so I was disturbed by what I saw in David. He was hyper-energized, even by his own standards, jumbling his sentences together, his words tumbling into one another in a stream of consciousness as we drew nearer to the growling thunder of artillery from the darkness beyond. 'You don't want to stay here any more than three weeks,' he told me, 'you gonna get jumpy as hell . . . it's bad . . . very fuckin' bad . . . nearly got tanked yesterday . . . gotta watch the planes . . . the artillery is something else . . . unreal . . .'

The sky ahead became a pulsing orange glow, while the sound of shellfire grew louder and louder. The trees that pressed on either side of us suddenly fell away as we entered Chernoreche, the southern outskirts of the city. Grozny was burning. The fires from the shelled buildings and ruptured gas pipes lifted the darkness from an infernal desolation of abandoned streets and houses, flickering shadows through the menacing emptiness.

Chechen fighters waved us down, telling us that the route ahead was sealed by Russian tank fire. Our driver, Sahid, was an ex-cop familiar with detours and back roads. He tapped the

Kalash across his knees and slipped into a confident U-turn to take an alternative route. There were shells falling everywhere, screaming in like freight trains, exploding in waves among the houses on either side of us or airbursting overhead, while volleys of Grad rockets streaked fire trails like comets across the sky. Severed tramlines hung across streets devoid of life but for the occasional stray dog or fighter – scuttling, Dantesque figures against the flame and smoke.

I had been in Grozny for five minutes. It was a bad moment to arrive. The Russians were launching their final attack on the Presidency and were unleashing their heaviest barrage to date on the capital.

The Volga skidded impotently at the base of an exposed hill, its bald tyres sliding uselessly on the packed ice. David and I scrambled out and began to push it, sweating and cursing in the cold, our feet skeltering away from under us like those of cartoon characters. It seemed the height of madness, getting out in that maelstrom of bursting shot and whistling steel to push a car further into the epicentre of it all. With a final OhfuckChristJesusmoveyoumotherfuckingbitch the tyres regained their grip and we leapt in and spun onwards.

From the top of the hill we could see the city centre below us. Para-illumination flares were suspended in the sky, bouncing their light into the billowing smoke and fire while the shell, machine-gun and small arms fire reached a new crescendo, the punch of the detonations shaking into us through the doors of the car. I had managed to effect my usual dullard's mentality under such extreme circumstances, my mind transcending any notion of responsibility, surrendering myself to circumstance and chance – the duo some call destiny, others the will of God. Their notions may afford more strength than mine, for I still could not escape the sensation of being scared nearly shitless.

We stopped abruptly in the lee of a large stone-walled house and unloaded my rucksack into an unlit hallway. Electricity and water supplies had long since ceased. The ground floor of the empty building had been requisitioned by the photographers as a sanctuary against the shelling. In one of the apartments candlelit faces turned to look at me, friendly and amused. I knew some of these faces from Bosnia. 'Hello, Anthony,' someone said calmly, 'would you like a whisky?' I loved that voice at that minute.

At dawn we emerged from our shelter having spent the night huddled in sleeping bags listening to the thunderous shelling outside, whispering and giggling in our uncertain security like children in a storm. The barrage had lifted just before first light, and other than the sound of tank and rifle fire towards the bank of the Sunzha River, which delineated the new front, silence hung over the city. Then a Russian voice, ghostly and detached, floated mournfully towards us: 'Lay down your weapons – you are surrounded. Lay down your weapons – your only hope is to surrender.' The repetitive thump of approaching rotorblades revealed the voice's source: a Russian helicopter cruised north of the river, speakers rigged to its sides. The Presidency had fallen during the night, and the gunship was flying on a psy-ops mission in an attempt to undermine the resolve of the Chechen fighters. It was wasting its time.

Resplendent in a tall fur hat and snow-smock, General Aslan Maskhadov, the Chechen commander, strode unperturbed down the devastation of Leninska Avenue at the head of twenty well-armed fighters. 'We decided to leave the Presidential Palace because it was becoming very difficult for me and my staff to work there,' he said matter-of-factly of the night's pulverizing bombardment. 'We now have an excellent defensive line. The Russians are little children if they think we will stop fighting.

They have no idea how to fight a war. This will carry on as long as they want it to, because we aren't going to stop.'

'*Allahu Akbar*,' Maskhadov finished, the posse of fighters joining in the chorus as they departed for the front line ahead, calling out to one another jovially. It was the sound of resolution that I never heard once waver in any conversation with the Chechens.

A former artillery colonel in the Soviet army, Maskhadov now led a force so small that it boasted only two other senior officers. Numbering a few thousand at most, his guerrilla army had been created at short notice, but its morale, unlike the Russians', was high and its street-fighting prowess had proved phenomenal. The original three regular battalions of Chechens had been badly savaged in the fierce fighting of the previous month, but volunteer units had flocked to take their place. Few of the fighters then in the capital seemed to have lived there before the war. Most were from villages in the countryside, rotating into Grozny in well-organized bands. Here they were supplied with small-arms ammunition, having first bought their own weaponry at one of the arms bazaars in the provincial towns.

They were not, it became quickly apparent, fighting for their leader, President Dzhokar Dudayev, nor for their Islamic faith, though their belief undoubtedly strengthened their courage and conviction in the struggle. They were fighting because they believed in their nation's integrity and independence. The previous month had concertinaed history in a way that only war can. In the Chechens' minds, figures and events from bygone eras were as fresh as if they had lived and occurred only last week; stories abounded of Shamil, the great warrior who led their nation against the Russians in the sixty-year war of the last century; of Baisangur, his one-armed, one-legged deputy who fought the Russians tied to his horse so as not to fall off: and especially of the great exodus of 1944, the year that Stalin deported the entire Chechen nation to exile in central Asia, where they were forced to remain for thirteen years for their alleged support of the Germans during the Second World War.

After the fall of the Presidency the respite in the Russian bombardment lasted for two days. It allowed both sides to collect their dead and breath. Under the guidance of my friends I was shown the rough disposition of the front, the detail so crucial to existing on a battlefield. Then that moment of stillness ended, seemingly swallowed in an instant, and the shelling intensified once more. There were no more lulls.

Having wasted so many men in their attempts to take the first part of the city, the Russians seemed determined to destroy the southern half of Grozny with massive concentrations of artillery fire before moving upon it. It was an act of mass murder. In Bosnia I had seen men guilty of attempting to take innocent life; in Chechnya I found the Russians as cold-bloodedly culpable in their complete disregard for innocent life. Basically they just blew the place to pieces.

No weapon frightens me as much as the shell. Bullets have a certain logic. Put a sizeable enough piece of concrete between yourself and the firer and you will be untouched. Run between cover, for it is difficult even for an experienced shot to hit a man who sprints fast. Even when people around you are hit the wounds seldom seem so bad, unless the bullet has tumbled in flight or hit them in the head. But shells? They can do things to the human body you never believed possible; turn it inside out like a steaming rose; bend it backwards and through itself; chop it up; shred it; pulp it: mutilations so base and vile they never stopped revolting me. And there is no real cover from shellfire. Shells can drop out of the sky to your feet, or smash their way through any piece of architecture to find you. Some of the ordnance the Russians were using was slicing through ten-storey buildings before exploding in the basement. Shells could arrive silently and unannounced, or whistle and howl their way in, a sound that somehow seems to tear at your nerves more than warn you of anything. It's only the detonation which always seems the same – a feeling as much as a sound, a hideous suck–roar–thump that in itself, should you be close enough, can collapse your palate and liquefy your brain.

There is a philosophical element to it all too: a bullet may or may not have your number on it, but I am sure shells are merely engraved with 'to whom it may concern'.

In Sarajevo there were times when we thought it was a bad day if a few hundred shells fell on the city. During the second half of the battle for Grozny the Russians sometimes fired over 30,000 shells a day into the southern sector. It was an area less than a third the size of Sarajevo.

And so Grozny had the life torn out of it by the second most powerful military machine on the planet and the lethal dynamics were breathtaking in every sense. A concrete killing zone, it was as if a hurricane of shrapnel had swept through every street, leaving each perspective bearing the torn, pitted scars, the irregular bites of high-explosive ordnance. The remaining trees were shredded and blasted horizontal, while the snow on the pavements became covered in a crunching carpet of shattered glass.

Artillery, tanks, mortars, rocket systems, jet aircraft, helicopter gunships – the permutations of incoming fire were endless. It left the dead plentiful: dead people blown out of their flats; dead pigeons blown out of their roosts; dead dogs blown off the street. Death became too frequent and too abundant to deal with, so that often the bodies were left where they had fallen to become landmarks in their own right: 'Turn left past the dead guy with the yellow shopping bag and his wife, then right to Minutka . . .'

Journeys of the shortest duration became a sort of ambulatory Russian roulette. Spin the chamber: beneath another grey sky I passed a dying Chechen soldier, croaking pitifully from his broken head, assumed he was the victim of a shell splinter, ran across railway tracks, suddenly under fire from a sniper, and reached the other side to be told that it was this same sniper who had shot the Chechen; fifty metres further on, along the route I would have taken had I known about the sniper, a shell turns five other fighters to red chaff. And always the emptiness, the blood in every street, the ravens pecking into the scarlet ice, the body scraps, the shells, and the fear, the terrible weight of fear.

Pathetic graves accumulated in the dismal parks and gardens as the thousands of Russian civilians who remained as troglodytes in the city, leading a subterranean existence in cellars, emerged to bury their dead whenever the opportunity arose. Bearing the brunt of the Russian army's fire, they were the wretched victims of the war, dying for what Moscow deemed 'salvation'.

'We are Russians,' a woman told me as her friend was lowered into a shallow scrape in the hard ground on a day unremarkable for its violence and misery. She had a gentle sing-song voice and clutched a small dog wrapped in a woollen coat to her breast. 'We don't have anywhere to go. It makes no difference to us whose flag flies above the Presidency. All we get from our own people is bombs, bombs, bombs. It is so cold. There is no water. There is disease. We are dying.' By the time Grozny fell a month later, 25,000 would be dead in the city.

Dying in abundance, too, were Russian soldiers. The army so laden with artillery assets still sent its troops, many of them teenage conscripts, to be gunned down in bungled assaults through the alien streets, or incinerated in their flaming APCs.

Dazed Russian commanders had already spoken to their own media of hideous confusion, of troops ill-prepared and unready, of vicious and internecine firefights between disorientated Russian units lost in the capital, of surprise attack and ambush.

Russian prisoners were plentiful, dotted through the city and countryside in various improvised detention centres. Though largely well treated by the Chechens, they told bleakly familiar stories, each an indictment of the Russians' disorganization.

'I was just told that my BMP would be part of a column,' said Sergei Martinets, the twenty-year-old driver of an armoured personnel carrier captured in the first days fighting. 'We had no idea where we were going until we got to Grozny. Once we were in the city the Chechens opened fire on us from all directions. The infantry got out and were running beside my vehicle. Then I was hit by shrapnel and escaped into a house with six other soldiers. There was so much fire. We were terrified. At dawn the Chechens shouted at us to give up and said nothing would happen to us, so we surrendered.'

The children of a warrior nation, the Chechens' tactics were simple: most of their time was spent beneath the city streets in cellars and bunkers sitting out the furious artillery barrages, while watch was kept for Russian movement by observation posts high in the buildings above. Word of an enemy move was brought by a runner, at which point the fighters deployed to defensive positions to combat the advance. Yet their war was far from merely defensive, and their raids and ambushes still created havoc among the already confused Russian forces.

Slamming into key points – the railway station, the Sunzha River and the arterial Leninska Avenue that linked Minutka to Freedom Square – then careering wildly into unsuspecting suburbs, the fighting pinballed through the city. Outgunned and, eventually, outmanoeuvred, the Chechens were driven slowly and expensively from their capital, bouncing back against their opponents in garrulous flurries of gunfire as the Russians tried to reorganize, then melting away beneath the suffocating weight of retaliatory artillery.

It became increasingly impossible to work. The city inched rather than slid towards capture and after a while the shelling all but paralysed our movement. Even when we did endure the frightful risk of the streets it was a disproportionate expenditure of energy, for the fear and horror of it all eroded our resilience like a poison. Too often the six of us who remained found ourselves apparently alone above ground in the desolation of a post-apocalyptic urban carcass. Then, sheltering in the squat from the bombardment one day, as we seemed to do more and more of the time, we heard a young Russian woman calling us from the street outside. 'Our house is hit,' she said simply. 'There are many dead and wounded.' She led us the short distance to an awful carnage.

Derbentskaya Street, Grozny. We stumbled out into the white desolation and ran slap into a thickset woman muffled in a coat held together by a string belt. She was shrieking hysterically, unhinged with rage, shock and grief. In one hand she brandished an awkward-looking club. It took me a few seconds to realize it was the severed leg of a man. With her left hand she tugged frantically at a sledge. On it lay the chopped bloody bundle of a corpse. Through some sacking the remaining leg dragged a scarlet wake in the snow. For long seconds she screamed her sound into us, the leg flying back and forth, boot to thigh, as we stood, stunned. Then suddenly she turned away and raged off into the wilderness dragging the sledge with its dismembered body behind her. Dumb with shock we next walked into a scene every bit as dreadful. In a nearby street shellfire from a Russian battery had landed among a group of old people. As we approached we could see their corpses sprawled in a random shatter of torn flesh and body parts.

Everyone was dead. We thought. But as I passed the body of an old man, one leg missing, the other a tangled mash barely connected to his torso, a hand twitched and grasped my ankle. 'My God, oh my God my legs,' he started to cry. I freed my foot and began to take photographs of him, so shut down in those moments that a part of me even noticed that the spread of the other bodies was too wide to allow for a strong composition. Then I knelt down beside him to put tourniquets on his wounds, though the blast seemed to have cauterized them already. It seemed better to do anything rather than allow your mind to soak up the impact. So I carried on anyway until one of my friends stopped me.

'Ant, leave him, there's no point, there's no point,' he said.

Across the ravaged city streets the giant tread of artillery fire continued. It seemed to be moving back towards us. Beyond the thumping concussions there was no sound but the old man's cries. I stood up and started mouthing a stream of cold logic like an automaton. 'There are no people and no cars: no place to take this man.' I might as well have been reading his death sentence. 'No morphine, and not enough dressings.' The incoming got closer. Our fear was tangible, a thick mantle upon us, heavier by the second. The old man sensed what was about to happen and grasped again at my ankle. He was crying loudly by then, begging us not to leave him. One fresh barrage, and we ran. We were gibbering with self-loathing and guilt, but we ran anyway.

Back in shelter we sloshed whisky down our throats and argued frantically with each other about what we should have done, or could have done. I felt terrible for leaving the old man, and that we had used our helplessness as an excuse to run at the approach of the shellfire. If only it had been as simple as run or die. It wasn't. We ran because we freaked out. I felt I was a pornographer, a voyeur come to watch. A couple of the others, who had been involved with wars for longer than I had, appeared not to question our actions. One even said that the Russian girl had only come to fetch us in the first place as she wanted journalists to witness what had happened. That was bullshit. She had come because she thought that as foreigners we might have had some way to help her with the casualties: a car to get them out, drugs, anything. We had nothing. All we had done was to take our photographs and leave the only survivor to die. It was one of those situations that war sometimes throws into your life. Whatever you do, you come out of it feeling degraded.

Next morning the bodies were still there. Stiff and cold in the stained snow.

For days later, whether my eyes were open or closed, I could see that woman shaking the severed leg at me: it was as if this accusing image had been burned into my retinas. She still comes to me sometimes now.

The incident seemed to break our resolve to stay in the city. I think we were all pretty traumatized by that stage anyway, and it finally became unsustainable to remain in Grozny. Nothing moved, nothing changed, other than the relentless shelling. Seizing a rare opportunity to share a ride out in a vehicle spacious enough to take our seven-strong group and its belongings, we drove to Goyty, shocked, tired, bedraggled and vacuous. As we left we passed through the site of a recent barrage. The shells had left wide brown whorls in the snow, like the blooms of flowers. A wounded dog was eating a bit of flesh at the edge of the street and a Chechen kid emerged from somewhere with a sledge. He sat down on it and pushed himself along with his legs, alone in the desolation, eyes completely empty.

Within three days my friends all departed from Goyty bar one, Jon, a photographer whom I had met in Bosnia a long time before. The others either left Chechnya or went to work the Russian side while Jon and I based ourselves in a fairly affluent Chechen household in the village, which had somehow managed to stay untouched by the fighting. The house was run by a middle-aged man named Magamet. For all his apparent riches he was a delinquent thug who used to attract the attention of his wife by throwing clods of frozen earth at her. His relationship with Jon and I was at best strained and he made us pay our rent in advance each day because, he told us bluntly, we would soon be killed. We saw him as a mannerless profiteer while he, a devout Muslim, objected to the way we drank and smoked. Things were not improved when one night he discovered me standing drunk and naked in my room pissing into an empty vodka bottle in preference to venturing into the blizzard outside to reach the loo. But we oiled our mutual disrespect with money, and although never satisfactory, it was a relationship of convenience that worked.

Jon and I hired a car and gold-toothed driver, and began to work the war in the countryside, while keeping one ear open for news of any significant development in Grozny.

One morning we saw a Sukhoi jet completing a bombing run on a distant village in the mountains, rolling back down over the target to rake it with cannonfire before swooping low away above us. Rather than lose ourselves trying to find the village without a guide, we headed for Shali, a small town south of Grozny, to see if they had brought any casualties to the hospital there.

We found many faces of President Yeltsin's war in the stinking wards: the burned; the blind; the maimed and disabled. Soon after our arrival some villagers entered carrying two little girls along corridors slippery with a muddle of used dressings, urine and blood. The children were sisters.

Marika was four years old. She was missing the lower part of her back and buttocks, but was still alive, just, and her pale, doll-like form lay motionless face-down on a table as a doctor removed large pieces of metal from her wounds, allowing each to drop on the table with a heavy clunk.

Her sister Miralya was a year older. I do not know what it takes to make a tiny child weep tears of blood, massive blast concussion I guess, but as she shook with noiseless terror it ran in thick lines from the corner of each eye, joining the scarlet streaks from a head wound to form a cobweb mask that covered her face.

The situation was very confused, and neither the villagers who had brought them in nor the exhausted hospital staff appeared to know what had become of the children's family. Then through the mêlée of casualties, fighters and nurses stepped a tall man dressed in a black suit, overcoat and wide-brimmed trilby. He was about sixty, and looked like Christopher Lee.

'Come with me,' he said mysteriously, in English. 'I shall take you to their village and you shall see everything you need to.' We got in the car with him and left.

After an hour's journey into the snow-covered mountains we arrived at the children's home. It was an isolated farm building overlooking a decrepit bridge that traversed a small mountain stream. The bridge was still standing. Nothing else was: the bombs had turned the earth black and transformed the site into a lunar landscape of charred domestic junk. The chassis of a car hung in a treetop.

We found the girls' family, their two sisters, brother and mother, in the nearby village little over a mile away. They were laid out in an empty house on a bed in bundles, none of which was bigger than a supermarket bag. The boy was the best preserved, the mother barely recognizable as human. Of the other sisters a small pair of legs emerged from a cloth, and the two heads lay at the end of the bed. Apparently their father had been vaporized. I remember that scene every time I hear a military spokesman use the phrase 'collateral damage'.

Jon stayed inside to take some photographs while I walked out to have a cigarette. I found our man in black addressing the men of the village who had assembled in the yard. About fifty of them stood in a silent semicircle, listening to him talk. Whoever he was he seemed to carry a lot of authority. The villagers may not have hated the Russians before but by the look on their faces they hated them now.

Jon reappeared and our strange friend spoke to our driver quickly, then bade us farewell as we returned to Goyty. The return trip was marred when our driver decided to stop the car on the bridge beneath the children's ruined farmhouse to pray. As it was presumably the intended target of the Sukhoi and we could still hear the sound of jets above us it was a most inopportune decision. Jon and I swore and shouted and threatened and cajoled but it was no good, the Chechen would not be moved. He clicked away at his prayer beads, murmuring softly as we sat in the back grinding our teeth in impotent rage, eyes rolling upwards to the skies in fear.

Jon left me a day later. He had to go to Ingushetia to ship some film and said he would be back but never reappeared. I cursed him for a while, little knowing that he had been arrested by the Chechen secret police as he tried to get back to me. Apparently he had picked a driver who was suspected of being a Russian sympathizer.

In his absence I hung on in Goyty alone as the war spread

through the countryside around me. I felt very isolated and more tired than I had ever felt before, but I still had a link with London via my satellite-telex. Somehow, until I heard otherwise, it seemed a point of honour that I should stay. I did not want to admit to having had enough, certainly not to a suit in London. Also, solitude is a state that has often lent me strength. I have an ability to deal with it that many others do not share, an asset that needs reconfirmation. But now, as each day passed I felt more and more unnerved, and had to fight with my mind to keep the images of the slain at bay. I had to sleep some time, though, and the children reappeared to me some nights after I last saw Jon, when I had surrendered my strength to the darkness.

By mid-February there were rumours in the village that the Russians had penetrated into the southern half of Grozny, and that the position of the Chechen forces there was becoming increasingly tenuous as they faced encirclement from the additional Russian advances in the south. I had only left the capital about ten days earlier, but knew that this news meant I should return once more. It was not a prospect I relished.

There are places, wars and ways to die. In war I had fantasized about my death many times with an almost prurient fascination: narcissistic visions of a swift and bold exit, thumping down painlessly beneath a bullet with my boots on, just enough life left to spit the blood out of my mouth and whisper no regrets before the big sleep – the ultimate hit. So the prospect of squealing around in the snow in Grozny smashed to pieces by a Russian shell, alone, in agony and terror, did not feature too high on my list of preferences.

I managed to track down an English-speaking Chechen fighter, Maksharip, and hired him as an interpreter. In his late twenties, he was a former English student well connected among the Chechen command hierarchy. Humorous and intelligent, he proved an ideal fixer. Hoping that I could close my mind down for one final horror venture, I planned to go back into Grozny and find General Maskhadov. Maksharip seemed enthusiastic enough, though he rather spoilt it by repeating 'maybe we live, maybe we die – only God knows' as we finished our discussion.

My shaken nerves were strengthened the day before our departure by the arrival in Goyty of two British TV journalists. They were both friends of mine and I greeted them as though they were the long-awaited relief for a beleaguered garrison, their fresh faces, smiles and rationality giving me the sustenance I so needed. One of them kept talking about his wife and kids in Wimbledon. Usually I would have smirked at such domestic banality. Now I stuck close to him, and urged him to talk more of his family, as if by his presence a little bit of Wimbledon would rub off on me: I knew no shell could reach me there.

Late in the afternoon the three of us walked towards Grozny with Maksharip as our guide, intent on locating General Maskhadov's headquarters. The situation was very confused. We encountered only isolated bands of Chechens – heading unnervingly in the opposite direction – who told us that the order had come for their forces to withdraw from the city.

Grozny had never been so quiet. Peering from among houses on a southern slope we saw the Minutka area, for a time the Chechen stronghold after the loss of the Presidential Palace, lying below us, a sprawling ruin, smoke from its numerous fires collecting with the gathering mist to form a grey shroud that floated gently above it.

We continued to move south as the light went, the glow from burning buildings casting strange shadows around us. For all the surrounding silence, we were heading towards the one area that still echoed with gunfire and received the odd artillery round. Near by, there was the ominous clanking of tank tracks.

Eventually we found a Chechen post that was holding firm. The fighters were wary of us at first, but soon relaxed in Maksharip's presence. They knew the location of Maskhadov's new headquarters, and we waited with them for the arrival of a commander to forward our request to visit. An APC appeared through the murk, moving towards us at speed. The Chechens initially had no idea whether it was one of their own or Russian and they ran quickly to firing positions at the edge of a building as we moved with equal haste to a fold in the ground. The vehicle was Chechen, and roared past into the darkness, leaving us laughing uneasily.

Then two particularly belligerent-looking warriors appeared, both of them wounded. They were members of Maskhadov's personal guard. The taller of the two, his eye and forehead serrated with stitches, spoke hurriedly on a walkie-talkie as his limping comrade took up position behind him. The general himself was on the other end. 'I have three English journalists here who want to see you,' the fighter said. There was a pause, then we heard an amused voice reply: 'What can I tell them? Bring them along.'

Maskhadov's headquarters lay in a linear cellar complex beneath a four-storey building. Once he had finished his meal, the first after the day's Ramadan fast, he received us hospitably in an impromptu operations room. Sitting at a desk beneath maps of the city, he looked tired though not dispirited and spoke with tremendous sincerity. 'I can only wonder at the strength with which my men fight. The Russians attack us with planes, then artillery, then tanks, levelling the houses before them. Yet still my men emerge from the rubble to fight on. But we cannot match the Russian weaponry, and will have to fight a different type of war. This is not a retreat from Grozny – it is a planned withdrawal. All we can do is fight on, to show not only that we want our independence, but that we are willing to die for it.'

It was not until the general marked the new Russian lines on my map that we knew the full extent of the Chechens' withdrawal. Except for our location in an emaciated urban finger to the extreme south of the city, and the access route's entrance around Chernoreche, Grozny had been abandoned to the advancing Russians.

Maskhadov reflected wryly on the imbalance of weaponry during the conflict. 'When this war is over every Chechen must sell his car and buy a Stinger missile,' he grinned, referring to the Russians' almost unrestricted ability to use their airpower. 'We don't have their munitions, but when one of my soldiers is given ten RPGs I expect eight tanks to be destroyed.'

He invited us to stay, and we saw that his mood of fatalistic optimism was shared by others in the building's cellars. Mad Max appeared to have met the Saracens: there were shaven heads; wild black beards; turbans; clanking layers of bandoliers; curved daggers and scimitars; the green bandanas of smrtniks emblazoned in Koranic script; flowing Afghan-style coats and snow-smocks; dancing and music in the wavering candlelight – an unforgettable scene; the brave and wild singing as their city burned.

Among the fighters, as laden as the others with assault rifle, magazines and RPG warheads, sat a thirteen-year-old boy. Esa had come with his father to fight the Russians in Grozny at the start of the war. His father had since been wounded and evacuated, while Esa had elected to stay. He was skinny, shaven-headed and pale, a dwarf beside the fighters around him. His features were smooth and childlike, but his pupils were indefinable in the blackness of his eyes.

'I can feel nothing when I fight on the front line,' he said wearily, claiming to have killed on a number of occasions. 'The worst thing is to lose your friends: nineteen of mine have died here. The next worst thing is when some men start to panic under fire. I did not go to Russia to fight the Russians. I am fighting in my country, for my country; for my village, my people and my God.'

As the revelry subsided the fighters snatched sleep wherever they could, or filed away to reinforce rearguard positions near by. We crashed out with one group against a wall in one of the rooms. None of us had much rest as the Chechens kept telling each other jokes and stories that they wanted us to be in on. It seemed more like a slumber party than the eve of defeat, and I wondered again how these people could possibly be beaten. 'Chechen people like the English very much,' one of my bedfellows kept informing me, giving me a powerful jab in the ribs each time to ensure he had my full attention. 'Lord Palmerston gave us guns to fight the Russians. English people good people.'

If the Cold War had not ended, I mused groggily, the West would certainly have given them a lot more guns, for if ever there was a cause which needed arming, this was it. But the justice of their fight had been sacrificed to the politics of the new world order.

At midnight came sudden word to move. Without dissent or confusion they all went about tasks, loading ammunition boxes and medical supplies into rucksacks, departing in groups into the darkness for a rendezvous far to the south-west. The shelling had come much closer as the Russians pushed forward, and it appeared that, rather than be caught in their loop, Maskhadov had decided to fall back towards Grozny's remaining gateway.

Our escape was one of protracted effort and confusion. Led by Maksharip, who was now toting a Kalashnikov, we joined a gaggle of soldiers and medical staff in a halting three-hour journey to Chernoreche. It was uncertain how close the Russians were – their signal and illumination flares appeared everywhere, forcing us into frequent stops. Each time I resignedly anticipated the eruption of gunfire around us as we tangled with the Russian noose.

Then a tank approached through the darkness. Lying in a ditch by the side of the road, we pressed our faces hard into the snow as it drew nearer. The night's smoke-laden mist dimmed the spread of its spotlight and the noise of its tracks until it was almost upon us and the boulevard's broken trees lit up on either side. I held my breath as the air filled with the sound of the grinding machine. Friendly or hostile: no-one knew.

It passed us. With softly murmured curses of relief, the twenty-strong band of Chechens stood up and moved off. However, the encounter had caused our group to become separated, and it was nearly dawn by the time we finally made the successful rendezvous at the new headquarters location, a former hotel in Chernoreche.

The four of us left the Chechens early the next morning. Maksharip was deep in contemplation. 'I never thought that I would see this happen,' he said of his city's loss. 'There will be much blood paid for this. The Russians have made a bad, bad mistake. But we did manage to hold out here for thirty-seven days – Berlin lasted only two weeks in 1945. This war shall continue, only now it shall be one without front lines.'

Back in Goyty my two journalist friends left me alone once more, and I found a temporary peace in the knowledge that I had returned to Grozny and caught its fall. In terms of nerve I was running on empty, and felt assuaged by the small personal victory of having fought my fear at such a bad time.

A message appeared on the screen of my sat-telex. It was from London. 'Return to Moscow and London as you see best,' it read. 'This phase of the story over. ENDS.' I was ecstatic with delight, hurling my belongings into a rucksack as fast as I could. I said farewell to the foul Magamet, silently wishing an air strike upon him, and rushed out to get my driver. He started whingeing about the price and risk of driving me to safety across the Ingush border.

'Take what you want, just get me the fuck out of here,' I jabbered, clutching at his lapels with one hand as I thrust a bundle of dollars into his face with the other. I must have looked completely demented.

Back in a Moscow hotel room, with less than twelve hours until my plane to London, I sat on the bed staring out of the window into the unsleeping city night. I had a bottle of vodka with me, which was disappearing rapidly, but as ever it was not quite enough. My brain was scrambling and flashing with thoughts like the warning lights in a cockpit consul when an engine burns out: damage.

Against this I weighed the attitude of the Chechens. It seemed that they had an almost complete disregard for death, backed by an absolute certainty in the justice of their cause, and the eventual victory that that would bring them regardless of the Russians' military might. 'You can break the man but not the spirit,' a fighter had told me once in Grozny as he strode into a battle. I am sure he had not read Hemingway, and I was cynical and faithless enough even then to have discounted his words as being those of blind machismo. Now I thought of them again.

Much of the Chechens' mentality had been forged by their upbringing. They were the product of a hierarchical society conditioned by values such as endurance and emotional reserve. A friend had told me that he had witnessed two Chechen brothers meet in a hospital. Both were fighters. One had had his legs and an arm blown off by a shell a day earlier. He lay in a filthy, blood-stained bed swathed in bandages. Only his face emerged through the swaddle of cloth; scabbed, scarred and blackened by the blast. He was conscious but could not speak. His brother walked in. It was the first time he had seen his sibling since he had been maimed. There was no touching, no display of sadness. The unwounded man took a chair and sat by his brother's bed for a while, talking to him softly. After a time he got up to leave. No sign of emotion had passed over his face at any stage. He said goodbye and just before he turned to leave there was movement from the bed.

The wounded man lifted his remaining arm from the blankets and raised his thumb in defiance.

Imagine the power of such men. Hail them, and fear them.

Before going to Bosnia I had seen war as a simple equation of physical force: add up the tanks, guns and men on both sides, throw in a few other variables, and if the discrepancy is large enough, you know who to put your money on to win. Increasingly, though, in the Balkans, and then latterly in Chechnya, I saw another ingredient, one that had a power totally disproportionate to any other asset on the battlefield: human will. The Chechens had it, and ultimately the Russians did not. While the match of weaponry and men was so unequal it made the chance of a Chechen victory seem ridiculous, it was to be will that carried the final victory.

If there was a positive lesson for me in that terrible place, then that was it. It suggested that the power of man can withstand the might of the machine, and it threatened the complacency of Western societies whose children, like me, are corrupted by meaningless choice, material wealth and spiritual emptiness.

A year later, in July 1996, the Chechen forces swept back into Grozny. They took on the Russian army head-to-head and recaptured most of the city within twelve hours. Defeated and humiliated, the Russians were forced to negotiate an end to the war and an eventual withdrawal from the tiny state. I returned to Chechnya at this time. One night, in a village north of Grozny, I found General Aslan Maskhadov with his inner circle of fighters. He was completely exhausted, having spent several days and nights thrashing out a negotiated settlement with the Russian special envoy, Alexander Lebed.

I spoke with him briefly and handed over the map of Grozny upon which he had marked our isolated position on the eve of his withdrawal from the city. He looked at it for a long time, then flashed me a smile of recognition. Taking a pen, he drew a large circle around the entire city before scrawling his signature beside it.

'These are our positions now,' he said quietly.

Returning from Moscow, I hailed a cab at the airport and collapsed into the opulence of the vehicle's seat, trying to find peace in this moment that I had dreamed of for so long in Chechnya. 'Don't worry,' I had told myself many times in Grozny, 'you're going to get out of this shit and by the time you are in a black cab it'll all seem like a bad dream.'

It seemed more like a waking nightmare. I still could not get the image of the woman and severed leg out of my vision, feared sleep for the return of the dead children, and had a kind of numb, shocked buzzing in my head that overlaid a sense of confusion and disorientation.

I had rented a flat in Shepherd's Bush from a friend. Lela was there to greet me as I arrived. She hugged me warmly in the darkness of the hallway, concern clouding her face as I walked inside and she saw me in the light.

'Fucking hell, Ant, you look shattered.'

I looked at my face in a mirror. Usually it never changed, whatever I had witnessed. On the rare trips home from Bosnia I had been annoyed by the people who noted 'how well I looked'. It was not the observation that angered me, for it was true enough – my face retained most of its babyish openness throughout the war – it was the disappointment in their tone, as if they had wanted to touch some element of the war without actually going there, and had been frustrated by the denial of my rude health. But the barely consumable levels of fear and death in Bosnia that had apparently so illuminated my complexion had been well exceeded in Chechnya. The face that looked back at me was haunted and furtive. I would normally have been vain enough to be intrigued by the difference, but now it barely interested me.

'I feel fucking shattered,' I replied and sank back into the sofa.

You cannot throw severed limbs, mortal terror, insane women and children's heads on to the floor of a London flat – even if it is the one you live in – in the company of a friend, however close you are to them. Lela coaxed me slowly into conversation as the darkness of the late winter afternoon closed in and the street outside metamorphosed into an orange glow of reflected lighting on rain-washed tarmac.

'Shall we go and see Leon?' she asked finally after a long pause, looking at me with the same interested compassion as a doctor who has found genuine sickness in one of the patients among a Monday morning surgery queue.

In his small West London flat, its walls a pastiche of his drawings, photographs and cluttered bouquets of domestic junk turned art, Leon welcomed us with the unsurprised smile of a tired guru.

'Hello, Ant,' he said quietly, looking intensely into my face, 'you look awful.'

He returned to his desk, turning the chair around to face us as we sat on the floor against the bed, like children waiting to be told a story.

Pulling a roll of foil out of a drawer, he tore off a strip, indenting a narrow trenchline down the sheet. A little white wrap appeared in his hand, and from it he tipped the gear, a small heaped pile no wider than a penny into one end of the furrow in the foil, then cooked it with an untrembling lighter. We took it in turns to run the small brown pool of processed opium up and down the foil, pursued by the hidden heat of the lighter beneath, chasing it corner to corner with a foil tube.

I sucked in the smoke greedily, and the cold wash of anaesthesia hit me. It swept over me, a wave that started at the tip of my nose, rushing across my face to encircle my head, running down my neck through my chest, crashing into a warm golden explosion in my stomach, my groin, a blissed sensation beyond the peak of orgasm and relief of nausea, as every muscle in my body relaxed and my head lolled gently on to my shoulder, every sense unwinding, unburdened of the crushing weight of pain I never even knew I had: the rush, the wave, death, heaven, completion. For hours and hours.

The hit. Sensual ultimatum. You can argue over every other aspect of heroin, but you can never dispute the hit. Get it right and you may never look back. Except in regret. As I write now, just thinking about it makes my skin crawl, and the saliva pumps into my mouth like one of Pavlov's dogs.

263

As my head rubber-necked upright the words began to pour from my mouth, the tales of horror released from me. Leon and Lela, their own sense of inherent calm and compassion heightened, encouraged me to talk more. Many hours later Lela and I ambled out into the night and back to the flat, where I fell into the first peaceful sleep for weeks.

The ceasefire in Bosnia was to last until the coming of the spring. So I stayed in London for most of the next two months. It does not take long to get a habit, and I ran in to get mine, hands outstretched, determined, like it was all I had ever wanted. Maybe it was.

MEETING MAJOR TOM

My dealer was away elsewhere, leaving his wife to conduct busi-
ness. We met at one of the usual places, trading the gear for the
cash over a cursory greeting. In the absence of words I had to look
deeper to work her out, drawing on details such as the way she
moved, if she smiled, whether she was rushed, late or relaxed.
Even the way she opened the door of her car thieved a little piece
of her anonymity for me. Today it swung from the vehicle's body
in a slow arc of deliberation, and she closed it with a cautious
thump, barely audible, as she walked towards me.

It was a three-bag day for me. Without the war to go back to,
my habit was gathering momentum like a runaway train.

'Anthony.' She touched my arm softly as she spoke. I think it
was the first time we had had physical contact so I turned to her
with some surprise. 'This is a strong batch, so be careful, right?' I
nodded and she walked away, then turned and approached me
once more.

'I've had two go under on me from this stuff, so watch it, OK?'

'Yeah sure, Cathy, don't worry. And, thanks.'

I raced back to the flat, eager to sample whatever it was that had so ambiguously 'had two go under' on Cathy. There was no-one else living with me at that time. Even Lela, her marriage with Alex finished, had fled London to live in a millhouse in France with Shimmy, exiling herself from the darkening cloud that gathered around those of us who remained.

Nevertheless, I shut myself in the bathroom as I unwrapped the gear and put the entire contents of the first wrap down on some foil. The days in which I had done it for pleasure were so far away; now it seemed more like an act of physical maintenance, like shaving and washing, something private you did not want to do anywhere but the bathroom.

I put the loo seat down, sat on it and did the first bag quickly. There was a bottle of Jack Daniels by the sink so I whacked some of that back and lit a cigarette, lolling back against the cistern.

Peace: the ground zero I had returned to where the memories of the past five years rushed repeatedly through my mind like a burning mantra; re-ripping and re-wrapping of their own volition as they tried to touch the sides of the empty new reality to make some kind of connection, some grounding to splice the past with the present. More than two years since Grozny, more than one since the Bosnian war ended, and I had never known such solitude. It was like walking through a battlefield when the fighting is all over: you just wonder where everyone went to. One minute there was such sound, movement, intensity and life, the next you may as well have landed on the moon: it's just you and a few confused-looking extras standing around in the silence.

Cathy was right. Good gear. After a timeless while my head lurched upright and I noticed that the cigarette had burned out *on the floor at my feet like a fat grey caterpillar, leaving a brown patch on a carpet already leopard-skinned with imprints from others that had gone a similar way. I lit another, and did the second bag as the evening drew in outside.*

It must have taken me the best part of an hour to co-ordinate starting the third wrap as I kept dropping the smoker, treading on it unwittingly, and having to compose another, itself a task beset with the problems of failing consciousness. Some people manage to look quite graceful on smack, ethereal and coolly composed. I was not one of them. The drug always left me twitching and sliding like a puppet with half its strings missing, eyes like frozen pizzas at the bottom of black shell-craters. Then again, I did not want grace in heroin. I sought not to gain. So I started on the third fuelled by painstaking deliberation.

Just after the second run the light seemed to snap off around me, and the world grew black except for a tiny point of fading glow at the centre, like the screen on an old TV in the seconds after you have switched it off. Eventually that too faded. I had the brief sensation of floating downwards, then nothing.

Consciousness came back to me through heavy veils, each a warm and cloying layer that delayed my resurfacing. I opened my eyes slowly, and stared for a long time at the deep blue wash of the ceiling, noticing the whirling brush tracks left by a bored painter long before. Eventually I rolled on to my side. Then stood up shakily. My face seemed to be covered in something cold and sticky. Looking in the mirror I saw that the right side of my head was plastered in a pale grey goo while a red-brown smudge of congealed blood smeared across my top lip, crusting around my nostrils. As I had tumbled from the loo I had crashed into the cabinet beside the sink face-first, the impact squirting me with thick coils of shampoo from an open tube: a domestic accident that left me resembling the victim of a snuff movie.

Looking out of the window, I saw a grey and cold dawn, herald to another hollow day. A sudden spasm of nausea pole-axed me to my knees. I flipped up the loo seat and puked into the bowl. Until the jets dried into bile and saliva, each racking convulsion had the power of a high-pressure hose. Projectile vomiting: it wouldn't have been so bad if it weren't for the splashback.

I rubbed my face dry on a towel and checked my watch. I had been unconscious for eight hours, which left another four to go until Cathy would be awake and I could score some more. So I found the crushed smoker, unwrapped it and had another hit. Slumping back against the cistern, my eyes again rolled upwards to the swirling blue paint of the ceiling. The tracks of the brush's bristles were like jungle fronds, a jumble of lush midnight-blue vegetation into which my dream wandered, back to a time long past . . .

The bar was made out of stacked bamboos at one end of an open-plan room, little more than a shack really, roofed with palm leaves that rustled with life even though there was no wind. The heat and darkness outside seemed to combine as a single entity, a thick blanket into which the clustering vegetation beyond the crudely boarded floor, so lividly green in the light of the sun, had all but disappeared. Yet the darkness had voice and life. The occasional grunt of a pig, or outraged shriek of a hunting or hunted creature in the jungle, drifted into the airless space, and fireflies danced green tangos like ships in a blacked-out harbour, all against the incessant throbbing chirrup of cicadas.

A couple of Indonesian fishermen sat at the one table playing cards and drinking Tiger beer, bodies wrapped in sarongs and ragged T-shirts, the skin of their arms sculpted with sinew, the smoothness giving way to the callouses and scars of their net-cut hands. A one-eyed youth lounged on a tilting chair behind the bar tapping a packet of cigarettes in a bored tattoo against the bamboo.

I sat alone, the only figure on the otherwise empty row of stools, like the surviving duck in a shooting gallery. The summer of 1985. I had left Australia a month or so before, travelling slowly through Indonesia en route for Thailand. A ride in a shabby minibus, its mechanical disrepair offset only by the dazzling murals painted on its bodywork, had ended up at this anonymous fishing village with the setting of the sun; and with the carefree attitude of those days, I had rented a beach hut for the night from an Indonesian without even bothering to ask for the name of the village. Having washed off the sweat and grime of the day's travel in the warm sea, giggling with the fearful pleasure of wondering what other creatures lurked beneath the deserted night waters, I walked to the only major source of light among the clustered bamboo houses, and found the bar. I dreamed happily of all that life had to offer me, fantasizing through a thousand loves and lives as those on the threshold of their life do, blowing my thoughts through smoke rings and cool gulps of beer.

Then Nemesis arrived on a red Kawasaki. She found me a willing disciple.

There was the distant roar of an engine, the beam of a light in the blackness, and the machine conjured itself out of the gloom, silent as suddenly as it had appeared as the rider killed the engine, kicking the bike back on its rest, before walking into the bar.

He was an unlikely individual for a fishing village, but must have been known to the men there for they greeted him with nods of recognition before returning to their cards. A young Indonesian, his cowboy boots, immaculate Levi's and black leather jacket were out of place in the cloying heat. He had a pair of aviator Ray-Bans tucked in his top pocket, and could have seemed a faintly ridiculous cliché of new Asian wealth. But there

269

was something about him that undermined any sense of risibility. His eyes had a one-dimensional coldness to them, and the skin of his face was the texture of marble, not even a pore visible.

He sat down beside me at the bar, ordered a drink and turned to me, confident and assured, friendly almost, but there was something missing.

'Where are you from?' He asked the inevitable first question, the preliminary skirmish in ritualistic conversations between travellers at that time and place. Route, destination, music, girls, dope: we wrapped up the essentials over a couple more Tigers, our dialogue reaching the point it always did, the moment when you had the choice to close it up easily with goodbye and good luck or see if there was something more on offer.

I was wary of him in a politely British way, but not overly so. In the emptiness of the bar I was an obvious target for talk to anyone who walked in, and there was nothing in what he said or asked to make me suspicious. It was just his dress, expression and the predatory ice of his eyes that cautioned me. I half thought he might be gay and on the pull, so got up to leave before there was the embarrassment of any misunderstanding.

'Do you want to score?' he asked me suddenly as I drew back the stool.

It is amazing how much thought you can cram into a second, and how much mistrust lurks behind the veneer of an affable conversation. He had the drugs and wanted some cash; I had the cash and wanted some grass. Was he a cop or an informer? Unlikely in this far-flung village. Would he try to rip me off or rob me? Maybe, but he looked too affluent and urbane to risk the aggravation of confrontation. If he tried it without a knife I could probably whack him and leg it comfortably enough. If he was armed I was not carrying sufficient cash on me to cry over its loss anyway.

Answer time (it's worth the risk): 'Yeah sure.' Then straight into buying guise: look confident and relaxed, but aware and direct; deliberate but unhurried; the bricks in the wall to shroud the vulnerability of your solitude.

Potentially it was a situation of no drama, or major drama. And there was a misunderstanding, but it was in my logic, not his.

We got on the bike and rode a short distance to a house on stilts at the edge of the village. Light glimmered through gaps in the walls, but there was no-one inside. He unlocked a padlock on the door and walked in. It was clean and sparsely furnished, a bedroom and bathroom adjoining the main room. His bike and clothes had led me to expect other visible signs of wealth, but an expensive stereo stacked in the corner was the only thing to differentiate the house from any other I had seen in the coastal villages. It was difficult to tell whether he lived there, or whether it was merely a temporary haunt.

He put on some Indonesian music as I took a seat at the table. Nothing was said as he rummaged in a suitcase lying beside the door, returning to the table with a large envelope. He tipped its contents out on to the table.

I had expected a few bundles of grass to roll out, and was surprised by the tumble of a half-dozen wraps, each a small envelope of folded paper about an inch long. Without a word he picked one up and opened it. A thick wedge of brown powder lay inside. Heroin. Suddenly all my self-assured rationale in coming to the house with him evaporated. I had not expected this. Smoking grass was almost a formality for foreigners in South-east Asia. So although it was a major centre for opium production too, it was easy to assume that it was marijuana that was on offer.

'I'm sorry,' I said. 'I misunderstood you – I thought it was grass you had.'

He was cool about it, apologetic even, varnishing what might have been an awkward situation into one of relaxed opportunism.

'No problem, no problem,' he reassured me, wrapping the little envelope up again and putting it back in the pile with the others. 'But if you want to try . . .' He left the sentence unfinished.

I thanked him anyway, said goodnight and went to the door. As I opened it a quadrangle of light fell from the room behind me into the night outside, perfectly delineated by the thick darkness.

I took about one step into it before I stopped, turned and walked back through the door.

It could have been minutes later that I stumbled grinning into the darkness, but maybe it was hours. I stopped briefly on the journey back to my hut to throw up deliciously into someone's yard, miraculously finding my way home in the darkness, lying awake throughout the night scratching and smoking, a dreamy smile fixed on my face. Somewhere in the night my wandering thoughts were given accompaniment by the soft notes of his bamboo xylophone trickling voluptuously into my consciousness. Lying on my bed in the dark that night I had no regrets at all, and wondered how I could have escaped sampling the delight of such a tranquil sensation before. Forbidden fruit: listen to the serpent, it tastes fantastic.

Yet by mid-morning I felt completely normal again, and had no great hankering to repeat the experience. The drug's addictive properties seemed greatly exaggerated.

People talk a lot of crap about addiction. It is hard to understand unless you have been there, but, God knows, once you see it from the inside your mind is taken to a whole new dimension of awareness. I for one would never have believed I would get a habit. In my early twenties I remember my incomprehension on the occasions when my anorexic sister stared at herself in the mirror, so thin it was painful just to look at her, and continued to deny herself proper nourishment because she thought the image that looked back at her was fat. I understand it too well now: another destructive compulsion that defies logic or reason.

I have lost count of the number of times I have tried to break the habit. With the exception of wartime, which hardly counts as cleantime, there have been dozens of half-hearted sallies where I manage to stay straight for a few white-knuckle days; a couple of intermediate struggles where I have managed a fortnight or so; and two notable occasions when I clocked a month without using.

Clean: it's always the same. When you come out of it and take a look around, the sight of wounds that you have left on the people who care for you makes you wince more than those you have inflicted on yourself. Though I am devoid of regret or remorse for almost anything I have done, if there is a corner for those feelings then it lies with that awareness. It should be enough to stop you from ever going back down there, but it seldom is.

You hope you will make it but you can never be sure, cleaning up is like trying to beat yourself at chess: just when you think you've won you realize it was all self-deception and the ground slides away from you as fast as it ever did. Like the way some people find God, you wake up one morning fragmented and incomplete, knowing that there is only one way to fill the yawning gaps. Run a stake through the Count a multitude of times, but spit blood on his ashes and Vlad the Impaler is at your side again. It is hard to fight a dream.

Smack – my most intimate and possessive lover, before whom any other dark angel would be a fool to tread. I would be hard pressed to explain the cravings to any outsider, those moments when my mind turns its back on rationality and wills my return to her arms again; and once in that embrace I do not want to leave.

It is nothing to do with willpower. Get a habit and the worth of your assets is inverted, your strengths becoming your weaknesses, your weaknesses your strengths. If anything, willpower only serves to keep you with the drug. To deal with all the shit, the sickness and isolation, to defy reason and hope in order to really fuck your own life up, requires a stamina and persistence most people could not begin to muster.

Even your sense of vanity turns on itself. You look terrible, you feel terrible, but what a delight it becomes to step outside yourself and cheer from the edge as the battered witness to your own destruction, more obsessed with your own sense of tragedy than the Serbs ever were.

The addictive chemical properties of heroin are well known, and many regard their effect on the body as akin to a disease that can perhaps be contained but never cured. I am not diseased, and I could defy the drug's physical pull. If I really wanted to. But the power of the dragon lies not in an inanimate powder, but in what it unlocks in your own psychology, that same force that led you to load up on it in the first place.

To clean up you have to weigh up what you want, and the best you can hope for at first is a fraction of a percentage in the difference between the desire to stop and the desire to plough on downwards. That is if you are lucky. The rub comes with the reality that the more you use the more you fuck your life up so the less reason you have to want to clean up. So a habit becomes self-perpetuating because of your need for it to cope with the damage.

No, not in the wildest dreams of my youth did I imagine becoming an addict, though the mechanical stages of that journey are clear enough now.

Once I had returned home from South-east Asia in 1985 it was not until after the army, in London in the early Nineties, that I used the drug again, and even then only irregularly. Yet as I sank *into the war, in itself unscrewing the lid on the darker side of the mind, so I began to use smack more and more during my sporadic returns to England. It was not just a complement to the war experience, and did more than merely splice wastelands together. As I found the adjustments between conflict and peace harder and harder to deal with I discovered that heroin ensured I never had to adapt to the change. In getting wasted in London I could simply transcend the whole contradiction, and with it all the questions it might have posed. Heroin atrophies your mentality to the point where you do not progress at all on any level. Which is probably why I cannot stop thinking about the war.*

There was only one other watermark of any significance, the point when I stopped scoring off friends and started buying alone. I suppose that, as much as anything, can be defined as the moment when the door on addiction really opened up to me . . .

Leon was away. I had given him a lift out of London, but we had had a last session together in his flat the previous night, caning it, so that our farewell was iced down with pinned pupils and sloppy grins.

I had gone back to tidy up his flat the same day. Whenever he eventually returned the last thing he would need to find, even if it was all he wanted to find, was a crumpled sheet of foil tiger-striped with burns to remind him of what had passed. For sure he would be checking the bins within two minutes of walking back through the door to see if there was still a trace of gear missed by the lighter's flame. So I emptied all the rubbish into black bags before slinging them out for the dustmen. I gave the flat a sweep out too, finding an unopened wrap behind the fridge as I did so. Bonus. The housework stopped as I went out to the dustbins to recover some foil to smoke it with.

I had a slight chill that morning, a light sheen of sweat covering

*my face like the onset of flu. It disappeared as soon as I had the
first hit.*

*Then the phone rang. I paused for a long time by the receiver
before answering. The street outside was empty, the silence of the
flat marred only by the insistent ringing. Then a motorbike
throbbed past the window. It could have been a red Kawasaki but
wasn't. I answered the call.*

*'Hello, is Leon there?' the voice, a man's, asked. I recognized
it from somewhere.*

*'No, I'm sorry, he's gone away for a while,' I said cautiously.
'Can I take a message?'*

*'Who's that, Anthony?' the voice challenged. 'How you doing?
All right are you?'*

*It was Leon's dealer. He was an addict himself, as was his wife,
Cathy; narco-refugees preserving their exile with a lifetime of use.
Together they ran a small dealership to a select syndicate of buyers.
It did more than just sustain their own habit, and their deals were
tight by London's standards. But while other dealers dealt in
larger quantities for better prices, the £20 bags on offer from these
two gave you some level of control by the nature of their size. Start
buying cheap grams off someone else and you sped down the road
to habit in no time: stick with this man and the milestones down
the same road were smaller and more widely spaced. Additionally,
he was always reliable. Leon would call, confirm the rendezvous,
get in his car and go, reappearing quarter of an hour later with the
gear. Fast-food junk.*

*Possession of their number was the gateway to a journey that
offered far more than just easy access to the drug. Knowing its
significance, Leon guarded it closely. Contrary to popular belief,
a lot of junkies keep their habit within tight parameters; Leon
might have acknowledged his own incarceration by the drug, but
he had no wish to see his friends freefall into the same trap.*

Some of us had exploited this fairly ruthlessly, piggy-backing our acquisition of smack by scoring through him as friends as well as second-degree clients. Paradoxically he did not begrudge this relationship either. Relying on a friend's use limited our exposure to the worst depredations of the drug, and he in turn got regular company to get wasted with. And company diluted the sense of one's own responsibility for the mess.

'Listen,' the man continued before I had the chance to say anything. 'I don't want no-one feeling sick or anything, so if you want to see me alone just give us a call, right?'

'Yeah right, what's your number?' The words were out of my mouth before I really thought about it. I took down the number and hung up. I stared at the digits for what seemed like an age. Their possession would alleviate some of the guilt I so often felt in scoring through Leon. Now the baton of self-control, of choice, was in my own hands. I laughed at the cynicism of the dealer's call. He must have feared the impact of Leon's absence on his financial situation, and trawled the flat with a phone call in the hope of picking up a new client.

Then I dialled the number.

'Hello,' I began, 'like how about now?'

He arranged to meet me at a near by newsagent in twenty minutes. I was there in ten. The rest you know.

15

Northern Bosnia, Spring 1995

The single shell came out of a clear sky as the sun dipped to the west and the shadows lengthened on Tito's Day of Youth. The Muslims still loved Tito, twinning his memory with a time of peace and prosperity. In every government-held town the graffiti scrawl of '*TITO VOLIMO TE*', Tito we love you, appeared with greater frequency as the war progressed: the spray-can sprawl of a desperate nostalgia.

In Tuzla the old town was packed with young people celebrating the traditional holiday of 25 May. Few had enough money to buy alcohol in the bars, so most sat outside in the fading sunshine of late May, talking and smoking on the cobbled streets. One of the last bastions of multi-ethnicity in Bosnia, the young Tuzla crowds were a mix of Muslims, Croats and Serbs.

There were only two foreign journalists in the town. Wayne

and Boris were hanging out in the Hotel Tuzla, a dreary creation in the new town whose drab fare was all that was on offer for outsiders passing through. The rest of the media were in Sarajevo feeding on the second-, third- and fourth-hand information handed out in UN press briefings concerning the fate of several hundred UN hostages taken prisoner by the Serbs in response to a NATO air strike. At least they were doing more work than I was.

I was languishing in Stara Bila, thoroughly disenchanted with events. More intent than ever on preserving its victim status, the Bosnian government had all but banned access to the front lines, where the rejuvenated Muslim army was having further successes against the Serbs, who for their part had always restricted the movement of the media. At times the combination of these strategies made the war feel almost abstract.

The seizing of the UN hostages was a massive story back home in England, which in itself annoyed me: hundreds of thousands had been killed, wounded or purged while the majority of the British public, duped by their government, was still ignorant of the issues at stake in the war. Yet the presence of a few score British troops among the prisoners had now provoked an enormous reaction, and the same politicians who for so long had mouthed dull and disingenuous platitudes about 'equal guilt' and 'inevitable tragedy' were suddenly branding the Serb tactics as those of a 'terror state', a term that had been noticeably absent while Bosnian blood had been shed.

The shell, fired by a Serb gun to the west of Tuzla, came in low. There were many places it could have exploded without causing casualties. Indeed, although the town had been sporadically shelled throughout the war, it was unusual for the detonations to exact too heavy a price, and the barrages had nothing of the intensity or accuracy of those elsewhere. But as the sun dipped below the horizon it landed in the old town's main square, thick with youth.

The explosion sent shrapnel scouring through the crowd and picked up the square's cobblestones in a cyclone of secondary death.

Inside their hotel room, Wayne and Boris knew nothing of the carnage. But they heard the detonation and, with little else to do, walked down to their Land-Rover as the final daylight went, and set off to find where the shell had landed. They were attracted to the old town by the sound of cries and sirens.

They got out of the vehicle in the darkness and pushed their way into the chaos of the square. In the narrow walled confines they were confronted with a scene such as few see in any war: the ground was slippery with blood and flesh, strewn with limbs and pulped bodies that still smouldered with the blast. Seventy-one were dead, nearly three times as many injured. The oldest of the dead was thirty-six years old, the youngest four.

As soon as they turned on the light of the TV camera they were kicked, spat at and punched. They retreated and entered the square from a different alleyway. The result was the same. As the grief and rage of survivors and rescuers alike redirected itself towards the two journalists, one teenage boy stepped forward and began to denounce the action of the others. Somehow he turned the mood of the mob, and Boris was then encouraged to film the scene.

Only when the last bodies were recovered did the pair send their footage from the TV station and return to the hotel. They washed the blood and human tissue from their boots in the shower and sat together in shocked silence in their room.

I found them like that the next morning. Having heard word of the massacre on the radio I had headed up to Tuzla in the Niva.

The square was almost empty when I walked in. The Bosnians had put curtains, cloth and sheets over the cobbles, so that the whole scene resembled a grotesque red-splattered patchwork quilt. There were still lumps of scarlet jelly all over the surrounding buildings.

I handed Wayne a bottle of whisky, sat back in silence and let them spill their story out as the bottle emptied. Boris, who was never short of a word to say and usually managed to come up with a quip at the most inopportune moments, just stared at his boots repeating, 'I never want to see that again, I never want to see that again,' as if by saying it he could wipe the memory from his brain. Wayne told me to look at the rushes, so I watched the scene on the edit pack in the corner of the room while he looked out of the window through a mist of tears, his South London talent for understatement failing him for once.

On the tape I saw most of what they had seen, the frightful mutilation and chaos, heard the pleading of the dying and the cries of the bereaved, only without the aggro of being punched and spat at.

We all wondered if it had been worth it the next day. Their footage was deemed unacceptable to be seen in Britain. They had been unable to edit out enough of the horror, unable to film a single body that was not too mutilated to be watched in a British home after dinner. Besides, Britain was not really that interested in the worst single massacre by an individual weapon in the war. It had its hostages to worry about.

The mass funeral was a clandestine affair undertaken in the dead of night. The Serbs had continued to shell Tuzla and the Bosnians were leaving nothing to chance. I would have thought their fears excessive had I not seen the funeral procession in Sarajevo machine-gunned two years before, and heard so many similar accounts of shell attacks on others elsewhere. Nothing seemed sacrosanct in the war and the Bosnians' air of secrecy was the result of bitter experience.

The ceremony began at 4 a.m. in the clearing of a wooded park, the site of a memorial to the partisans, on a hillside above the centre of the city. For hours a large crowd of Bosnians had struggled to dig the crowded graves in the grass slope, the steam of their sweat lifting into the lancing rain, given ghostly illumination by dim spotlights that hung in the surrounding trees.

Lightning and rolling thunder played in the distance, the sudden forks of light throwing the faces of the labouring men, creased with physical strain, into stark relief. One of them, a Bosnian soldier, paused and rested his chin for a minute on the handle of his shovel as a NATO jet rumbled unseen overhead, the noise of its engine merging with the tumult in the heavens.

'I've hated the sound of those jets from a long time ago,' he said. 'It was as if they were taunting us before. So much power, yet they only watched as we suffered.'

It took more than an hour for the coffins to be put into position on slats over their respective graves. First each had to be passed by hand up the hillside along a double file of men that stretched from the clearing into the darkness a long way below. It was a deeply moving sight: the silence, concentration and effort as they staggered beneath the weight of their dead, hand by hand in their grief, feet sliding in the mud. There was a real dignity there, a triumph of grace and humility in this response to death. On each grave lay a wooden marker: green wood for the Muslims, brown crosses for the Serbs and Croats.

The rain stopped as the bereaved families arrived, accompanied by soldiers, dignitaries, imams and priests, about five hundred people in all, gathering silently in a circle around the vast jumble of earth, coffins and tilted headstones. There were brief prayers from the Islamic and Christian faiths and then the silence of the crowd broke as they surged forward to lower their dead into the ground and fill the graves.

The pervading sense of grief was of such intensity as to be smothering. The sound of weeping rose above the thumping of earth as it fell upon wood, while clusters of people clutched at each other over the rent earth sobbing together, Serb, Muslim and Croat, in paroxysms of sorrow at their collective loss.

I walked away with Wayne and Boris as the earth levelled beneath the feet of the living, and the first glimmer of dawn through the dark bruises of the clouds brought the crowd's dispersal.

Several weeks later Wayne was in a pub in London. He got talking to a Scouser who had by chance been present at the Bradford City stadium disaster, when so many fans died in the fire. Fuelled by drink they each became furious with the other's apparent inability to relate to the scale of their respective tragedies. The dispute rolled in a flurry of fists on to the street outside. It was not the most glorious of Bosnia's battles, but few of the war's fights were marked by anything other than futility. Some colleagues later sneered at the brawl, fought between men in their thirties, the Bosnian corner represented by South London, the Bradford corner by Liverpool. For myself, I knew exactly where Wayne was coming from, and if his foe could not tell the difference between mass murder and accident, then that was his problem. Wayne gave the Scouser a good and righteous kicking then legged it while still ahead, so I guess the question remained unresolved, though not through any lack of effort on Wayne's part. It was a conflict borne of the gulf between different experiences. We should never have expected anything more from those who had not been there.

*   *   *

The sunbeams broke through the forest canopy in rods of light, spangling the dried mulch of dead leaves left by the previous winter with golden shards that shivered in the gentle summer breeze. The air was rich with birdsong and the hum of insects; only the distant thump of shellfire in the valleys to the north and south, and the occasional nervous finger-tapping of an HVO trooper on his assault rifle gave an indication of the tension.

The Bosnian-Croat troops were manning a trench that was a relic of their eleven-month war with the government army that had ended the previous year. At the forward edge of the Croats' Kiseljak pocket, the trenchline fronted the Serbs around Sarajevo to the east, and the Muslims at every other point of the compass. I walked down it now with a party of five HVO officers. As we followed the trenches' slow ascent the bunkers became deeper, freshly turned earth indicating recent work. A sudden turn in the defence line marked an otherwise invisible boundary. Less than two hundred yards away, across no man's land, were the Serbs. We slid silently into position, pressing our bodies into the earth above the firestep, and waited.

Hours before, a dawn barrage across the front lines north-west of Sarajevo had broken two weeks of mounting tension. BiH forces were massing in the area of Visoko and along the Čemerska Planina, the aptly named Mountain of Grief. It signalled the start of the government army's long-awaited push to break the siege of the capital and I for one had a particular stake in the outcome of the operation.

An HVO officer beside me glanced down at his watch, then caught my gaze and grinned. H-Hour, and the silence shattered with a continuous rolling of gunfire. Assault rifles, machine-guns, anti-aircraft fire, RPGs and mortar rounds, tore into the Serb positions before us. BiH infantry troops, fleeting figures in the shattered foliage below us, scrambled parallel to the Croatian line to take on their Serb enemy beyond.

The Croats simply watched. In Kiseljak they had co-operated heavily with the Serbs throughout the war until the new politics of the Croat–Muslim federation forced them into new alliance, and their part in this offensive was limited to artillery support of the Muslim fighters.

'Look, see the Turk sniper.' One of the officers pointed to a man crawling slowly through the undergrowth. He crouched upright for a second, fired, then dropped down into cover. Bullets ripped back in response through the branches around us, and we pressed our faces into the warm, rich smell of the ground as before us the Serbs were driven back.

A week earlier I had got Sinbad to fix new licence plates on my Niva. The federal cops were getting far too organized for my liking. Gone were the days when I could just brush off questions concerning the car's origins with a couple of cigarettes. Too often now the police wanted to see documentation. The peace dividends of the Muslim–Croat détente were not all good as far as I was concerned. I did not want to lose my wheels to law and order, so bought some hooky papers off a drunken cop one night with plates to match.

Sinbad was a mechanic in Zenica. He was cool, and well used to fixing my car without asking questions. He greeted my new request calmly and offered me a beer. We sat and drank while one of his men bolted on the plates. I commented on the row of Bosnian army staff cars in the yard.

'Yeah, I've had a lot of work from the army recently,' Sinbad said even-handedly.

I looked at him. 'Something I should know about?' I asked.

'Something you will find out about,' he replied.

The job done, I drove into the town to look for a young Muslim couple I knew. The centre of Zenica was as I had never seen it before. Every bar and café was closed, and the streets were empty of young men. I found Mirela. She told me that her boy had gone to ground to escape the conscription gangs that had been trawling the streets with mounting urgency over the past week.

Next I drove to Kakanj, where I found Azera. She was the daughter of a senior Bosnian commander, and young wife of a field officer. Pretty in a gap-toothed kind of way, she must have been bored of her small-town life even before the war took away most of its pleasure, as well as removing her husband for long stretches at the front. She called me up to her bedroom where I found her in front of the mirror putting on different shades of lipstick to pass away the hours.

We talked and drank for a while as I manoeuvred the conversation towards finding out where her husband and father were. She liked to talk. I left her a couple of hours later. She had told me that both were away on the fronts facing Sarajevo, that they would be away for some time, that a massive offensive was imminent to relieve the city.

Mechanics, draft-dodgers, bored girls: they were the little pools of information from which I drank that summer in the void left by the government's restriction on movement to the fronts. I was not left too thirsty.

Returning to Zenica I dropped in on Nehru Ganić, the Bosnian officer I had last seen when Vareš went down the pan. He was now head of the BiH officers' military academy, and remained as charming and articulate as ever. I trusted him enough to ask him the question directly:

'I know of the offensive,' I said, playing for a reaction, 'can you tell me anything more?'

Ganić was silent for a long time, then leaned forward on his desk and stared at me intently. 'If you have ever loved anything of this country, then I urge you to speak no further to me now on this subject, and repeat to no other what you have already heard.'

I was left in a quandary. As a journalist the story was potentially big, and safe in my hands while the rest of the media shacked up with the UN in Sarajevo. I felt sure that given another twenty-four hours I could get some real detail on what was going on – probably from the HVO, who always played a duplicitous game – and the structure of a good story.

Yet what of the war? Did I want to blow the whistle on the Bosnians' plan before it even kicked off? Did I want to think that even one government soldier may die because Serb gunners had been given extra time to prepare their artillery and fire plans by a story in a British newspaper warning of an imminent Bosnian offensive? And what of my friends still stuck in Sarajevo, their lives in grey menacing limbo: did they deserve to have their chances of relief affected by a story?

My answer came with Ganić's words still ringing in my ears. It was easy enough really. I said nothing. I wrote nothing. It was hardly the first time I had kept my mouth shut in order to allow events to unfold naturally.

Then five days later, having dropped in on a UN base in Visoko, I saw a Canadian officer blow it all. He was standing in front of a TV camera, answering mundane questions from a correspondent concerning 'life as a peacekeeper in Bosnia'. Prompted solely by his expanding sense of self-importance and the desire to keep talking, the officer suddenly blurted out, 'Well, we are expecting the situation to change now real soon ... yep we estimate at least thirty thousand Bosnian government troops ... that's right thirty thousand ... to have gathered over the last few weeks in order to break the siege of Sarajevo ... recent developments make us think that an offensive is now imminent ...'

287

I watched the correspondent register the significance of what was being said and walked away, shaking my head with disbelief. The story was out, so I ran with it, feeling uneasy nevertheless. Perhaps, with hindsight, I should not have been so worried. All sides were so counter-penetrated with each other's intelligence that the Serbs must have had word of the attack long before I did.

I used my few remaining contacts with the HVO to get to the line near Kiseljak on the first day of the offensive. Subsequent access dried under me and, I believe, every other foreign journalist as the operation turned into a familiar fiasco. The government army may have been stronger than at any stage in the war, but it was still painfully ill-equipped to respond to the Serbs' heavy weaponry, a deficiency that was not even offset by the limited support of Croat guns.

The BiH stopped publishing the death notices in Zenica after a week. A few days after that I picked up a couple of hitch-hiking Muslim soldiers near the road outside Visoko. They were very young, and stained deeply with the mud and filth of the front. Returning home to Kakanj for two days' leave, they looked absolutely numb with exhaustion. After a while I asked them how the offensive was going.

One gave a kind of bitter dry bark that I suppose was a laugh. 'It's going. That's all,' he said. The other stared out of the window in silence. After a time I noticed he was crying.

16

Zagreb, Autumn 1995

I bundled the porter out of the room with a wad of Kuna, my hands fumbling with the notes for clumsy seconds in my haste, before dragging the cases in from the corridor myself, each impossibly heavy. The sweat was beginning to pour down my face and tiredness crunched my limbs like the crushing weight of a physical load. Sleep. Christ, I felt my brain would combust if I remained awake for another minute. I stumbled back to the door as an afterthought, wrenching it open and hanging a 'Do Not Disturb' sign on the handle, three years too late. I pulled a bottle of whisky from a bag, swashed down a couple of DFs, tore open the neatly made sheets and threw myself into their embrace fully clothed. My consciousness left me in a juddering exhalation of foul-smelling breath.

The garden was on a small incline overlooking a meadow and some woodland, bordered by tangled hedgerows heavy with summer foliage. An earthen path rambled through a profusion of untended flower beds, whose blooms emerged from a combative mêlée of weed and creeper. Tumbled walls, their stained bricks heavy with lichen, spoke of a rockery long abandoned. The path led away from a cottage, a building warm and slumbering crouched beneath overhanging branches like a newly baked loaf, towards the fields beyond, which it entered through a small wooden gate split with moss and decay. It was as if one of Constable's paintings had come to life: a rural English paradise into which I had suddenly fallen.

From the direction of the cottage a Bosnian soldier walked down the path towards me, Kalashnikov swinging lightly at the end of his right arm. He was a fighter from the 17th Krajina Brigade, the refugee troops that I had met so often in central Bosnia. I thought I recognized his face as that of a slain fighter I had seen lying on frost-hardened ground outside a village long ago. It was an unsettling moment that was often repeated in Bosnia where the theatre of war sometimes seemed so limited that the players could play corpses one day, living the next.

'Hi,' I said, shaking the man's hand. 'You were dead the last time I saw you.'

He smiled and patted my shoulder. 'Yeah, it was so cold out there. Here, let me show you something.' I followed him down the path, and we moved out of the dappled sunlight into a shaded corner of the garden where undergrowth spilled over a wall onto the overgrown grass of a lawn. The soldier pointed into the shadows. 'Look, the wheel.'

A carousel stood on the furthest reaches of the grass, barely distinguishable from the reach of the trees beyond it. It had a radius of about twenty feet, and was made entirely out of dead wood, each branch lashed to others with rope so that the profile of its circumference was more pentagonal than circular. Human cadavers hung thickly from each rung between the two sides of the wheel, so closely packed that they overlapped like mackerel in a fishmonger's stall. Men, women and children, the old and the very young, each was strapped to the wood by either their wrists or ankles, and the corpses swung gently as rare fruit. They were in varying states of decay; in some places slime-green flesh glistened between the ragged tears of clothing, in others eye sockets gaped darkly and bones emerged in dirty grey; there were creams, blues and red: the brilliant bouquet of death.

'They are all our criminals,' the soldier told me. 'Serbs, Muslims, Croats, thieves, killers, black marketeers, prostitutes, soldiers, civilians, the lot.'

As he spoke one of the bodies moved, and disentangled itself from the ghastly bunches of torsos around it. The corpse jumped down to the grass. It was the red-haired soldier who had discovered the girl's ear in his ammunition pouch over two years before. His flesh was a little pale but he was otherwise intact, and walked up to us smiling.

'What are you doing here?' I asked him.

'I killed many civilians and cut off their ears,' he replied with a shrug. 'But I was a brave fighter so I am allowed to walk in the garden sometimes.'

'But you didn't cut off the girl's ear,' I told him. 'It was the Croat soldier that did it, remember?' But he said that he did not remember and began to walk away to the meadow. I called out to him again, 'It was the Croat that cut off the girl's ear. You just found it, remember?'

My guide began laughing beside me. 'No, Anthony, you don't remember. It was he who cut off the girl's ear and killed so many children. Here, come and meet the judge, he will explain everything.' We walked back up to the cottage and stepped inside.

There was only one room, long and rectangular with a floor of bare earth. It was empty except for three items of furniture: a wooden table and stool, and a long bench that ran along the length of the wall opposite. The roof was low and dark, and the only light trickled weakly through a small window beset by shrubs.

A midget, his back contorted and deformed, sat on the stool, resting his elbows on the table, his hands clasped together as if in prayer. He looked at us thoughtfully as we walked in. A white cap sat above the grizzled brown skin of his forehead, seeming to denote some kind of religious denomination. Two dead women sat propped on the bench behind him, their shoulders resting against one another. Both wore traditional Muslim dress and headscarves.

A dull dread began to grip my stomach, the herald of so many screaming nightmares before it, the first symptom of the black, unmouthable terror that I knew always followed. I had to get out of the room but when I turned to leave the door had gone. My guide stood by the wall laughing, his humorous demeanour at odds with my panic.

'You cannot leave,' the midget spoke behind me. 'Your trial has been outstanding for far too long.'

I awoke with the sound of my own cry still hanging in the room, staring blindly at the unfamiliar surroundings, rocketing out of the dream into the cold arms of full-blown withdrawal. I dragged myself out of the bed and over to the whisky bottle. I had been asleep for nearly twelve hours and was in a very bad way. The pain of the cramps in my legs, back, stomach and kidneys was offset only by the intensity of the despair in my mind, a rushing wave of sorrow and anguish that had me sobbing. I downed another couple of DFs and crawled back to the sheets. With a habit, your life becomes full of animals: you have the monkey on your back, a dragon to take you in and a turkey at the other end. They squawked and roared and jibbered at me now as I curled into a ball, hallucinatory visions of foil and smokers slipping in and out before my eyes, which themselves seemed to be dripping with sugar.

Time inverts when you are coming out of the drug. Go in and each day slips past in a slick blur of matt light, its details so fuzzed that you barely distinguish one from the next, so that whole weeks can be unzipped into the void. Come back out and each minute stretches into an hour, each hour into a day, and the days pass like months, fat with the promise of pain.

There were worse places in which to withdraw, though, than the Hotel Esplanade in Zagreb. The one-time headquarters of the Gestapo in the Second World War, its winding corridors were always shrouded in a heavy silence, and the light was somehow softer than the glaring buzz given out by most hotel strip lamps. You had the sense that you could lose yourself in the building's more distant rooms, remaining there undetected for days if necessary. And days were necessary now.

My recovery was slow but unfaltering. On day two I finished the bottle of whisky and the DFs, so started on the drink in the mini-bar. On day three I had my first crap for nearly a fortnight, on day four my fifteenth. I tried on my flak jacket while sitting on the bed. It felt so heavy that I was not sure if I could stand up. I took it off again and lay down.

In July Srebrenica, a government-held town in an eastern Bosnian enclave given 'safe area' status two years before, a condition that should have meant UN troops would fight to protect its population from Serb attack, had been over-run by the Serbs. The entire Muslim population was purged from the town, the women and children sent westwards to Tuzla while the men, possibly as many as 10,000, were slaughtered. Dutch troops from the UN contingent in Srebrenica stood by and did nothing. Srebrenica's fate unmasked the UN's culpable impotence as much as all the previous debacles of the organization's involvement put together.

In the six weeks that followed, the war in Bosnia had undergone some of its most decisive moments. In response to continued Serb attacks on safe areas, NATO planes and artillery had smashed Bosnian-Serb positions around Sarajevo, as well as their communication centres, barracks, ammunition dumps, roads, bridges and armour elsewhere. The Serbs were unrivalled specialists in screwing themselves up as well as everyone else. Having held all the cards for so long, they had insolently ignored the new climate of anger in the international community resulting from their hostage-taking of UN personnel earlier in the summer, and were now getting their richly deserved come-uppance.

NATO powers were attacking the Serbs not on account of their crimes in Bosnia, but because of their humiliation of the UN and its resolutions. However, the missiles were manna in my mind and, whatever the logic behind the attacks, the result was the same: the Serbs were getting the shit well and truly kicked out of them after three years of doling it out to everyone else.

In London, after a long summer in Bosnia, I had not begrudged missing out on the NATO action. It was a remote war of bombardment, as distant as the fall of Srebrenica whose first-hand horror had been denied to journalists; unwitnessed due to the hermetic sealing of the front lines by the Serbs.

A few days after the air strikes began a French plane was shot down near Sarajevo. The crew baled out but were captured. It made headlines in the next day's papers, and I sat reading them in a friend's office in London.

'I hope the Serbs bomb New York,' a heavily accented voice

said behind me. I looked around. A very tall, very beautiful girl stood at the reception desk staring at me angrily.

'I hope NATO bombs Belgrade until it's flat and smoking,' I replied. It was an exchange of escalating response. She was a Serb from Vojvodina. A couple of days afterwards we screwed each other in her flat: proxy war repackaged as love. Then we got wasted together and hung out for a while. I wanted to bite her, scratch her, hurt her, fuck her, love her. I adored her. She was one of those. But she revoked her application for UK refugee status and left the country a fortnight later.

In September the Bosnian army decided to take advantage of the Serbs' disarray and launched a massive offensive of their own. I packed up my things and left for Zagreb. It was time for real war again. Once I had wanted a drug to click me out of the war. More each time now, I needed the war to boot me out of the drug.

On day five in the Esplanade I finished off the booze in the mini-bar. On day six I checked out, a little unsteady, but hacking it pretty well all things considered. I hired a car and drove to Bihać, back to Dudaković and the 5th Corps.

Firelight lifted the darkness from the gathered faces of the soldiers, the soft shimmer of flame emphasizing their exhaustion in a shadow play of sunken eyes and hollowed cheekbones. Government troops of the 502 Tiger Brigade, they had been in action for thirty-five continuous days, advancing more than sixty miles across the undulating terrain east of Bihać, spearheading the biggest Bosnian operation of the conflict, the autumn's final act before the Dayton peace deal finally brought the curtains down on the war.

But now, on the eve of an attack, the omens of disaster and defeat clustered thickly around them like malevolent spirits.

The brigade commander, Hamdu Abdić, 'The Tiger', listened

carefully to the reports of his officers. His fame in Bihać had reached near-legendary proportions since I had last seen him shortly after he had duped the Serbs and autonomists with 'Operation Tiger' the previous summer. A tall man with a humorous face, he sat at one end of the fire, biblically resting his arm on a stave, while a soldier turned a spitted calf over the flames. Distant artillery rumbled through the darkness beyond as one by one his subordinate commanders spoke.

Under Hamdu the brigade had displayed the freewheeling courage and initiative embodied by these officers, and was deployed as a shock force with good effect against the Serb forces. However, tonight their message was unambiguously despondent. The troops were exhausted, they said, and it would take twelve hours for artillery munitions to arrive to replace their diminished stocks. Meanwhile the Serbs were using a forced-labour gang of 120 Muslim civilians to dig trenches on the planned objective of the assault.

Yet the attack was to go ahead regardless. Higher command in Sarajevo insisted that the 502 was to advance that night to the end of a narrow twenty-kilometre-long salient and at dawn strike south-eastwards with the aim of rolling up the flank of Serb units defending the west Bosnian town of Sanski Most. In Dayton, Ohio, the Americans were pressurizing all three sides to come to a peace agreement. The possession of territory was both a bargaining tool and de facto insurance in these negotiations; and as there were potentially only days of the war left to run, the Bosnian government was set on having its army grab back as much land as it could while there was still a war left to fight.

The fighters accepted the news stoically enough. Handicapped by the arms embargo, their supply options strangled until only a month previously by the encircling Serb forces, they were accustomed to fighting in the face of apparent folly. Due to the shortage of vehicles they had covered the ground over the last month entirely on foot. Many had their disintegrating boots held together with little more than blood-soaked bandages, and seemed almost stupefied with fatigue.

The Tiger gave his orders and the tension of the moment subsided a little. We drank beer and ate some veal. There was a fat Bosnian *Gastarbeiter* at the fireside wearing a combat jacket and cowboy boots. Rejo was one of those bizarre characters that appear in war from time to time, so incongruous they appear surreal.

He had arrived after travelling the rutted battlefield tracks in a new black BMW, its boot stuffed with bundles of Deutschmarks and uniforms: donations from expatriate Bihać Bosnians who had elected to sit the war out in Germany. Now he sat by the fire, hands over his belly like a degenerate Buddha, and leapt out of his skin every time a Howitzer went off. He had the gift of the gab, but he was not quick enough for the cynicism of the soldiers around him, and after a while sat silently as Juta tore him to pieces.

'How nice of you to come, Rejo, it's so good of you,' Juta said, smiling wickedly. 'You've brought some new uniforms and cash for us, have you? Now you want to see a little bit of war, huh? Well fuck you, Rejo, fuck you. We've been fighting and dying like dogs since ninety-two while you've been getting fat in Germany. Now you decide to turn up with some presents as things look a little better. Where you been all this time? See any of us looking fat, do you? Have a nice war tour, Rejo. Fuck you.'

Juta was about forty years old, a little over five foot tall, and skinny. He had the look of a gypsy, dark eyes and a Romany nose peering from beneath the brim of an American helmet. He seemed to have spent the whole war on one front or another, leading a company of fighters known as 'Juta's babes', since most of them were under twenty-one. Juta softened his tone as a group of these troops arrived through the blackness, and once their excited chattering diminished to silence he briefed them almost paternally on their tasks in the dawn attack. 'Remember,' he closed, 'our cause is just. We are on the side of good, and so we're going to be all right, we shall win.'

He turned towards me as his armed youths filed away into the night. 'You are with us and share our hardship,' he started simply. 'You see that we are not savages. We are not fighting for Islam. We are not fighting for fascism. We are fighting for sovereign Bosnia. We are fighting against a genocide against our people.' Through the tainting nihilism of the conflict, his sincerity shone a humbling light, the core of romantic idealism that was all but dead elsewhere in Bosnia.

I was with three friends. We left our packs and vehicle, a high-tech armoured Land-Rover, at a hamlet named Vrh Polje and moved off with the Tiger into the night amid columns of his troops, their black silhouettes hunched beneath the weight of weaponry and munitions. The atmosphere of impending disaster pressed around us more closely than ever, in spite of Juta's words, and I walked with the fighters laden with thoughts of death, wondering once more how my nerve would serve me, an outsider, in the coming battle. Yet there was no question of turning back. I was in company that I knew and trusted: again I would not be the first to say 'enough'. Besides, we were guests of the 502 and I still believed in the Bosnian cause with enough passion to make a refusal of their invitation to join them in battle almost inconceivable. My motivations were also fuelled by other things: these were the last days of the war – I did not know if I wanted to be around when it ended.

'If this was a dog in a race I wouldn't put any money on it,' murmured one of our number in the darkness. Within twelve hours everything was in Serb hands and we were the running dogs.

Juta was not alone that autumn in believing that righteousness meant eventual victory. His general, Dudaković, nursed a theory of 'cosmic justice' which suggested that the same power that cast Rwanda's genocidal Hutus into refugee oblivion on a volcanic rock on the Tanzanian border would also come to his aid in fighting the Serbs.

After three years in Bosnia I was not about to laugh at either of them. The course of the war had flowed like a river, sucking new alliances, new weapons and NATO air strikes into its currents of spasming violence. But by September 1995 it had condensed into a contest of strength of belief. The winners would be those who believed most strongly and were prepared to suffer most for the perceived justice of their cause. There would be no peace deal until one side broke on the battlefield. And it was the Bosnian government troops, at last, whose endurance in the face of repeated military catastrophe was to be rewarded with victory.

Croatia had retaken the Serb-held Krajina in August, releasing the Bihać enclave from its isolation. NATO air strikes had shattered the Serbs' communication links, and the Bosnian 5th Corps had seized their chance and catapulted eastwards out of Bihać, driving back the Serb forces in a continuous running battle, regaining territory hand over fist. 'I'll say this for the 5th Corps,' noted the Croatian commander whose troops had broken their siege, 'they asked us for bullets before they asked for bread.'

In Bihać, a natural base from which to cover the fighting, I had met up with old friends among the journalists who had gathered there, including Aernout. Nicknamed 'the Baron', he was a titled

Dutchman, a former captain in the marines known personally to General Dudaković after his exploits reporting on the fighting there the previous year. A tall, rangy figure who moved in stalking motions like a heron, he was given to easy laughter and his bravery and outspoken, uncompromising views on the war had endeared him to the Bosnian government. It was largely thanks to his introductions that I was given Dudak's permission to move with the 502, and we found ourselves together on the battlefields in the weeks ahead.

Brigadier Fikret Cuskić, acting commander of the famed 17th Krajina Brigade – the refugee unit I had known in central Bosnia during the Croat–Muslim war – let us accompany him on a trip to brief his officers at a forward command post in an abandoned hamlet captured only the day before. We took some incoming almost as soon as we arrived. The soldiers called it 'harassing fire', but the shells that crashed about them with unnerving irregularity wound up our nerves beyond the level of mere harassment. Ćuskić concluded his orders with a little more alacrity than he may have done otherwise. 'We're fighting our way home,' he added as he rolled up a map. 'We're going home at last.' We slopped down some brandy and together with the troops scuttled outside to our vehicle as ceiling plaster from the latest detonation dusted our shoulders.

In a clearing among the woodland on a nearby hill we found a group of refugees. They were not as others, broken and wretched. These were a new face of the Bosnian war. Troops from the 17th, their brigade had recently added 'Knights' to its title, a battle-honour gained through repeated operational exposure, they were loaded up with weaponry, their uniforms battle-tattered and torn, their mood buoyed and jubilant. I recognized one of them, whom I had seen disgorged across the Serb front lines at Turbe in central Bosnia back in '93 after months in a concentration camp. He grinned at the irony of his new predicament and twirled a revolver expertly around his right hand, a very different man from the stunned figure I remembered.

'Home' was the word on all their lips, and in the recent action many of them had already found the houses from which they had been purged so long before. The rolling green valleys around them echoed with combat. Across hundreds of kilometres front lines held by the Serbs since 1992 were being swept aside by similar men, no longer the ragged and ill-armed victims of yesteryear.

We spoke with the refugee fighters for a while longer before moving forward into the zone of action. The day became crowded with the sounds and images of Bosnia's war: tank shells punched through the battleground in sudden explosions of white heat and sprayed earth; Weber rockets flashed duelling fusillades between each side in air-whooping salvoes as a half-dozen different firefights chattered through the hillsides and men ran crouching and ducking through the colossus of the battle about them, partially shrouded by the drifting grey clouds of smoke from burning hayricks that always seemed to delineate the front.

Through the thickening haze, truckloads of reinforcements arrived, a grinning human skull and antlers mounted upon the lead vehicle. Mobitel radios jabbered with the desperate voices of men in combat – at one point the voice of Dudaković himself swept others aside to direct his artillery fire: 'The Četniks are breaking their lines, drop the range two hundred metres and just keep firing, just keep firing . . .'

And on the hillside a teenage Krajina soldier with frozen blue eyes stood upright, shouldered his machine-gun and together with his platoon broke cover, moving forward to whatever waited before them – 'Ciao, bambinos,' he turned and called back to us, 'see you later. Maybe.' Hollywood could not even come close.

Fear was with me but not to the point that it whited out my perceptions. Instead it rose and fell inside my stomach, a tactile chill as each new danger appeared; a natural, almost thrilling instinctive clutching that I felt I could control and override if necessary.

If I felt personal triumph then its details were earthy. Pinned down by tankfire late in the afternoon I realized that I was desperate for a piss. The choice was either to roll over cravenly and piss where I lay or take the risk of being blown away by standing up to do it. I crossed my legs and agonized over this for a while, then stood up quickly, cursing to give myself fortitude as I slashed against the wall before sprawling on the ground again. It felt like a major victory at the time. Maybe it was. Don't knock it until you have tried.

One of my three companions was having a bad time of it, though. He was very frightened and at one point said that it was 'madness' to move from our cover in search of another fight.

'Well, it's war so everything we do has to be a bit bloody mad, that's the idea,' Aernout said with rare unhelpfulness, lighting another cigarette and looking all the more insane for his composure. The fearful man did go forward with us, much to his credit. Yet I could see that even when we finally broke from the battlefield to return to Bihać with the coming of night he was looking distant and strained. I pitied the loneliness I knew that he must be feeling, the naked transparency of his fear. I had been there so many times. I thought about trying to talk him down from it all, then rejected the idea in case I made him worse. You can only really work it out yourself anyway.

✳   ✳   ✳

Glorious days followed, a halcyon time in which we saw war by day, grinning inanely at each other on account of the signed authority from Dudaković that permitted us drastically to multiply our chances of being blinded, maimed or killed alongside his troops, and got smashed out of our faces in Bihać at night.

There was no other place in the world that I would have preferred to be; no other company I would have chosen; no event I could more have wished to witness than the one I watched. There can be few instants in life that a man is lucky enough to feel so at one with his time and place. It would have been a good moment to die.

I cannot apologize for enjoying it so. Sure, the face of war is a base one: suffering, destruction, brutality and incalculable grief. There is enough misery waiting upon each of us without seeking it voluntarily. But I felt I had stood in line often enough – laden with dread as likely as not by every possible outcome – to justify revelling in the more fear-free periods when they occurred. So I took the freedom and light that the fighting offered, feeling truly earthed with the Bosnian war once more. It was like falling in love again, a heady sensual rush that I wished only to clasp unquestioningly: at the time it never felt like the end of an era.

Then the Tiger asked us if we would like to be in on the attack for Sanski Most with the 502, and the bubble of our fortune burst messily in our faces.

For all of about half a minute the attack appeared to go well. Going in at 10 a.m., five hours behind schedule due to problems in deploying the exhausted troops in time for H-hour, it kicked off to a cacophony of gunfire that smacked into the hillside beyond as Tiger troops breached the Serb line there so the rest of the 502 could move through.

Aernout and I were hanging out in an abandoned hamlet at the distant end of the salient with Nino and Chenga. Bosnians from Sarajevo, the pair were famous among journalists in the city for their courage and skill and had been sent in to replace Aernout's previous camera crew. With us too was Hamdu Abdić, flanked by his bodyguards, Saba and Nefi, two young hoods from Bihać tooled to the eyes with hardware, and the rest of the 502 headquarter group. I was tired after the night's march and dozed and smoked indolently in the morning sunshine waiting for the word to move, turning over in my mind the thoughts unique to those special moments just before action.

Chaos descended upon us by stages. No sooner had the Tigers' breach group taken their objectives than the Serbs put in a big attack of their own. Aimed at the base of the salient and backed with a heavy barrage, it shattered the lines of Bosnian reservist troops holding the area far behind us, and within minutes we were as good as cut off. The radio traffic became jammed with distraught calls for reinforcements to support the crumbling rear lines, and the 502, off-balance, was turned to face the new threat, its assault halted almost before it had even started.

Through the confusion the voices of Serb soldiers began intercepting the armija radio channels, swearing and laughing. 'Hey, Turks,' one hissed, 'we're coming to get you, kill you all and fuck your mothers.' At first the Bosnian troops raged back at them, but as the gravity of our situation revealed itself they became pensive and subdued, their derogatory responses replaced by lengthening silences.

The morning dragged itself away as to a man we chain-smoked our way into the warm autumn afternoon while the Serb artillery broke the Bosnian lines on our narrow flanks. As the angry crackling of gunfire crept closer the valley reverberated to the sound of a Serb Galeb jet flying ground-attack missions overhead, sending its payloads into the 502 on the hillside beyond.

The Tiger left, taking with him a group of troops to counter a Serb incursion near by. Before departing he told the men remaining at headquarters to hold their position until he returned. But he never came back, and in his absence the doom-laden atmosphere intensified. The soldiers' talk ceased altogether as we listened intently to the radio, trying, through the garbled pleas and breathless directives, to make out details of the disaster that was rolling inexorably towards us.

'Can someone tell me what the bloody hell is going on?' Aernout asked no-one in particular. It was the third time he had uttered the question in as many minutes, and I could not help but feel a stab of anger towards him. You did not need to be a fluent linguist to work out that we were in a very bad situation which had all the promise of getting worse. Yet in not understanding the language Aernout seemed almost oblivious to the danger and, noting his calmness, I wondered bitterly once more how much of an advantage I had really given myself by learning Serbo-Croat: Aernout's blissful ignorance looked more enjoyable than my enlightened fear at that moment.

'Well, Aernout,' I replied cruelly, hoping for some kind of reaction, 'I'd say it's going to be time to run away fairly fucking soon.'

'Oh,' he said, looking no more than vaguely curious, while I ground my teeth.

The soldiers' eyes began to change. The dull sheen of simple fear and exhaustion seemed to drain away, leaving stares as vacuous and empty as those of babies. Hard-faced men of war with the gaze of infants: it was frightening just to see it happen. It was the look I had seen in my father the last time I saw him – the eyes of helpless surrender. The moment seemed to reach each of us in the same instant, and ended with similar brevity as the void was filled by the squirting retina-spangle of dread. Never before had I so strongly felt the sensation of other humans' fear, and when I saw the eyes metamorphose I knew that the end was inevitable.

It was not long in coming. As a fresh gunbattle erupted on the crestline above, a young soldier ran into the hamlet warning that final line around us had broken, that the last Bosnian troops had fled, and that the Serbs were upon us. Maja, a junior officer, argued with the man for a frantic minute and called him a liar. Then someone said something on Maja's radio. Maja's face paled, and panic seized us like the grip of fever, a virulent contagion that burned through our brains leaving scarcely a man untouched.

The brigade disintegrated around us. We were under attack from three sides and all but surrounded. The majority of the forty or so troops around us simply turned and fled, barely faltering as Maja yelled at them to keep their heads while a battalion commander stood dumbstruck beside him. My heart felt as though it was about to pump itself out of my chest cavity. It was a fight just to keep control of any rational thought. I did not really give a damn whom I ran with – Maja, the rabble, or alone – I just wanted to start running.

There was one vehicle, a low, long-wheelbase jeep, already laden with mortar tubes and ammunition. As it tried to pull away a young Tiger soldier implored its crew to take with them the body of his commander, a cousin slain by a single bullet. They refused. The fighter took hold of the driver by the elbow to reiterate his request. He looked desperate, close to tears even, for to abandon the body to the advancing Serbs would leave it at the mercy of their knives: mutilation of the dead with blades was an established battlefield favourite among some units. Yet once more the driver refused, shaking himself free of the boy's grip and swearing at him.

'*Dobro*,' the young man said, 'good,' picking up his RPG and stepping quickly in front of the vehicle's bonnet. 'Go as you wish, but leave without him and I will kill you.' He spoke softly but with such certainty that there was no doubting his threat, quite aside from the way he shouldered the RPG. Two men jumped out, slung the body over the side of the jeep, then spun away in a cloud of dust, the stiff's boots kicking rhythmically over the tailgate with each bouncing rut in the track.

As the Serbs closed upon the edge of the hamlet we began our escape, leaving with Maja, the Tiger's bodyguards and about ten other fighters. It was a small, concealable group of veteran troops who in spite of their fear seemed infinitely more level-headed than the terrified mob. I fell into their company more by chance than choice, but once with them some of my logic returned, and I knew my chances of making it out were as good as they could be.

Spurred on by a burst of anti-aircraft fire that lanced through a tree beside us – the universal language of its cracking impact at last communicated a sense of what was going on to Aernout: he gave an enthusiastic 'Right, let's go' and sprinted off like a grey-hound out of the traps – we started to tear away northwards. There were about six hundred yards of open ground to the nearest treeline, our only escape route unless we followed the rabble fleeing the field in the opposite direction, attracting mortarfire as they did so.

Speed was our only hope. Although we did not know if an ambush was waiting for us in the treeline, we had to get clear of the open ground before the Serbs charging into the hamlet organized themselves and poured heavy fire into us. So we stumbled forward in frenzied desperation, as the bullets began to crack and zing through the air around us, slinging our excess gear into the grass as we ran. Even a flak jacket was sent spinning to the ground; 25lbs of body armour would be of little value against the anti-aircraft fire and only hinder the run.

I knew the rules of this battlefield. This was not a war of prisoners. Everybody knew what had happened to the Croats the Serbs captured in Vukovar, and to the Muslims taken prisoner at Srebrenica: they were slaughtered. Killed too in this conflict were many, many journalists. My press card would not save me from a shared and shallow grave if I was caught. On the battlefield the Serb troops would most likely have regarded me as a male of combat age with the Muslim side. Even if I managed to survive the first few minutes of capture, I couldn't imagine how explaining I was a journalist would improve my chances of staying alive: the Serbs hated what the foreign press did almost as much as the foreign press hated what the Serbs did.

Media coverage of the war had widened the scope of the international community's reactive involvement in Bosnia. It was a fuzzed and contentious relationship, which at its simplest had resulted in the United Nations feeding the enemies of the Serbs, enemies who would otherwise have been starved into submission. More recently it had progressed to the Serbs being bombed and shelled by NATO forces. The Serbs regarded journalists as a hostile force that was losing them the war. They were certainly right as far as I was concerned. So I was running particularly fast that day.

It was a terror that I shared with the Muslim soldiers and was related more to the fear of pain and humiliation than of death alone. Too often in the war a single bullet came as a relief to prisoners; castrated men tired of sucking on their amputated dicks or clutching at their flayed skin with fingerless hands. How many times had I heard stories of soldiers, surrounded and without hope of escape, killing themselves rather than take their chances with the mercy of captors? So often that I was bored of dull torture tales and suicide glories. Bored, that is, until I found myself running across the field knowing that the Serbs were all around and in vengeful mood. Then every tale was resurrected in my mind with each fall of my frantic feet, and suddenly I found envy for the pistols of the soldiers running beside me. Such was our panic in that field that there was no question of stopping for the wounded. Our pounding legs seemed to pump of their own accord, the adrenalin wave and desire for self-preservation carrying us beyond the boundaries of our brother's keeper. I trusted the fighter next to me to give me his gun if I was wounded and could go no further. The soldiers had already been speaking about it as we first fled the hamlet: pistols and grenades for the wounded.

For long lung-busting minutes I cursed everything: my predicament, my job, my choices, the Serbs, the shooting, the amount I smoked. I invoked the name of every deity I had ever heard of, promising them all, again, that if only I made it out of that situation alive then I would never go back to a front line again. Never.

War terror always brings out the religious slut in me: on a bad day one bang and I am anybody's. Born-again Christians have got nothing on me. I find some sort of god or another in every firefight.

Our pace was like something out of a bad dream. One second I was hurtling over the soil faster than the speed of thought, the next I was the robo-slug going nowhere fast except down, just waiting for shearing metal to blow me to the ground.

It seemed impossible that we should not be mown down as the fire picked up. I thought I would get hit for sure, probably in the arse – it was all the Četniks must have been able to see of me as I diminished doubled-up towards the trees. Though I did not know it at the time, Chenga had sorted out a grenade ready for such an eventuality. Then some kind of calm descended upon my mind. I felt almost ready for the bullet.

We reached the treeline, sprawling panting in the undergrowth; ten soldiers and four journalists. Of the rest I did not know, other than there was a lot of artillery and machine-gun fire ploughing into their route.

For four hours our little group made its way back to the government lines through an eerie landscape of slaughtered livestock, abandoned hamlets and toppled icons, our thoughts gelling once more. During this time I searched furiously for some symbol of luck that might indicate our survival, but all I seemed to see were dead pigs and fallen crucifixes. We lived, so perhaps I should re-evaluate them as auguries of fortune.

We reached the BiH lines as darkness fell. Fresh troops were arriving, and officers were turning the retreating forces back into the hills to face the Serbs. The rout had stopped. Some wounded fighters stood beside a bridge smoking, waiting for evacuation. Near by the young Tiger soldier whose cousin had been killed began to cry.

Much later the government troops recovered the bodies of two men taken by the Serbs that day. They had been bound together with barbed wire, had their eyes cut out and been torched alive with flaming petrol. The grenade option gets my vote.

The thing about near-death experiences is that you only get to appreciate them after the event. For three consecutive mornings after the rout I woke up laughing, and stayed high on adrenalin for the rest of the week once the last vestiges of dread had gone. War is like hard-drug abuse or a fickle lover, an apparently contradictory bolt of compulsion, agony and ecstasy that draws you back in the face of better judgment time and time again.

The 502 were withdrawn to Bihać to recuperate, where the

more optimistic among them made the tower blocks ring with the sound of happy fire. The attack on Sanski Most was delayed for another week. Aernout left Bihać, among other things to explain to his bosses the absence of the armoured Land-Rover, captured by the Serbs in the retreat. For a time I was concerned that without him the Bosnians would feel embarrassed to have had their defeat witnessed by me and discourage further voyages to the front. But on the contrary, they seemed delighted, poured a lot of brandy down my throat, and laughingly agreed that it had been an amazing day.

Rejo found it a little difficult to agree with these sentiments. He reappeared in Bihać more dishevelled than ever, stranded without a passport having had to abandon his BMW, documents and money in the Serb attack and make good his rhinestone escape crawling down a ditch. 'War? You can fucking keep it,' he remarked morosely.

One evening shortly before the rout I had been trying to chat up a Red Cross officer. We were talking about war and death and missing people. Almost as an aside, I mentioned that I wanted to trace Irma, the wounded mother from Velika Kladuša whom I had helped on the day the 5th Corps captured the town from the autonomists. I was sure it was a hopeless request as I did not even have Irma's family name. But within twenty-four hours the Red Cross woman came back to me with an answer. By an amazing coincidence, one of her staff had looked after a woman of that name for several weeks as she waited to see if her daughter, Dina, survived treatment in the hospital in Bihać. She gave me the family name, and the location of a village near Velika Kladuša where Irma was now believed to be living.

It took me less than a day to find the village. As I approached I could see Irma working in the fields. She took one look at me and burst into tears, then led me to her house. A beautiful blond-haired little girl stood in the doorway: Dina. She stared long and hard at me, mute with surprise.

'She remembers that day,' Irma said.

That Dina was alive was incredible in itself, that she was not brain-damaged nothing short of miraculous. At the hospital in Bihać X-rays had shown that the bullet in her head had fragmented into fifteen pieces. They treated her as best they could but thought it too dangerous to try to remove the fragments. She recovered anyway. The only legacy of her injury was that sometimes, if there was a major pressure change preceding a storm, she would stumble and fall as the metal moved fractionally in her brain.

Everybody wept with the memory of that day in Velika Kladuša. I felt very happy. It seemed like the war's supreme wonder, the only time when anything I had ever done in Bosnia really made a difference to someone else.

After the failed attack on Sanski Most I found my nerves in ragged state, in spite of the consoling company of Gilles and Ron, who spent an inordinate amount of time draining the fears from my mind. Gilles was no stranger to this: he was the man who had sorted me out in central Bosnia in 1993 after I had freaked out in Travnik, returning two years later like a medicinal godfather. As for Ron, he had taken the photograph of the Serb fighter kicking dead Muslims in Bijeljina, the shot that angered me when I had seen it in the papers in London in 1992. In their company I had a sense of my journey drawing to its conclusion like a twisted ring, and it was largely thanks to their reassuring influence, as well as the dark encouragements of a death-charged lover, that I asked Dudaković for permission to return to the front. To my unease, he agreed, giving me another carte blanche ticket to hell accompanying the 502 with the wiggle of a pen on paper.

Under different circumstances I might not have made the effort, but in Dayton, Ohio, the final efforts were being made to secure a deal stopping the war. Time was running out for the Bosnian troops' operation to secure Sanski Most and Prijedor beyond. I did not want to sit out the final battle in Bihać. Access to the front was like gold dust to journalists. If you got it, you went. So seven days later, whisky covering the cracks, I got in the battered Peugeot that I had hired in Zagreb, whacked Ennio Morricone on the stereo to acclimatize myself to the thought of spaghetti death and headed east into the hills towards Sanski Most.

I met up with a real Bosnian eccentric on the way in. A self-styled 'Doctor', Pazić was a thin, middle-aged fighter who mixed mysticism, philosophy and brandy with Kalashnikov politics, and was coincidentally on his way to link up with the 502 for the fighting. I had seen him standing at the edge of the road with his gun, so gave him a ride.

As the light faded we had joined a vast column of Bosnian troops heading east to the front. Mules pulled carts laden with munitions that jostled alongside tanks, their turrets crowded with tired infantrymen; horsemen rode beside artillery pieces; old men touted assault rifles and knives as they walked beside fighters barely midway through their teens. It was an amazing sight, a mediaeval and contemporary war crossover, a people's army sucking the draught of victory, snaking for miles through the dusk in a rumbling column, thousands strong.

Pushing ahead to the vanguard we were shelled badly by a Serb tank, and the seraphic smile I had worn as I left Bihać lay with dead and wounded by the edge of the road on the approach to town. I started to have second thoughts about the venture before I met Hamdu. His ecstatic mood was as contagious as the panic that, days earlier, had forced me to run across the fields to the south.

By the time I arrived the fighting had already subsided to isolated skirmishes on the most eastern outskirts of the town. It had been a battle between two specialist units: Hamdu and his men against the Serb paramilitary warlord Arkan. Bodies lay in the darkened streets, making the car bounce sickeningly as I drove towards a hotel in the town centre. The day before it had been under Arkan's control, but now it was Hamdu and the 502 that drank Serb wine in the foyer.

He had had a good fight and a big win. Around him commanders clustered for another candle-held orders group, though very different in spirit from the one I had seen a week earlier. Captured beer stocks flowed as jubilant chatter echoed across the blackness of the square outside and tired but smiling runners arrived with news of advances on the flanks. This time it was the Serbs who had been routed. Two of Arkan's men had been blown away in the foyer, but their bodies had been removed for the evening's celebration. Best of all, the 502 had liberated Aernout's armoured Land-Rover. It was parked proudly by the hotel entrance full of ammunition and rockets, temporarily on loan to the brigade.

Hamdu and Dudaković had argued about who should sleep in Arkan's hotel suite, but the general had departed for Bihać to receive further orders from Sarajevo and it was the Bosnian Tiger who slept there. I crashed out in a room above, but before my eyes closed I heard on a radio that an immediate ceasefire, beginning at midnight, had been agreed in Dayton.

For two days there was little evidence of any ceasefire. Artillery duels clashed as infantrymen fought it out in the hills, and Dudak, linking with General Mehmet Alagić of the Bosnian 7th Corps, swung his forces northwards towards Prijedor.

Ron moved up and joined me, and together we found ample evidence of the Serbs' venom at their retreat. Muslim and Croat forced-labour gangs lay rotting on the battlefield, murdered in their dozens by the withdrawing forces. In one gutted house we discovered twelve bloated bodies of Muslim men whose heads had been pulverized by something like a sledgehammer: it seemed the bestiality knew no limit. I know that I was in that house. I know that I saw that horror. Yet all that I can remember of it is Ron gagging into his neckscarf.

He and I spent the night before the final action with the 502 on the edge of Sanski Most. They were tired beyond belief. 'Another day, another day of war,' an officer mumbled as he walked ashen-faced into the briefing room, formerly a café. 'How much longer?' All of them appeared to have suffered personal loss, not only that of fallen comrades, but mothers, sisters, children. I never heard one of them doubt their cause, but they were exhausted, sick of it, their energies depleted by the years of fighting.

Hamdu returned from Bihać the following morning, angry at the orders he had been given. Word had come from Sarajevo, in the corpulent form of the overall commander, General Rasim Delić, to halt all military operations and abide by the Dayton ceasefire. Streams of 502 troops poured back to Sanski Most as fresh soldiers took over the lines. It was over.

The war was over.

Over?

I returned to Bihać, gave my lover some flowers from the front and a hand grenade, and started going to soldiers' funerals. They buried the first five of the 502's most recent dead in the cemetery outside the town a day later. The unit had suffered heavily. The day before the ceasefire twenty had died in a single Serb ambush. Others were MIA, and many more still had to be recovered, lying sprawled in inaccessible swathes of no man's land along various areas of the new front. The graves of Bihać's fallen reached far across the grass-covered slopes, laden with red flowers whose blooms wounded the green of the surrounding fields.

Beside one grave sat a young Muslim woman whose grief had drained her of all movement and colour. As soldiers, among them Doctor Pazić, dug the soil from the graves and the women wept, she crouched motionless beside the turned soil, staring through the gathered mourners into distant horizon, her pale face framed by scarlet cloth and a falling tumble of dark hair. Ghostlike, chilling and beautiful, she seemed like the bereaved epitaph to the legions of war dead.

'We never wanted this,' Senad, one of the 502 commanders, said quietly beside me. 'We did not want it, and we were not ready for it. Look at our loss. Yet the dead here aren't even ten per cent of those who have died from Bihac. No-one came to help us. The West thought that as we were Muslim it was our problem, and that we were somehow guilty. You see what became of us? Not in my wildest dreams could I have perceived this.'

17

Responding to a request from Petar's family in London, I left Bihać and drove down to Sarajevo to get him out. He had always resolved to stay in the city while the war was on. Now that it had finished it was time for him to leave. Life would be difficult there for Serbs in the future, no matter whose side they had been on. He had been living alone for over a year since Yelena had got out in a convoy of Serb civilians during a ceasefire the previous summer. She had eventually reached her daughter and family in London, who waited hungrily now for the arrival of Petar.

Momćilo? His devil's luck had not deserted him: I heard that a Serb officer he had known prior to the war came and baled my droog out of jail. He got out of Bosnia immediately, before the army could get hold of him again, and linked up safely with his wife and son in Vojvodina, Serbia.

There were already dark rumours circulating in the capital that Serbs trying to leave the government-held zone were being 'disappeared' as they passed over Mount Igman on their way out. The stories were probably more the figment of paranoid imaginings stretched by over-exposure to the whole tortured machinations of the siege, but no-one could be sure. Petar's daughter had asked if I, as a foreigner, could escort him from Sarajevo to Zagreb and try to get him a visa for England. It was the least I could do after all they had done for me in Sarajevo. I felt more than duty-bound by the request. The role of guardian had now fallen on my shoulders. It was a matter of honour that I should fulfil it.

I found him in the flat at Đure Daničića, bags packed and ready to go. It was four days since the Dayton ceasefire had been signed, and already the city outside seemed to buzz with the sounds of a new vitality. Yet inside the flat was still, the dim-lit rooms heavy with the ghosts of our past conversations, the atmosphere as sad as dawn upon a party.

We had to leave as soon as possible, as the visa for Croatia that Petar had somehow acquired was due to expire in four days: the British embassy in Zagreb would be closed for two of those over the weekend.

Leaving the empty flat to its uncertain fate the next day, we drove out to Dobrinja, the front-line suburb at the edge of the airport that was our gateway out of the city to Mount Igman beyond. Yet at the final Bosnian army checkpoint we were halted. Government troops told Petar that his papers were not in order, and that we must return to a headquarters inside the city for authorization to leave.

Predictably, back in the city centre, we were waved away by the staff at the HQ, who said that they did not have the relevant authority to grant Petar clearance, and that it was a matter for the army in Dobrinja. This game went on throughout the day, as Petar's cool detachment faded and his protestations grew more frenzied. He had endured everything that the war had thrown at him, and now it seemed that his tiny window of opportunity would be closed through bureaucratic wranglings over which no-one seemed to have any control. It was unclear whether the army wanted paying off to allow us out, or whether the whole debacle was just the result of confused intransigence.

As we shuttled pointlessly back and forth between Dobrinja and the city centre, the mood of hope that we had had in the morning dissolved into one of increasing desperation. It was the kind of problem that in Bosnia could only get worse. In dealing with officialdom you became like a bluebottle brushing against flypaper: the more you struggled with it, the tighter its grip upon you, until finally it became better to lie still and do nothing at all.

I felt as imprisoned by the circumstances as Petar. There was no way I could leave him, and in the growing sense of hopelessness I considered taking our chances and accelerating through the checkpoint. It would have been ironic for both of us to die in no man's land on one of the first days of peace after the ceasefire. Indeed, the final peace accord would only be signed in a fortnight's time. The dormant war could technically have us yet.

As the day closed I urged Petar to abandon his dealings with the headquarters. We drove back to Dobrinja and waited in the car by the kerbside some distance away from the checkpoint. The sun lowered over Igman in the west, throwing its light into our eyes and that of the soldiers ahead, transforming the broken buildings around us into an eye-squinting yellow glare of rubble. At that moment a dull roar approached us, growing in volume as it approached: a UN military convoy, a circus of lorries and armoured personnel carriers, was passing us to leave the city, throwing clouds of dust about it which caught the light of the setting Bosnian sun as effectively as a screen of smoke. Our moment was upon us. If I could ever have believed in divine intervention, that was the moment. We spun the car into a narrow gap between two trucks, keeping tight behind the bumper of the first as we moved with their flow.

We passed through the checkpoint at speed. In the rearview mirror I could just make out the silhouette of a Bosnian soldier in the swirling dust, body half-cocked at the hip as he leaned forward as if he had noticed something of interest in the grinding column of passing vehicles.

We were out. Accelerating past the column, we took the winding road up Mount Igman alone, passing the collapsed carcasses of burned-out vehicles that lay as rusting monuments to the former danger of the route. As we climbed, Sarajevo stretched out below us, crisp and still in the dying light of autumn. Beside me I could feel Petar staring down upon the city which had been his home for nearly thirty years, which he was leaving now with two suitcases, for ever, for the chance of an uncertain future in a country he had not even visited before. I had never seen him look sad on any occasion in the war. His mind was stronger than any of ours had been, and he had walled out the damage with his mathematics and stubbornness. But as I watched now I saw his face ripple for a second, while invisible clouds raced over his eyes, irises deepening in dimension like extended telescopes. The moment passed, and we drove in silence over the crest of Igman.

Twenty-four hours later the British embassy in Zagreb gave him a visa. I put him on a plane to London that evening. He was met by his family at Heathrow. It was the first time he had seen them for four years.

The first Bosnian I had ever known: in taking him out at the end of the war it seemed as though somewhere a circle had closed. I never saw any of them again. I know that they live quite close to me in London, and I think of them often. We had shared something together in Sarajevo so intimate and incommunicable, a humility and compassion among individuals unconnected by blood tie, which I have never found elsewhere. Some would call it the human spirit. Whatever it was, to discuss those times in London seemed an unbearable prospect: the needless wounding of a walk back into loss that I just could not face. I hope that they understand.